THE COVENANT: A READING

By Jonathan Bishop

Will two walk together, except if they have agreed?
— Amos 2:3

The Spirit and the bride say, come.
— Rev. 22:17

Te totum applica ad textum: rem totam applica ad te.
— J.A. Bengel

Templegate Publishers
Springfield, Illinois

Templegate Publishers
302 East Adams, P.O. Box 5152
Springfield, Illinois 62705

ISBN 0-87243-113-4

PREFACE

We always reflect on the conditions
of possibility for a reality which we
have already encountered.
— *Karl Rahner*

This book begins with a scheme for dividing up the world — which could seem merely pretentious or eccentric. Within the economy of the argument, though, it is meant to function as a convenient language in terms of which to read certain portions of the Old Testament and then of the New, with a view to identifying the major repetitions of a single pattern, that of the covenant. The philosophic polarities provide the scaffolding, as it were, for a structural re-reading of these texts.

So far the book would be a somewhat schematic exercise in Biblical criticism. But there is also, in the final third of the whole, an assemblage of instances to illustrate the same covenantal possibility within contemporary circumstances; that is, within what must be called the Church. There are accordingly chapters on

1

the Eucharist, marriage, the practice of charity, and private prayer. These are meant as contributions to a theory of the spiritual life which should make that venture too at least intellectually consistent with an adequate reading of scripture. The observations that present themselves are therefore ordered in terms of the same general scheme with which the book begins.

The result is a sequence of contexts which the book proposes may be understood as essentially parallel to one another, so that what can occur in an inner-city soup kitchen, for instance, or a modern marriage, or simply to a wanderer on a beach may still be interpretable as exemplifying the same kind of relation that can be seen to obtain within a Biblical narrative or argument. The tracing of these likenesses allows me to call the whole an attempt at theology as well as interpretation.

The specifically Biblical chapters, then, are not meant as a contribution to scholarship, though the work of the relevant community of inquiry has I hope been reviewed as required, and debts are at least informally acknowledged along the way. For the most part I presume what has become the "consensus" view of the texts and their history, though well aware that this is now subject to challenge. I have tried to respond by emphasizing the inevitable tentativeness of all hypotheses. It would probably be fairest to identify this bulkily intermediate portion of my argument as a species of literary criticism, the kind in which I was trained. To read the Bible both critically and as revelation is to attempt to clarify a complicated context out of which a universally applicable message *may* be read. In our world texts are usually read as if the Bible (in this sense) could not exist. Occasionally other texts are read as if they were the Bible. I have done my share of that elsewhere. But if the Bible exists at all — in the sense proposed — it must always be possible to read it as if it were the only text there was: and so as the very type of the meaningful.

The last "Book" of this book, which traces the covenantal principle in the midst of this world, turns out to be largely autobiographical, at least in the sense of drawing on the experience of a single person in the various situations adduced. A discussion of the Eucharist, which bridges the gap between the Bible and ourselves, need not be more than one more analysis of that sacrament; but marriage cannot help being a private experience, from which one learns what one can. The intention in that chapter is to elicit the covenantal implications from one more accidental set of modern circumstances, with the help of so much fiction and generalization as may be required by the usual moral considerations — themselves, of course, part of the larger topic. There need be less verbal inhibition with respect to the example which stands here for the possibility of charity. One's sense of what prayer might consist of is also necessarily dependent upon whatever one may have learned might be the case. All these contexts together are meant to illustrate the possibility of the Church; that is, that state of affairs within which the covenantal relation *might* obtain here and now. For if this relation is in fact the absolute relation from the beginning, as the stories affirm, and is now accessible to all, as Christians believe, then it should be detectable within the experience of each and every one of us — at least as a constant opportunity.

Book Three is therefore an idiosyncratic specification of a possibility which could be actualized in a variety of other ways — including some which might seem more consistent with the style of the first two Books. It could easily contain other chapters besides those devoted here to marriage or the works of mercy or prayer (though it probably could not do without a chapter on the Eucharist). And even assuming just these topics, the treatment might be as various as there were persons or couples or communities. Book One *has* to be about the Old Testament and so in the mode of exegesis, for that is where covenant begins. Book Two *has* to interpret the New Testament in the manner of theology, for that is how covenant is generalized. But Book Three cannot be determined ahead of time. Usually indeed it is left out — or placed in some other volume by itself. But if it is included at all, any version of it, including this one, need only claim that the matters assembled will represent one more specification of the universal possibility within contemporary circumstances. That is enough to sustain the covenantal case in the mode of spirituality. If a further defense of the autobiographical style is needed, it might be found in the suggestion, which I have seen attributed to Gerhard Ebeling, that the history of the Church is the history of hermeneutic. If this is so on the scale of the collective, it should also be true on the scale of the individual; in which case a repetition of a Biblical structure in some contexts of an illustrative life would simply spell out the implications of the general argument in the form of narrative; which is, after all, frequently the method of the Biblical texts themselves.

Generically then the book is an acute case of *bricolage,* or the putting together of things the best one can. Genre is the Law in literary contexts, and some readers may find their expectations obstructed by this mixture. It is certainly in conflict with a "Deuteronomic" understanding, of the sort that once prohibited linsey-woolsey, or the yoking together of an ox and an ass. I am obliged to take refuge in the "Priestly" analogue, where a single tabernacle could be put together out of heterogeneous elements — like the *Torah,* or the Old Testament, or the Bible as a whole. Composition, after all, should follow differentiation, and both are modes of definition, which together with polarity and repetition make up the angels of this enterprise. Meanwhile I do not undertake to assemble every piece of evidence, or

5

out-argue each authority. That would take a couple of academic lifetimes I have not lived. So the reader is assumed to have arrived at his or her own reasonably knowledgeable engagement with the matter of Israel. Nor do I quite assume an explicitly Christian commitment, in spite of the Catholic coloring here and there.

It follows that the book cannot fall into the category of preaching, straight or sneaky, for which another kind of authority is required. The second half of the title calls it a "reading"; a word that can cover a variety of interpretive activities from the analytic to the contemplative. One needs a term capacious enough to include philosophic discriminations, literary recapitulations, and autobiographical anecdotage without embarrassment. Perhaps the whole might be called a meditation. For meditation, though not the same as prayer, as I shall eventually be arguing, may sometimes be included within it. That disposition could make this book an act of intellectual discipleship at least.

So coarse a mixture will of itself illustrate a major purpose, to exhibit the prevalence of covenant as a form capable of articulating not only the meaning of scripture but experience in general. In fact the meaning of scripture *is* experience in general — by way precisely of the covenant. With respect to the Bible itself the idea is almost secure: students of the Old Testament at least have within the last scholarly generation enjoyed several opportunities to test the power of covenant as an organ-

6

izing principle in more than one version, historical or theological, American or German, Christian or Jewish. With respect to the New Testament, unfortunately, there has been much less professional interest in the theme. And to my knowledge the impact of covenantality upon modern theology or spirituality has been marginal at best. Yet if the relation can be shown to hold for the major texts it should by definition be recoverable within other contexts too. Hence the philosophic scheme with which the argument begins and in terms of which it continues. For it is by understanding covenant as a structure of possibilities rather than just a textual preoccupation or an event in history that it becomes plausible to universalize the scope of the idea both backwards and forwards: backwards upon (that much more of) scripture, forwards as far as the rest of the world.

This enterprise could accordingly resemble that of those Puritan theologians of the later sixteenth century who re-thought Christianity in terms of covenant for their generation. Within the Reformed tradition from Bullinger through Olevian, Calvin, and Cocceius the idea of covenant maintained itself for some generations as an interpretive principle. Perry Miller and others have shown how much this effort could mean in at least one corner of the American earth for a century and more. The churches elsewhere and since have been the poorer for allowing the apparent exhaustion of this attempt to discourage equivalent reconstructions in other idioms. But it is surely not accidental that Eichrodt, the chief re-originator of covenant thinking within post-critical modern theology, should have appeared within this filiation of thought.[1]

To think covenantally, to re-read one's master texts in just this sense, and thereby to re-order the relevant actualities and possibilities in the light of the form disclosed is most generally to presume and consent to the intuition that reality is essentially relational. To that extent this argument may be taken as descending from the style of thought originally associated with Buber and Brunner in theology and MacMurray in philosophy. For covenant is simply the Biblical name for relation as soon as this becomes absolute; as soon, that is, as it is conceived as taking place between me (or my collectivity) and Somebody Else to the infinite degree. And if relation is indeed absolute, it must also obtain for the reader in his or her own circumstances as well as for the scriptural persons imagined in theirs. The histories I read may then become figures of my own situation, insofar as that situation is also the absolute situation. If

---

1. I learn this minor fact from D. G. Spriggs, *Two Old Testament Theologies* (Napierville, Ill., 1974), p. 98. Let me take the opportunity of this footnote to announce that there will be only two others, both omnibus notes to list some of the principal secondary books that have been especially useful. This abstinence will be a formal sign of my necessarily amateur status. All other specific debts and references will be made within the text itself.

This is also a convenient place to mention that I found the Latin quotation from J.A. Bengel on my title page in A.H.J. Gunneweg's *Understanding the OT* (Philadelphia, 1978), p. 65. It is identified there as the motto for the Nestlé edition of the Greek NT.

these histories report the covenant as the articulation of that situation, then I may be included within it even as a reader. For if the literary situation too is recast in covenantal terms, the composition of the Biblical texts would have to be classified as a service performed on one side and the reading of them as a gift received on the other. Whoever I may be as a Biblical writer, I am writing for God in the end; whatever I read as a reader of the Bible, I read in the end as coming from him; or rather, I write so that another person like and unlike myself may read the same words as coming from God, directly or indirectly. "Inspiration" too may be understood covenantally.

The present text though must obviously remain un-inspired; if only because it so often stands outside the situation it addresses itself to. This is of course to misrepresent the true state of affairs. The actual cove-nant is a relation to be entered or refused, not a com-plication to be explained. Of this truth the matters taken up in Book Three are as it were a miming at a certain distance, which is one more reason to include them. The book as a whole, then, which incorporates so many forewords, is therefore in the nature of its special case something of a foreword in its entirety. The ideal reader, though, to whom any book is silently addressed, may as silently make the necessary adjustment, so as to see through the balance of errors to the truth beyond. With that person even this writer may covenant — to do at least common justice to the thoughts that present themselves.

In conclusion I would like to thank Joseph Brennan, Warner Berthoff, Michael Colacurcio, John Gatta, Sandor Goodhart, Thomas Jeffers, Sandra Siegel, Anthony Yorke, and at least one other whom I should not name for various kinds of help. The Hull Fund of Cornell University has generously contributed to the costs of publication. I am most grateful for this assistance, and for the hospitality I received at St. Bernard's Seminary and St. Joseph's House.

I should finally warn all actual readers that the translations throughout are my own. I have tried to make them as uncomfortably literal as possible.

Ithaca, New York — July, 1981

BOOK ONE

The Old Testament

And they read in the book, in the
law of God, distinguishing, and
placing the sense, and caused
them to understand the reading.
— Neh. 8:8

PART I
The Categories

The initial instances of covenant are to be found, of course, in the Old Testament. But I should like to begin my approach to this material with a move which may seem at first either an anticipation of a future argument or a step backward into the preface. Let me propose a philosophic reconstruction not of the Old but of the New Testament; or rather of the "world view" presupposed within that collection of texts and easily enough educed from them. This will provide a scheme of possibilities in terms of which to organize the rest of the Biblical specifics, "old" and "new" alike. Part I of this first Book then, may be read as outlining a form for all the content still to come. The appropriateness of this form to that content should appear as we proceed.

The starting point for such an arrangement of possibilities is the familiar NT distinction between the Flesh and the Spirit, *sarx* and *pneuma*. Linguistically the NT is not original in this respect. The world of the day, Jewish as well as Hellenistic, was markedly dualistic in temper and agreed upon much the same structure, though variously disagreeing as to what went where. Given this distinction, everything is either on one side or the other. On the side of the flesh would be all natural bodies, including our own and all their members — but also (and here the NT *is* original) every kind of cultural product insofar as any of these may be considered an invention of man, and so as persisting in an apparent independence of God. The loftiest intentions and thoughts are therefore no more "spiritual", from the NT perspective, than the most shameful lusts or disgusting weaknesses. On the side of the spirit, then, is really (according to the NT) nothing but the Spirit with a capital letter: God himself and the works of God, especially as these have just been revealed in the deeds and words of Jesus of Nazareth and those of his followers who have received the privileges of the Spirit through him. That the so-called "spiritual" is in fact only truly so when it presents the Spirit may indeed be said to be the special NT contribution to the distinction it adopts from its culture. The familiar line is drawn at a new point. To "preach the gospel" is then to re-draw that line through differences where the persons addressed would *not* have thought of drawing it for themselves. And to read the NT *as* the gospel is to continue this project; which indeed we are still trying to do here, intellectually at least, by extracting and repeating the basic distinction in abstract terms.

The principal differentiation within the NT as a whole, then, is between the flesh in general and the Spirit in general. But within specific texts or pericopes it is often necessary (as we shall see later) to sub-divide this major difference into what may be identified as four subordinate categories, two on either side of the primary division. There are often distinctions within the sphere of the flesh which it is important to recognize. That between the body and soul, for instance: both are absolutely considered *sarkical,* to be sure, but the first is more immediately and the second more subtly so; which is why, indeed, the latter has so often been confused with the Spirit. This anthropological distinction can then be seen in its turn to parallel a variety of other contrasts which can be crucial to the sense of a specific NT argument or story. The difference between Gentile and Jew, for instance; or between the crowd and the disciples; or health and sickness; or innocence and sin. In each of these contexts the realm of the flesh may be found to have its own specifiable modes or conditions.

And there is at the same time an equivalent distinction within the realm of the Spirit. There is a difference between God himself, or absolute Spirit, and the various modes through which his power is manifested on

14

earth, which collectively are all signs of the Spirit without being Spirit altogether. Obviously that is still infinitely far off in heaven — while the others may be present in the shape of some miracle or cure or exorcism or ritual or proclamation or prophecy then and there taking place. Jesus himself is of course the central instance of this possibility according to the NT, who explains all the others.

Once the need for these secondary distinctions becomes clear, it is convenient to arrange them as a pattern of categories. The first category, reading from left to right, would include all those pre-existents which are on the whole taken for granted within the NT — as indeed they must be taken for granted in other texts too. It would include, for instance, the natural and social scene in Palestine at just that time and place in all its largely irrelevant and virtually irrecoverable detail. It would include, therefore, the ground or metaphoric "vehicle" for all the parables, including seedtime and harvest, lamps and bushels, cockles and wheat. It would include Jesus' personal appearance, about which we do not hear, and his relatives, about whom we hear very little. Biographically it would be represented by the years before the baptism by John, about which we are at first not invited to be curious, though presently retrospective anecdotes accumulate. In the miracle stories it would include, for instance, the five loaves and two fishes as they happened to be around; or the stone jars full of water before a new use was made of them. Morally (and so more significantly) it would include the state of innocence, either as a theoretical precondition to any story of sin and redemption or as an identifiable period in anybody's life. In modern terms we would call this the category of nature or the Past.

The second category, of flesh qualified by the possibility but not yet the actuality of Spirit, is a good deal more prominent within the various stories and arguments, all of which are addressed to those who find themselves in this category whether they like it or not. This is the category of Sin, and therefore of the Law; of sickness, possession, and death, and so of every effort to conquer sin, possession, and death, effective and ineffective alike. It is accordingly the category within which the national struggle against Rome may or may not be carried out, with or without violence, for it is, in the NT as elsewhere, the category of individuality and collectivity, action and passion, choice and expression — and so the category within which faith may or may not obtain. In modern terms we should call this the category of Culture, or the present moment.

If the first and the second categories, or the Nature and Culture, exhausted all the possibilities of existence, redemption, according to the NT, would be impossible. Sin and death would determine the horizon of possibility. It is of course the function of these texts and the tradition out of which they emerge to declare that in fact liberation from the entropy which dominates the categories of the flesh has now at last become possible indeed, for the Spirit has once more entered this world to bring its powers to an end, already in principle and very soon in fact. The kingdom of God, or regime of the Spirit, is now "near." Jesus, proclaims the NT, has been sent to make this variously evident by words and deeds which in one way or another exhibit the Spirit. Everything he can be reported to have done or still be doing in or after his ministry as an individual or through the community that inherits and extends the power with which he has been endowed is therefore a miracle in the sense of being a sign of the presence of God even when it is not also literally a wonder. The things Jesus and his apostles do and say are therefore to be ranked within what we have got to call the third category, or the first sub-category within the realm of the Spirit. One must observe of course that this category, like the fourth and last, simply does not obtain at all except in faith and obedience — outside the NT as well as in. To the unbelieving of any time the events which may be ranked within it can always be interpreted in one set of fleshy terms or another: "this is the carpenter surely, the son of Mary, the brother of James and Jose and Jude and Simon? His sisters too, are they not here with us?" (Mk. 6:3)

Finally would come the fourth category, or Spirit unconfined. This would be the category of the absolute

17

future, that "time" when the kingdom of God would not only be "near" but have altogether "come"; the time therefore of harvest as contrasted with the time for sowing, when at last we shall see God face to face and no longer in a glass darkly. Apocalyptic outlines the way from the third to the fourth categories with a scenario of fantastic images (as if the homelier ones of the parables could not suffice) and hope anticipates fulfillment as best it can. But all expectations are understood at least in principle as visionary projections, however well or dubiously authorized. "Times and seasons" are really unpredictable, even by Jesus; the only sure member of the fourth category is God himself without condition, in whom all the categories dissolve together with their contents.

2

There will be more to say later in local illustration of this manner of organizing the NT evidence in Book Two. For the present my purpose is simply to lay out the structure presumed within the NT with just enough particulars to allow me, in the first place, to enforce the contrast between the situation presented there and the situation as one would normally understand it outside that perspective. For if one uses the same categories to comprehend the way things are divided up outside the NT, either in those days or ours, it is clear that only the first two are required. Between them the first and second categories would normally take in all the *other* contrasts in terms of which it has ever seemed reasonable to divide up the human world. For that world, ancient or modern, would from a NT perspective be Spirit*less*.

The most all-embracing of these everyday contrasts, we have said, would be that between Nature and Culture, of which the differences between animal and human, body and mind, country and city, feeling and reason, etc., etc., would be familiar sub-species. The unconscious is obviously on one side, and consciousness on the other; or, in another order, existence and action, or life and language. In terms of temporality, the past is primary and the present secondary; in which case the future is ambiguous: it may either be an intention within the present, and so a member of the second category, or what is bound to happen anyway, in which case it would still be a member of the first. Life and Death are mythological names for all the possibilities in question; the second category might indeed be defined as the human use of death, literal or figurative.

In the context of art the gross distinction, presumed or denied, between matter and form makes another contrast with the same double weight. Romantic and Classic might be similarly placed. Within the social sphere the imaginary columns might be extended to include the traditional differences between the "feminine" and the "masculine," as these have been either accepted or contested; or between the child and the adult, or the primitive and civilized. At the lowest level of economic activity, the same general difference would appear as the contrast between the things which money can buy and money itself; at the highest level, this is therefore the relation between the "base" and the "superstructure" of Marxist theory. "Low" and "High" in all contexts would ordinarily have the same meaning.

In terms of the possibilities of identity, I have argued elsewhere, the first and second categories would correspond to the subjective differences between Everybody and Somebody; that is, between ourselves as human beings and as persons, or the first person plural and the first person singular. *We* live our lives within the first category, like it or not; but *I* may sometimes act within the second to carry out an intention as well as fill a

20

need. Such distinctions of identity are also useful in filling out the third and fourth categories along the same line once these have been counted in, for if Everybody is in the first category and Somebody in the second, it follows that Somebody Else would be either in the second too or in the third, depending on whether the other person in the situation in question were realized as infinite or not. God may accordingly be denominated Somebody Else to the infinite degree.

Philosophy has regularly generalized the ontological bearings of these persistent distinctions and others like them, evaluating them according to school and purpose. The empiricist or Romantic will value the first category as original or fundamental; the rationalist or moralist the second as intentional or differentiated. *Sein* is Heidegger's master term, for instance, for being is a first category idea to him; but for Sartre the *pour soi*, a thoroughly second category conception, takes ethical precedence over an *en soi* which it "transcends". Saussure and the influences which descend from him similarly "valorize" *langue* over *parole*. Derrida, rationalist of rationalists, has more recently proposed a "deconstruction" of the claims of speech in favor of writing and of "presence" on behalf of "difference", thereby undoing at least the metaphysical claims of the first category altogether, so that the second and its "textual" contents would amount to the totality of all possible worlds. Even Derrida though is obliged to assert this acutely critical doctrine against the doubleness traditionally presupposed, and like the alternative or Romantic position represented within his polemic by Rousseau or Levi-Strauss must include within his perspective the very contrast he means to subvert. Meanwhile older differences between existence and essence, phenomenon and idea, or the aesthetic and the ethical can represent other philosophical deployments of the same basic distinction.

All these distinctions, traditional or contemporary, presuppose that the pair in question exhausts the relevant possibilities; which in turn has meant that the possibility of the Spirit, which for the NT is quite other than *either* fleshly possibility, has had to be ranked within one or the other of them as soon as the question arose. Thus the spiritual has regularly been identified with the social, imaginative, or rational (which would place it in the second category) and less frequently with the vital or erotic (which would place it within the first). In either case the four NT modes would be reduced to two, both (from a NT perspective) on the fleshly side: the basic contrast between Flesh and Spirit would be treated as if it were equivalent to what might be called Flesh[1] and Flesh.[2] In which case of course the revelatory witness of the NT would be eliminated *a priori.*

But if all culture is differentiation, the specific message of the NT would have to be understood not as a repetition of the familiar differences in some new lan-

22

guage, Hellenistic or contemporary, or even as their abolition in some apocalyptic paroxysm, but as a re-alignment of them all in terms of the ultimate difference between the Flesh and the Spirit. The "gospel" or good news is the drawing of that line: *not* Flesh *but* Spirit. And Jesus is understood in the NT texts as the one who has drawn it. That is what makes him the "word" of God.

3

To realize the absolute difference the *gospel* makes is thus at the same time to reorganize the relative differences that make a difference in the culture which happens to be our own; a culture which, such a re-arrangement obliges us to recall, is in fact "placed" just as definitely as the apparently very dissimilar culture of the NT authors. We shall be following some of the consequences of this reflection in the Third Book, where the spiritual possibility we call the Church is reviewed under some characteristic heads. For now though I should like to return to the idea of the covenant, which this display of the categories may seem to have left behind.

If the system of possibilities presumed by the NT is articulated in this way, then the relation between Flesh and Spirit proposed within these texts would take place as an equilibrium between the first and the fourth categories, or Man and God, by way of a complementary pair of elements disposed within the second and third. In the NT, this "new" covenant is of course sharply differentiated from the "old," which is interpreted as more or less obsolete. Within *this* version of the relation between our common Flesh and absolute Spirit, faith has become the key element within the second or cultural category, and the various "gifts of the Spirit" the corresponding elements within the third.

There will be more to say in specification of the newness of this new covenant in due course. At this stage I want only to observe almost in passing how the proclamation made by the NT may be seen to fall into a structure of which the categories would be an outline. And I want besides to propose that these same categories and the possibilities they generalize will also serve to put in order the covenantal information with which we are variously supplied by the Old Testament.

Such an affirmation is of course the perennial Christian gesture. Only the Christian is obliged to read the OT through the NT; or could boast that he or she had done so. But the Christian is obliged as well to read the OT through the NT without disturbing the integrity of the OT in the process — or by implication that of the "other" religion which has descended from it. The difficulty — some have found, the impossibility — of meeting both these conditions at once is implicated though in a pair of complementary advantages. It is only by reading the OT through the NT that one could connect the two "testaments" at all in a *theologically* significant manner. And it is only when the two testaments are brought together in such a way that it could become not only possible but normal to connect the Bible "as a whole" with other possibilities of experience in a religiously significant manner without injury to *their* integrity. It is one half of my argument, then, to affirm that by means of the covenant and in no other way can one thoroughly accomplish this double connection. The other half claims as well that the desired connection is most advantageously accomplished when one sees it as the repetition of a single structure — which is to see it in terms of a system of possibilities. And any system of possibilities can be organized as a set of categories. By way of the covenant, then, the Bible as a whole can be read as saying, God may be (at least theologically) comprehended; by way of the categories, it is here proposed, the covenant may be (at least philosophically) explicated. Nor need this prove an arbitrary schematizing: by way of the categories, the covenant is universalized; which is at least a cognitive reflection of the essential Christian event — through which indeed, it is proclaimed, the covenant has been universalized.

It would follow from such a view of the matter that the serious difference among the religions would not be between those for whom a covenant, "old" or "new," is already the authorized articulation of the relation between Somebody and Somebody Else to the infinite degree. The real difference would be between those for whom the covenant is the type of relation and those for whom it is irrelevant because "religion" does not mean relation in the first place. In these traditions religion does not mean relation because for them infinitude does not cohere as Somebody Else. Religion means an identification with the powers of life and death in this world. Within the horizon of that enterprise the numinous will be located behind rather than ahead, under rather than above. It will be felt as illusively immanent within instead of distinctly transcendent of the flesh.

If this is the important difference, it would continue reasonable to draw a decisive live separating the religions of revelation, which in practice would have to mean the religion of the Hebrews and its collateral descendants, from all the other religions of natural piety. Some of these may be "authentically" archaic; others have had to be continually re-invented, from the reactionary elaborations of Sumer and Egypt to the banalities of contemporary popular culture. The simplest versions focus naively upon apparent sources of vitality within the first category. These will be the religions Everybody practices. Obviously they need not all go under that name to function as such. They may appear in our day as a therapeutic cult, an erotic complicity, a communal allegiance, a musical taste. What they all have in common is some attachment within the first category. More refined versions absolutize the first category as a whole, as in the different species of mysticism; or they elaborate its contents as myth — or they seek liberation from its constraints altogether. In any case the infinite possibliity remains essentially antecedent and inherent — or else empty.

The difference between all varieties of "paganism,"

then, primitive or civilized, and the religions of revelation would confirm the difference between the Flesh and the Spirit generally. And that difference in turn may be appreciated as equivalent to the difference between the principle of identity and the principle of relation. All modern ideologies, it would not be too rash to affirm, presume identity of some kind as ultimate. That is the mark of the flesh upon them. But all ancient religions (except those which derive from the encounter of Abraham) are equally determined by the same principle. So the religions of relation stand over against both the ancient religions and the modern ideologies that serve the same function. The Bible is distinguished from other texts precisely by virtue of its declaration that relation is ultimate across the board. Relation is what revelation reveals. And the covenant is the means of relation, as soon as that has been explicitly consented to. Once relation is admitted, I may still obey or rebel, believe or deny, neglect or serve; but I cannot help becoming Somebody "before the face of" Somebody Else to the infinite degree. And in that case whatever I do will become comprehensible in terms of the possibilities organized by the categories. It is what we vulgarly call the "Judeo-Christian tradition" that gives philosophy something serious to do.

PART II
Covenant in the Old Testament

Gather to me my devoted ones
Cutters of my covenant upon sacrifice.
— *Psalm 50:5*

The idea of the covenant has been neglected in New Testament studies, which can seem a scandal; but it has been very prominent in modern scholarship on the Old Testament. The covenant may indeed be considered virtually the dominant concept within the long sequence of books and articles which make up the chief modern effort in the "field." This project may now be coming towards an end, intellectually if not professionally. Neutral reviews of earlier stages in the enterprise like D.J. McCarthy's indispensable *Old Testament Covenant* (Oxford, 1972), or deliberately "controversial" critiques like B. Child's *Biblical Theology in Crisis* (Philadelphia, 1970) or G.F. Hasel's hectic *OT Theology: Issues in Current Debate* (Grand Rapids, 1972)have (perhaps prematurely) presumed as much. They have also helped a late-comer organize a plausible sequence for the work they survey. I am indebted to these and other reviews of the academic "tradition" for what follows.[2]

---

2. I promised no more than two proper footnotes; let me make this one reasonably comprehensive. The full titles of the older books about to be mentioned are *An Introduction to the Literature of the OT,* Meridian edition (Cleveland, 1956) and *The Theology of the OT* (New York, 1904).

The principal "fathers" of modern OT theology in their English editions are Walther Eichrodt, *Theology of the OT* (Philadelphia, 1961) and Gerhard von Rad, *OT Theology* (Edinburgh, 1962). Other standard German contributions would include Albrecht Alt, *Essays in OT History and Religion* (Oxford, 1966); Klaus Baltzer, *The Covenant Formulary* (Oxford, 1971); Walter Beyerlin, *Origins and History of the Oldest Sinaitic Traditions* (Oxford, 1965); and Martin Noth, *The History of Israel* (New York, 1958) and *The Laws in the Pentateuch* (Philadelphia, 1967). Walter Zimmerli, *Old Testament Theology in Outline* (Atlanta, 1972), is a summary of this discussion.

The key American scholar for the covenant is George E. Mendenhall, whose principal book is *Law and Covenant in Israel and the Ancient Near East* (Pittsburgh, 1955). M.L. Newman, *The People of the Covenant* (Nashville, 1962) and D.H. Hillers, *Covenant: The History of a Biblical Idea* (Baltimore, 1969) are also useful. John Bright's standard *A History of Israel* (Philadelphia, 1959) and Frank Moore Cross' *Canaanite Myth and Hebrew Epic* (Cambridge, Mass., 1973) have been laterally interesting. On the covenant of David, R.E. Clements, *Prophecy and Covenant* (Napierville, Ill., 1965) and *Abraham and David* (Napierville, Ill., 1967) would come first.

My impression that the modern covenantal "moment" of which these books are standard exemplars may have come to an end is shared by others besides Childs and Hasel. John L. McKenzie's *A Theology of the OT* (New York, 1974) is elegaic as well as acerb, and the acute intelligence of James Barr renders a similar judgement: see especially his *Old and New in Interpretation* (London, 1966).

A fair number of other books and articles have contributed less obviously to the background of knowledge presupposed in this argument. The relevant bibliography is best consulted in D.J. McCarthy, *Old Testament Covenant* (Oxford, 1972), already cited, and in the same author's *Treaty and Covenant,* second edition (Rome, 1978), which surveys the topic up through 1976. More recent works such as J. Bright, *Covenant and Promise* (Philadelphia, 1976), R.E. Clements, *OT Theology* (Greenwood, S.C., 1978) .A.H.J. Gunneweg, *Understanding the OT* (Philadelphia, 1978), W.C. Kaiser, *Towards an OT Theology* (Grand Rapids, 1978), or W. Zimmerli, *OT Theology in Outline* (Atlanta, 1978) do not seem to me to alter the general picture, through the sociological hypothesis of N. K. Gottwald's *Tribes of Yahweh* (Mary Knoll, 1979) may be read as indirectly supportive. T.N.D. Mettinger's *King and Messiah* (Lund, 1976) and J.D. Levenson's article, "The Davidic Covenant and its Modern Interpreters," *CBQ* 41 (1979), 205-219 have been especially useful reviews of the Davidic covenant. J. Coppens' "La Nouvelle Alliance en Jer 31, 31-34, "*CBQ* 25 (1963),

30

The old nineteenth century effort to reconcile criticism and faith may be taken to have concluded as far as OT studies in English were concerned with S. R. Driver's summary *Introduction* to the literary problems and A. B. Davidson's topically organized *Theology* at the turn of the century.

Thereafter for a long generation critical theology of the OT seemed almost suspended. Scholarly effort went into textual and historical studies. Theology proper revived in the middle thirties with a renewed German endeavor to make sense of the complicated critical inheritance which by then had accumulated. The task was to find a central theme in terms of which it might be possible to interpret the texts as they had come to be understood. The first major step in this modern enterprise set the problem for the discussion thereafter. Eichrodt's massive *Theology of the OT* put covenant forward firmly as the concept that unified the OT. This proposal received unexpected support from archeology in the middle fifties when Mendenhall published a famous monograph on the Biblical significance of certain Hittite treaties. According to him the earliest Hebrews had borrowed a formula to express the relation between the new nation and its God from the "suzerainty

---

12-21 was my starting point for that text. I have found the work of M.G. Kline stimulating, especially his *Structure of Biblical Authority* (Grand Rapids, 1975). U. Cassuto's extraordinary commentaries on *Genesis* (Jerusalem, 1964) and *Exodus* (Jerusalem, 1967) also deserve special notice: they have persuaded me, if not that the "documentary hypothesis" is wrong, at least of the stature and artistry of the final redactor of the Pentateuch.

31

treaties" with which Middle Eastern monarchs of the period were accustomed to establish relations with their vassals. This discovery seemed to confirm an old American preference for a historical as opposed to a German bias in favor of a conceptual theology.

Both of these initiating proposals have had their successor repetitions, qualifications, and rebuttals. Mendenhall's case for a deliberate employment of the treaty formula at Sinai has seemed less convincing as evidence has accumulated to support a Deuteronomic date for Israel's literary borrowing of this international form to express its theological situation. And Von Rad among major German theologians was in any case to argue at a length equal to Eichrodt that there was in fact no central theme to the OT at all, only different theologies, each independent of the others. Instead of a unifying paradigm, there was in his view a *Heilsgeschichte* — by which Von Rad could seem to mean ambiguously the story told in the texts, the possible "real" history of Israel behind that, or the equally hypothetical process by which the texts themselves were assembled. The influence of this "traditio-historical method" has been immense, though (I believe) inhibiting to theology. For it assumes the ancient Hebrews shared the modern conception of history as a recapitulation of a probable past in a merely mental present. Such a view is altogether of the flesh, in the terms just explored, for it leaves out the pressure of the future on any actual present, which *is* the Spirit, and so upon the apparent structure of those events in the past which have come to seem worth repeating. Von Rad's perspective omits eschatology, without which relation is out of the question *a priori*. His theology fails to find covenant in the past, in effect, because it falls short of rediscovering it in the present; without though, necessarily annuling it as a possibility in either context. For what could a properly "holy" history amount to, if not a narrative spelling out both sides of the relation as they had once obtained because they always might? *Torah* is narrative before it becomes law, says J. Sanders in his influential *Torah and Canon*. But this can only be true to the extent that the events rehearsed illustrate a possibility which is and will be to the end of time. A proper "creed" can sum up nothing less.

Meanwhile other theologians have offered alternative ways of finding unity in the OT texts. Their proposals too can seem from a certain distance assimilable to a covenantal perspective. Vriezen put forward communion as a key; a theme with its own obvious links with covenantality. Smend looked for a formula that would unite God and Israel — but the covenant already is that formula. Vischer and Jacob make Jesus Christ the center of both testaments, which in one way or another has got to be a Christian truism; but who is

Jesus the Christ, in just that view, but the mediator of the covenant, if not the covenant himself? More recently some scholars have begun to remind themselves that if the OT can have a center at all, it must be God. This view occurs in Walter Zimmerli and is repeated by J.L. MacKenzie and Samuel Terrien, whose *Elusive Presence* finds the concept so entitled the key to the Bible in explicit contradiction to the covenant. But to experience this presence *or* its absence is still to be in relation; and the Biblical form of relation is still covenant. Such determinations are not really alternative but complementary to any theory of covenantality. The same could be said of R.E. Clements' recent emphasis on *torah*, for in what other context could divine instruction, succinct or elaborate, ever become relevant? W.C. Kaiser's stress on the importance of the "promise" can be taken as exactly balancing Clements' preference, once covenant provides the frame for both: *torah* is what man must obey to remain in relation with the God who promises blessings. It would not seem wrong, then, to understand Eichrodt's initial hypothesis as still implicitly standing behind these alternative renderings, as it has served to reinforce the dogmatically grounded reassertions of covenant in such modern representatives of the Calvinist tradition as Jacob Jocz and M.G. Kline.

There seems good reason, then, to continue with covenant as still the most satisfactory clue to the OT even if one does not go beyond the ever-expanding circumference of the professional discussion. That discussion can also serve to remind the amateur student that even at its most ingeniously applied covenant will not explain everything in the OT. Wisdom is apparently outside it, for instance; and Wisdom is obviously a major factor in the whole complex. It would almost be fair to say that if covenant is removed, Wisdom is what is left. But a Bible containing a Wisdom so reduced would be no more than "the Bible as literature" indeed. Covenant may not help much with Apocalyptic either, though with an effort that unstable genre might be brought within its scope as a mutation of Prophecy and an anticipation of fresh revelation. Prophecy itself is secure within covenant, as we shall have no difficulty confirming later. And it will also take in the Cult, as I shall presently be arguing. If the system of worship too can be aligned with the covenantal structure as outlined by the categories, we would have a way of reconciling ethical and liturgical modes of worship, and so the otherwise opposed scribal and priestly traditions.

Critically, as Eichrodt began by proposing, covenant also makes it possible to connect the OT as we have it and the stories it tells with the various reconstructions which have been worked out to establish "what really happened" either in the history of the nation or in the development of the text. The paradigm can therefore in principle reconcile scholarship with faith, since covenant can be located at the center of both the imaginative

35

and the critical versions of what would then become in-deed one story. And finally, as we said earlier, covenant provides a way to get from what it meant once upon a time to what it means now (to repeat a formulation which Krister Stendahl has made current); that is, from whatever is depicted as having happened in the past whether in the text or in some scholarly reconstruction to whatever might still become the case for Somebody here and now. That sort of connection, it is always worth recalling, has been in request from the beginning, whether one thinks of that beginning as in the garden with "J," at Horeb with "D," on the slopes at Sche-chem (as some moderns have hypothesized), or in the square under the falling rain in Jerusalem as a later or-thodoxy would in effect presume. It has always been ne-cessary to interpret the tradition in such a way as to make it re-apply within the present. If our fathers cove-nanted once upon a time, so, to the extent we can take what they did seriously, must we be able to covenant now — whoever we are. Interpretation is repetition, as in the liturgy; indeed, interpretation, rabbinic or schol-arly, redactional or critical, is ideally the cognitive equivalent of liturgy. To write about the covenant is then is some sense to participate in it.

What seems to emerge indeed from the complex mixture of knowledges assembled in modern scholar-ship taken as a whole (a virtually canonical "OT" in its own right) is the inference that the covenant may best be realized as a succession of moments within which a single fundamental action is repeated over and over, a deed the purport of which in every case is to reconstitute the absolute relation. It is encouraging to recollect that this is also the way in which the last redactor of the Pentateuch appears to have seen the same tradition from his earlier but still very scholarly perspective."P" (if that can still be his proper name) and modern scholarship do not always have the same moments in mind, but they both see the history of covenant as a repetition of a form. The moments of course differ chronologically, like the post-Exilic or contemporary modes of inquiry and re-composition which rehearse them, so that one covenantal moment cannot help but appear before or after another either within the text or in some hypothetical history outside the text — which is itself a text of another kind. This need not mean though that we have to see a "development" from the "earliest" to the "latest" version. Some have, among them Eichrodt; some, like Mendenhall, have seen a declension. The principle of repetition though need not of itself imply either valuation. Of itself repetition would rather imply that all actual (and therefore all possible) covenantal moments are *finally* equivalent; a suggestion with its own clear bearing on the relation between the parts of the OT and between the OT as a whole and the NT. The imagined predicament of the tribes at Sinai with Moses or the inferable state of affairs at Schechem with

37

Joshua are not "literally" the same, thought they are enough alike so that the language of one can apparently be used to describe the events of the other. The circumstances of the new monarchy celebrating its conquest of a hitherto pagan Jerusalem and those of the little band of theocrats assembling in the ruins of the same city after the Exile are surely very different. What eventually happens among a few disciples grouped in an upper room either in reality or in any of the versions which recall it can seem still more remote from any of the previous moments — and is evidently intended to be. And there are great differences of medium as well as circumstance. Oath and cult are *not* the same even if they can be reconciled. None of these differences, though, need seem absolutely disabling — if the focus is kept upon the structure of the relation. Covenant *is* that structure, as soon as it is comprehended. And the categories, as we have said, will be the means of that understanding here.

2

A good introductory survey which draws on the whole of the scholarly "tradition" like B.W. Anderson's *Understanding the OT* can help underline the extent to which the final editor of the Pentateuch expected a reader who would understand the history of the nation he hoped his own editorial work would help to re-constitute as an intelligible sequence of covenantal moments. It is likely that "P" (as I shall call him here) meant us to read the aboriginal relation with Adam, as "J" had already handed down a rendering of this, as essentially covenantal in character. (Later theologians may have been a little surer of this than the text will quite support.) If so, Genesis 2:16-25 would be the significant passage. It would not be too difficult to locate the relation there displayed within the structure we have outlined. Do *not* eat the tree of knowledge, the first half of the characteristic commandment would then go, but *do* eat of all the other trees — including, it would seem "J" has already decided, from the tree of life. Adam might thus have become an immortal vegetarian. The triple blessing corresponding to these already very "Sinaitic" comandments within the second category would then be revealed in the food provided, the dominion over all other creatures — and especially in the gift of the woman as a helpmate. All these would represent the third category to him.

Covenantal language is used more explicitly a formal ten generations later to define the case of Noah. In this context there is no earlier author to complicate a last redactional intention. The flood is explicitly a punishment for wickedness, not just a natural disaster. Noah is saved because of his exceptional and representative righteousness. Though him, then, God proposes to renew the blessings of Adam, which would otherwise be nullified by the destruction of humankind, in the form of an explicit covenant (Gen. 6:18). Noah is commanded to build an ark and to fill it; and is repeatedly said to have done precisely what he was commanded. His obedience then represents his righteousness, which is his participation in the relation. In answer God re-creates the whole world. And the first thing Noah does in response is offer sacrifice. Pleased, the Lord promises never again to curse the ground (Gen. 8:20-21) in spite of man's invariable propensity to evil. All this is already implicitly covenantal; but in Chapter 9 comes an explicit balance of elements, with the *word* "covenant" repeated seven times to mark the meaning of the event. Noah is *not* to eat blood or kill other human beings. To these negative commands a new positive corresponds: he *may* eat flesh, which was not permitted to Adam. The explicit promise within the third category in this context is the repeated assurance that God will not destroy the world again. The sheer presence of that world, therefore, and the rainbow as the sign that being will continue trustworthy, are accordingly defined as gifts to Noah and all his descendants — who in principle include the whole human race. Creation, with which "P" began his sacred history, has been renewed as explicitly covenantal.

After Noah comes Abraham and the crucial covenant before and even after Sinai. The Abrahamic story begins in Chapter 12 with "J's" account of Abram's call to leave Haran and a sevenfold promise of posterity which is immediately linked with that command. The essential blessings for Adam, to be fruitful and multiply, is repeated, Cassuto points out, for Noah ten generations later and for Abraham ten generations after him. Fertility is the first gift. The second is the land. Having arrived in Canaan, Abram passes through it from north to south. At Schechem, in the middle of the country, the Lord reveals himself to promise the land just passed over to Abram's seed. Like Noah, Abram responds by building (two) altars. Then comes the brief descent into Egypt, the return to Schechem, and the separation from Lot. The Lord again formally renews the promise of the land and descendants to enjoy it (Gen. 13:14-17). An Aramaic war follows, with the mysterious episode of Melchizedek. In Chapter 15 a son is promised, to specify the seed, with descendants like the stars. Then comes the famous response: "and he trusted in the Lord, and he counted it to him as righteousness" (Gen. 15:6). The first six verses of Chapter 15 may be from "E"; verses 7-20 supplement this version of the exchange with what would apparently have been the original "J" version of the central covenantal moment. A heifer, a she-goat, a ram, a turtledove, and a young pigeon are (except for the birds) divided according to instructions and the Lord himself passes between the halves in the darkness as a flame of fire. This acts out the invocation of a covenantal curse against himself should the promises not be kept. The double gift of the land and posterity is in this case answered only by Abraham's obedience to the several instructions received, which in effect specifies the faith here credited to him. The preparation of the sacrifices is then a ritual demonstration of this trust, as the flare of fire is a complementary sign of God's presence within the third category.

Genesis 17 is "P's" own reinforcement of the implication of these earlier versions. As in the story of Noah, the language echoes that assigned to the story of creation in the first chapter. This time both parties acquire new names by virtue of the new relation, *El Shaddai* and Abra*h*am. As with "J" the covenantal intercourse begins with the promises which are to be kept within the third category: a son, now named Isaac, will be born, and after him many generations of sons, and to them as to their father a land will be given. These promises will be kept forever, *l'olam* — a key "P" phrase, it is regularly pointed out, for like the fire-curse it guarantees that the divine contribution to the relation cannot be invalidated by any deficiency on the human side. This constant element in the patriarchal version of the relation turns out to frame Sinai in anticipation, as if to answer those among "P's" fellow exiles who might have wondered what could still be hoped by a people who had disobeyed the Mosaic stipulations and could not presume on a renewal in those terms. In the second category, to correspond, is circumcision, a new specificity as specific as the naming of the promised son. Commentators usually observe that circumcision is not part of the covenant but a sign of it, like the rainbow for Noah. This may be giving up too easily; but if the rite is indeed functional within the relation, it is still necessary to decide whether it should be understood as an instance of the negative or the positive commandment. M.G. Kline has suggested in his *By Oath Consigned* (pp. 42 and 87) that circumcision functions as an oath-curse, like the splitting of an animal. In that case it would mean, let it be done altogether to my sons and their sons as to this member of mine should I ever break faith. The language of Gen. 17:9-14 suggests to me though that we should rather understand the practice as typifying the way in which the covenant is to be "kept." If so, it could be taken as the relevant positive commandment for this context, balancing the outlawry imposed upon the *un*circumcized. In that case it would most acutely specify the "faith" of "J's" version in Chapter

43

12. Sacrifice is faith acted out in terms of the body. Circumcision would then be that sacrifice which may be accomplished within precisely the context that most closely corresponds to the anticipated son. The idiom of *this* convenantal moment is literally genital throughout.

It is only after the covenantal structure has once more been made secure by a new element within the second category to match the new element in the third that "P" goes on to include the subsidiary stories about Sarah and Lot and Abimelech with which "J" (and "E") have supplied him. The next important episode is the near-sacrifice of Isaac. This has already been assimilated to the familiar structure in "J's" language: "because thou hast done this thing, and hast not withheld thy son, thy only one, blessing I will bless thee, and multiplying I will multiply thy seed . . ." (Gen. 22:16-17). An all-but-entire sacrifice within the second category once again matches an all but infinite blessing in the third. So a new "work" threatens to complete the castration enfigured by circumcision by doing away with the son of the promise. But a ram is substituted, as the foreskin stands in for the procreative member and before that for the self. The Lord accepts a *symbolic* demonstration of faith. And presently the blessing too is rendered concrete in the form of a cave in which to bury the mother of the son who had just been offered and restored. As the son is to the future nation, so the cave is to the land.

The complex moment which all these stories concerning Abraham represent, with their variously specified counterparts of faith and blessing, is itself repeated through the next two generations. The promise is rehearsed to Isaac in Gen. 26:2-4, balanced there not by a cultic request but by the memory of the father's obedience: it will hold, the son is told, "because Abraham listened to my voice, and kept my charge, my commandments, my statutes, and my laws" (Gen. 26:5) — a strikingly Sinaitic formula attributable, it has been supposed, to the intermediate "JE" redactor. There is another repetition in Gen. 26:24-25 which prompts the erection of an altar at Beersheba. The tribal story of Jacob and Essau is indirectly assimilable to the relation by way of the birthright or blessing for which the brothers contest. Of these secondary repetitions the most prominent is the story of Jacob's dream in Chapter 28, where the Lord announces himself as the God of Jacob's grandfather and father, and repeats the usual double promise of progeny and land with an additional assurance that he will be with Jacob and bring him back from Haran, where he goes to seek a wife. This triple gift within the third category is then matched by a triple response within the second when Jacob arises to anoint the stone on which his head has rested as a pillar of remembrance; to vow acceptance of the Lord as his God too; and to promise a tithe of everything that will be given him. The folk-tale struggle in Chapter 32 with

45

the "man" at Penuel is harder to fit in: it seems as pre-covenantal in its treatment as its context is pre-Mosaic. But this archaic *agon,* more "primitive" in its assumptions about men and gods than any of the stories about Abraham, can also be read in parallel with the other versions of the patriarchal relation. Jacob's superhuman strength in *his* version of faith in this context, and the blessing he extracts a decent version of the one he stole from Esau. Encounter is inarticulate covenant, in or out of scripture.

Through all these patriarchal tales the covenantal theme is carried towards the grander story of Sinai, where the relation can become at last collective and legal as well as individual and cultic. By combining these moments as he does, "P" is working like the "second-generation" OT scholar he already is as much as any modern attempting to repeat his editorial steps in analysis and imagination. For us now Adam and Noah are "mythical"; but so, it should be remembered, would they have been for "P" too. For him Abraham is historical; for later scholarship he is at least legendary or tribal; and perhaps even historical as well, if on a less cosmic scale than the text narrates. Whatever the proportions of fiction and fact, the covenantal structure can be seen to obtain; which for "P" as for any of his readers must remain the important consideration.

The Exodus is of course historical not just for "P" but for "J" and "E" as well, the sources the final redactor is assembling or confirming the assemblage of. Sinai is accordingly the central moment of covenant for all concerned within every cycle of re-telling from the most ancient to the most contemporary. Deuteronomy, which this last redactor accepted as a whole as what was then the final version of "the scriptures" was being put together, associates the contents of this essential covenant with Moab, where Moses is represented as repeating Sinai on the verge of the promised land. Scholars disagree whether there was in fact a covenant "cut" at Sinai, though on the whole the consensus seems to assume that there would be no compelling reason to doubt it. Of course it is usual to suppose that whatever happened in the desert was a good deal more limited in scope and detail than the elaborate event depicted in the composite text. Some have also hypothesized another unreported convenantal moment at Kadesh, where desert tribes besides those which had taken part in the escape from Egypt can be supposed to have joined the nation first established at Sinai. If something of this sort did occur, though, it would still have amounted to a repetition of Sinai politically and therefore theologically.

Actual narrative and supposed history would combine to indicate another major moment at Schechem soon after the conquest. This is represented directly in Joshua 8:30-35 and 24 and indirectly in Exodus and Deuteronomy, for the Sinai covenant, it has been argued, is now rendered in language which may once have been borrowed from rites which later repeated what had begun at Schechem. Some like Martin Noth or G.W. Wright have accordingly proposed that the original covenant of the Mosaic type would have taken place at that site, where all twelve Hebrew tribes could have taken part, including those who had never passed through either an Egyptian or a desert phase. Once the covenant was constituted or re-constituted in the promised land, there is further evidence that the essential action would have been repeated ritually every seven years. The warriors of the tribal league may be imagined as gathering with each new "crop" of young men to swear once more to keep the bond with the Lord which their fathers had sworn before them and attest their readiness for holy war in defense of the land. Patches of language in the final version of the Pentateuch could than be read as rehearsing the liturgy of this ceremony in the mode of narrative. The later New Year and Tabernacles festivals would accordingly be interpretable as ritual repetitions of this "original" feast of harvest, consent, and military assembly. Such a primitive congregation could have moved as circumstances dictated from Schechem to Bethel, from there to Shiloh, and finally to Jerusalem in David's time. But these suppositions have been heavily contested.

With the beginning of the monarchy there is somewhat stronger evidence within the texts for still another version of the relation, in which the human agent would once again be reduced from the nation as a whole or its tribal leaders to an elected individual, in this case the king. There is possibly a covenant renewal ceremony at Gilgal, for instance, on the occasion of Saul's accepting the kingship — though the account in I Sam 11:14 - 12:25 is not unambiguous. If so, the fact would confirm a guess that a serious renewal of the covenant was associated with a change in leadership, especially the *form* of leadership. With the accession of David this becomes prominent, for new promises of an everlasting dynasty and a holy city are explicitly added to the blessings imported by the relation. The subsequent "Zionist" version of the renewal liturgy would thus have included a special role for the monarch and an opportunity for the people to make an act of homage to him as well as an oath to the Lord. How large this royal role may have been is a bone of contention between the Scandinavian school and the rest of the learned world, who have not been quite so ready to see even a possibly "heretical" covenant with David sink into Middle Eastern King worship. According to Mowinckel and Weiser and those who have followed them, several of the psalms should be read as fragments from the liturgy of this revised or royal service of renewal.

The text of the "Deuteronomistic history" from Joshua through Second Kings and modern historical scholarship alike are agreed that the monarchy, united or divided, slid into idolatrous compromises out of political vulnerability as well as personal and public weakness. Revivals of the covenant in the pristine mode took place under Hezekiah and most prominently under Josiah, a "moment" associated with the discovery of what most authorities since the beginning of modern criticism have agreed must have been at least the core of the present book of Deuteronomy. The nation was accordingly reassembled once again, though under the leadership of a king still, to reaffirm its commitment to the Lord alone and to pray that punishment for previous infidelities would not include total annihilation. But Josiah died in battle, and Judah followed Israel into exile. The liturgies of renewal had to cease. But in Babylon the various texts now assembled in the Pentateuch were re-written in their final form. The "Deuteronomistic history" was edited, and oracles of the pre-exilic prophets collected. Prophecies of a "new" covenant which could replace or reconstitute the old were promulgated. A full *literary* recovery of the older covenantal documents was completed. What for us are inferable "pre-texts" then became for them and us both *the* text upon which all future versions of community and consciousness alike would depend. The first of these was the act accomplished by the band of returnees under Ezra. This seems to have intended as a deliberate repetition of what had occurred under Joshua at the time of the first entry into the land and afterwards in the renewal under Josiah. It was the old covenant made new once

50

more.

It is remarkable that each of the major acts of covenantal renewal after the establishment of the monarchy seems to be associated with a significant stage in the development of the essential text. The Davidic revolution is closely linked with the composition of "J's" version of the Sinai event and its patriarchal preliminaries. The Josian reform is connected with the "invention" of Deuteronomy, itself apparently a repetition of older traditions from the lost northern kingdom presumably connected with the "E" version of the earliest history. The renewal under Ezra is similarly associated with acceptance of a final version of the essential *torah*. The same coincidence, we may observe, obtains with respect to the next major covenantal moment, the one associated with Jesus. In each instance a change in the canon accompanies a change in the style of the relation.

These covenantal moments are not just chronologically sequential inside the Bible or out of it. They may be linked as well in logical families. On one side would be the conditional covenant of Sinai as the master instance of its type for both the "D" and "P" filiations. "P's" account of an implicit covenant with Adam and an explicit covenant with Noah makes them virtual anticipations of Sinai, as we have seen. Deuteronomy repeats this version literally and forcibly as Moses' last testament in Moab. Whatever was actually done at Schechem would certainly have been a repetition of this

51

version of the covenant, if it was not as some have thought the initial establishing of it. Josiah's revival is another stage in the same line of descent, and so is the renewal under Ezra. On the other side is the (apparently) *un*conditional covenant with David, which may in turn be linked, both thematically and (it has been proposed) historically with the covenant with Abraham. This version appears as well in several of the Psalms and in Isaiah among the prophets. It is clearly this second kind of covenant which has been taken up in Christianity, which has defined itself from the beginning in opposition to the "legal" style represented by Moses and Ezra. The difference between a conditional and an unconditional idea of the relation may be traced back, Newman has proposed, into the desert period and the differences of tribal experience at that time. This may be over-ingenious historicizing; but the difference is still clear between Judaism and her younger sister down to the present, where indeed it reappears in comic form as the clash between scholars like Mendenhall who despise the "Constantinism" of David in order to uphold the "protestant" authenticity of the original tribal union and scholars like Clement or Murray whose sympathies are clearly more tolerant. The conflict between Law and Faith has had many odd reflections.

B

As songs have been to me thy statutes
In the house of my sojournings.
— Ps. 119:54

Our review of the chief covenantal moments as these can be read out or hypothesized has already been attentive enough to the patriarchal versions to bring out their respective balancing elements in reasonable detail. We need to pay an equivalent degree of attention to the major Old Testament representatives of the two later filiations, the covenant of Sinai and the covenant with David. Sinai obviously comes first, in every sense. The central passages for this master instance for the relation, it is agreed, would be Exodus 19 and 24:1-11, and 33-34. It is also agreed that Chapters 19-24 are predominantly the "E" version of the story, though blended here and there with "J" passages. Chapter 33-34 would be the full "J" equivalent. The pre-exilic "JE" editor has apparently combined the two by making the second version a repetition of the covenant after the golden calf episode had annulled the first attempt. In this way justice is done to all versions of the essential tradition. The final redactor could have approved this combination as incidentally promising a happy ending to the period of exile and estrangement within which he was himself putting together a last version of the whole story.

M.L. Newman's *People of the Covenant* can be useful in arranging the differences between the "J" and "E" variants. If the passages attributable to either are separated out, it can be seen that "E's" version of Sinai involves all the people. The relation is firmly conditional. All the participants share in whatever is going on. God is enthroned upon the mountain. The theophany when it comes is audible: a thunderstorm and the blast of a *shofar*. The people are sanctified by a sprinkling of blood. In the "J" version, on the other hand, Moses plays the role of mediator. The covenant is apparently unconditional. There are bounds to the mountain which the people are not allowed to cross. God descends upon the mountain from heaven. The theophany is visible: a volcanic cloud with lightnings. The reception of the covenant is testified to by a communion meal. The "E" story would then have been closer to its successor Deuteronomy in tendency, with the familiar "democratic" and moralistic emphasis of that text. The "J" version seems contrastingly priestly and cultic. Thus one might already find in embryo, thinks Newman, the division between the two principal types of covenant and in due course, the two kingdoms — not to mention, later still, the two religions.

But within the context of the Sinai pericope as we have it such a separation is artificial. As B.S. Childs points out in his recent commentary, Chapter 19 as it stands deliberately interweaves the two "sources," if that is what they really are, so as to stress that every tradition testifies to what from all possible points of view would have to be essentially a single action. (In the OT, the "gospels" are already harmonized.) The result of the combination in this case is to throw the weight decisively on the side of the "E" tradition. It is therefore predominantly that version one has in mind when one refers to the covenant of Sinai. It is certainly this version that is offered in Exodus 19:5, which J. Muilenberg and Childs after him find the key to the whole narrative: "and now, if listening you will listen to my voice, and keep my covenant, then you will be to me as a treasure from all the peoples, for to me is all the earth." The characteristic "E" (and "D") stress is clear: *if* the obligations are kept, then God will be with his people. The third category promise is made explicitly dependent on the performance of a second category duty.

The Decalogue, which follows immediately in Chapter 20, is so positioned within the structure of the narrative as to specify the conditions anticipated in general in Ex. 19:5 as well as to typify all the commandments to be elaborated thereafter through the remainder of the pericope. We have recalled that Mendenhall found the literary structure of this sequence powerfully reminiscent of the suzerainty treaties prevailing at the putative period of the Sinai covenant and for centuries thereafter. He concluded that we should understand the Decalogue as the text of a formal treaty struck between the Lord and his new vassal Israel. In the last two decades the historical component of this hypothesis has gradually worn away, until most scholars would apparently agree with D.J. McCarthy that the treaty form as such should probably be thought of as a Deuteronomic innovation. The Sinai event was probably, he thinks, cultic in style rather than diplomatic — though no less covenantal for all that. An oath of some sort though seems virtually presupposed by the nature of the case presumed: nations are founded on words as well as sacrifices. And covenants as M.G. Kline has pointed out invariably call for documentary evidence of their own prevalence. The story of the two stone tablets would seem to register the antiquity of a textual element in the event. This need not mean we now have that text as it may once have been inscribed. The language of the Decalogue as we can read it is clearly late. But the moral structure it articulates would have had to obtain for any version of the relation in which an exchange of promise for duty was central. The present introductory verses do as they stand seem to reflect the treaty formula's way of articulating this covenantal combination. The superior party first identifies himself ("I am the Lord your God") and then recalls a gracious favor already granted ("who brought thee out of the land of Egypt, from the house of labors"). Next come the obligations which typify the half of the relation which concerns the subordinate member. The assembly are ad-

56

dressed in the second person singular, as if they were one individual:

There shall not be to thee other gods before my face.

Thou shalt not make for thyself a carved image or any likeness of that which is in the heavens from above or which is in the earth from below or which is in the waters from under the earth . . . .

and so on, through the rest of the "ten words."

Most of the specific commandments are in the negative: do not bow down, do not take the name in vain, do not murder, or commit adultery, or steal, or bear false witness, or covet. Two, in this final version, are in the positive: keep the Sabbath, and honor thy parents. It has been argued since that these positives must originally have been in the negative too, so as to keep all the basic instructions in the same style. But the possibility of a positive commandment is not as such impossible, as much of the rest of the Law show. An implied general positive throughout is clearly: keep these commandments. It is a degree more evident that some of the individual directives must have been expanded and perhaps others curtailed. Originally, it has also been supposed, they would all have shared the same rhythm. But all these negatives, short or middle sized or expanded, may be reduced to a still briefer general command: do not sin.

Thus the Decalogue provides a sharp instance of the negative/positive substructure which can be regularly fitted into the second category so as to govern whatever may be done there by whoever is addressed. The first thing that might happen within the second category, given the relation, is sin: in this case idolatry, disobedience, neglect of parents, murder, adultery, and the rest — including "coveting," which as Paul was later to realize may be fairly understood as summing up the principle of all the others. The second thing that might happen within the second category is a reception of the negative commandment: do *not* sin. This negative would be expressed personally or nationally in a deliberate turning away; if after the fact, then as repentance on the scale of the individual or as punishment on the scale of the collective. The third and last thing that could happen within the second category would then be the fulfillment of the positive commandment: keep this Law. We are now in a position to chart the sub-possibilities within the second category that form the human half of the covenantal act:

Second Category		*Third Category*
Do *not*		
sin	AND	I will be with you
but keep		
obey		
worship, etc.		

58

The AND can represent the logical link between what may be done by the person addressed and what will be done by God provided the stipulations are kept. That God will be with his people is a formula which will cover all possible gifts within the third category, including those already provided: in effect the promise reads, I will be with you in the future as I have already been with you in the past.

This scheme though obscures a significant feature of the Decalogue in particular. The commandments are in the imperfect tense and directed to the second person singular. They are therfore "apodictic" rather than "casuistic" in form, to repeat the distinction first put into currency by Albrecht Alt. A casuistic law is in the "if ... then" form in the third person: if a man does such-and-such, let so-and-so be done to him. This, it has been observed, is the usual form for ancient Near Eastern law generally, which the Pentateuch uses for most of its detailed provisions. The form in effect defines the law entrusted to it objectively, as a norm that should apply to Anybody. It evokes for its enforcement whoever is authorized, impersonally. The apodictic form which appears in the Decalogue is by contrast wholly subjective. It is directed by the speaker, who is alternately God himself or his mediator, to — whoever is listening. And whoever is listening is addressed as an individual. The crowd as such is not commanded, however many people may be present, but the individual *in* the crowd —

who represents, on that scale, the whole of the collectivity assembled. We learn accordingly that the typical commandment within the covenantal relation is addressed absolutely by Somebody Else in the infinite degree to Somebody in particular: that is, to me personally. They are not addressed, as in the narratives of the patriarchal versions of the relation, to some third person other than myself. Nor are they directed to Anybody in general, though the structure in which they appear must be understood as if they were. Nor are they addressed, *a fortiori*, to Everybody back in the first category. Everybody may as well ignore them, indeed; except insofar as they have to be objectively enforced as the conventions of some world in which We will go on living as best We can. For Everybody is still in Egypt, theologically speaking.

The commandments of the Decalogue establish a relation, then, between Somebody who has just started to listen and Somebody Else in the infinite degree who has just started to speak. The fact that something is said at all is revelation. The fact that I am addressed as an individual means that the revelation is to me. The fact that the revelation takes the form of a command means that I *might* obey; I have the power to do what is asked as well as not to do it. Either way, I am in relation in the mode of action. It is thus, I discover, that *I* exist at all. Israel, that collective singular, understands itself as founded by virtue of the covenant, and in no other way.

The content of the revelation presumes that I could not have known what it required before. I may have honored my parents and avoided adultery but I could not have known that neglecting my mother or sleeping with another man's wife mattered ultimately. If I practiced these or the other virtues, it was presumably by convention and according to interest; if I failed, it was because they had become inconvenient. But the Decalogue establishes a few specimens of bad behavior as indirectly but decisively implicated in the absolute relationship. Ethics *is* religion, it is thereby revealed. To discredit, kill, steal, or "covet" are all species of selfishment; and selfishness is in principle infinitely contrary to relation as such. Adultery and false witness obviously contradict relation in the private and public life respectively. In all these cases the relation in question is apparently finite; but within the covenant, we are hereby told, a finite relation represents the infinite relation. Within the covenant there is therefore no way to be simultaneously immoral and religious.

The tradition has had trouble numbering the "Ten Words." But in principle there could be an indefinite number of such stipulations. The other commandments might themselves be interpreted as additional specifications which might in principle be elaborated as far as necessary — and were, in the oral tradition. The number doesn't matter, except liturgically. The commandments are representative, not exclusive. What counts is their specificity, not what they happen to be specific about. They are polarized into acute relevance by the absolute character of the relation they illustrate.

The apodictic form is the appropriate rhetorical manifestation for such a reorientation of ethics. Most of the laws listed in the compilations which follow the Decalogue are in the casuistic form. But every casuistic law could conceivably be put back into the apodictic as an absolute commandment addressed to the second person singular. Here and there in the casuistic sequences, in fact, individual orders can be found in the apodictic style: "a witch thou shalt not let to live" is one memorable instance. *If then* is always capable of being turned back into *thou shalt;* and must be inwardly, if it is to be obeyed religiously as well as socially. For if I receive the Law only objectively I may seem orthodox but at best I become a Pharisee in the disparaging sense the New Testament gives that term. I am no longer Somebody but Anybody; in which case I am no longer really in relation to Somebody Else in the infinite degree. Instead I am at best identified with a system in the second category; and so out of the covenant without knowing it. But this need not happen. If I once again receive the Law apodictically, I accept it as and for myself. Then I am in relation after the mode of the covenant again — and the promise can be kept.

Exodus 24, the next crucial part of the Sinai story, is the ratification of the covenant, still predominantly in "E's" version. The people swear to obey the ordinances proposed — which by this time include the detailed instructions assembled in the so-called "Book of the Covenant" as well as the Decalogue — and so by implication the whole of the Law which was ever to extend and apply these initial orders. "All that the Lord has said we will do and keep." Thus Somebody individually *and* collectively promises to obey the positive command already implied by the apodictic negatives. Whereupon a sacrifice is performed. The young men offer holocausts and communion sacrifices of oxen. Moses dashes half the blood upon the altar. The rest he sprinkles on the people. In the "J" version, a portion of which immediately follows, the elders of Israel ascend the mountain to eat and drink with God. If these episodes are read in parallel, the sprinkling in one version would correspond to the eating and drinking in the other. Both would be third category acts of communion to match the second category sacrifice. Or if one understands the sprinkling as the collective equivalent of the dashing, the people are being invited to participate in the sacrifice along with Moses. Some of the sacrifices are communion sacrifices anyway, so there is sacramental eating and drinking in "E's" version too. In either version, then, there is a bodily action corresponding to and expressive of commitment within the second category, together

63

with a bodily action corresponding to and expressive of the blessings already received and hoped for within the third category. The cultic act may have been central to the original establishment of the covenant at Sinai, as McCarthy believes. But in the text as we have it the cult is comparatively subordinate. By the time one reaches the "J" version of the story in chapters 33-34, for instance, one can understand why the "JE" editors chose the "E" version to lead off with, and used the other to express the renewal of the relation after the golden calf episode. There is a "Decalogue" of sorts, with commands for the second category to match the promises in the third, but in this version they are all cultic, and scattered and irregular as well. Do not covenant with the peoples of the land, or bow down to other gods. Remember that all the first born belong to me: that is, sacrifice them, except for the first born of an ass, which may be redeemed with a lamb, or the first born of thine own sons, who must be redeemed. Observe the Sabbath, even in harvest time. Appear at the festivals three times a year. Do not seethe a kid in its mother's milk. Such a collection looks vague and disorganized after the comparative succinctness of the "E" version. Without a parallel moral action the cultic material seems unanchored and random. For the Sinai covenant, then, the "E" rendering (and so the northern tradition) dominates; in part, no doubt, because it did in fact so dominate throughout the tribal period. Therefore the editors, early and late, made sure that the final text would reflect what for them would have been the essential emphasis. As a result Sinai *means* a conditional ethical covenant; *the* covenant, as it were, strictly so called.

One would do better to look back rather than forward within the present order of the text for additional examples of the fundamental relation in this moral style. The "E" version of Moses' call, for instance, in Exodus 3 anticipates the covenant to come with the nation as a whole on the scale of an elected individual. First comes the gift, as usual: God reveals himself in the burning bush as one with the God of the fathers but also as now disclosing the whole of his nature and so (for "E") a new name. "I will be with you" is the essence of both, and thus the master phrase for everything within the third category which is to follow: the miracles in Egypt, the rescue, the guidance, the theophany, the commandments themselves, and the feedings and waterings in the desert; not to mention, in due course, the gift of the land and a progeny who should inhabit it, according to the patriarchal promise. All these are implicit in and summed up by the holy name, which predicts everything to come that could ever give evidence of the truth of itself. For the secret of the third category in all contexts is presence: God makes himself felt within some occasion which then and there presents him. The "name" is most simply the literal expression of this constant possibility. For in spite of W.F. Albright's ingenious connection of the tetragrammaton with the idea of creation by way of a possible causative form of the verb, it seems simpler to agree with von Rad and the other authorities who have interpreted the holy name as a promise of future accompaniment. I AM THAT I AM might as well be understood therefore as equivalent to "I will be (the One) who will be (with you)." In the third person, this becomes *Yahweh:* the One who will be with us is the one who will be with us. Such a rendering would be locally confirmed by Ex. 3:12, immediately previous to the verse introducing the name, which says "certainly I will be with thee," *ki ehyeh imak,* and by Ex. 4:12 and 15 not long after, where God promises that "I will be with thy mouth," *ehyeh im pika.* Similar expressions occur elsewhere in the Pentateuch — and beyond. Hosea 1:9, for instance, reverses the promises of Exodus for prophetic purposes: "I will *not* be with you," *lo ehyeh l'chem,* is the response of an angry God to his sinful people. To read the name in this way would also consist with the "E" belief that it originated with Moses; that it is therefore *the* name of God associated with the covenant, for it defines in advance all the possibilities within the third category which it is the special purpose of the Sinaitic covenant to assure. In the less dramatic "P" version of Moses' call, which in the present text follows the "E" version in Ex. 6:2 ff., God repeatedly asserts himself in his name: "I am the Lord, *ani Jahweh:*" that is, I am indeed he who will be with you. The name is renewed, in this version, in order to reveal that the second half of the promise made under the name of *El Shaddai* to Abraham and the other patriarchs is now about to be fulfilled. The difference between the former and the latter name would then correspond to the difference between sojourning in the land and living there by right. "P" could thus understand the Exodus event and the Sinaitic covenant which it includes as a fulfillment of the covenant with the fathers; the third category is now to be wholly filled up and to complement this within the second category, Israel will be able to "know" the Lord by way of a set of specific instructions, ethical as well as cultic.

In the concrete of this context and the ones which follow in the narrative of the plagues the presence guaranteed by this name is manifest in various signs and wonders. And to correspond with these and (at the moment of the call) to the holy name which reveals the principle of them all would be the specific instructions which Moses himself receives. These constitute a "Decalogue" for him then and there. *Torah* is direction: to approach the burning bush (what better image for a third category *pneumenon* could there be!); to remove his shoes; to proceed to Pharoah and convey the Lord's message to him and to the elders of Israel; and so forth. Whenever Somebody is called, he receives *his* version of the "ten words." These particular instructions disclose what Moses can do to confirm his side of the relation. This combination of duty with blessing already effects an implicit covenant, which prefigures the explicit determinations still to come on the collective scale.

And as the instructions to Moses represent another set of positive commandments within the infinite relation, so Pharoah can stand for the possibility of sin. His resistance to God's will is therefore repeatedly evoked and as repeatedly punished. The negative commandment is elaborately enforced against him and his people so that the complementary positives may be carried out by Moses and Israel. What becomes explicitly moral at Sinai is thus acted out narratively by the national antagonists. The first born is slain so that the "first born" may escape; Egypt sins that Israel may go free. This is as it were the fairy tale version, in which You are utterly bad in order that I may be utterly good — a primitive differentiation which reappears in just this form in several of the psalms. Once the people are in the desert, though, they become capable of sin on their own account, and fall victim to the appropriate punishment as a result. In either version the story enacts what presently becomes the structure of the relation. Von Rad, followed by Alt and Noth, has argued that the Exodus and Sinai traditions should be considered as having developed separately. But there is no need for such a hypothesis as long as the basic structure is kept in mind: then the narrative is simply a diachronic version of what appears synchronically as the covenant. The Exodus dramatizes Sinai, and Sinai organizes the Exodus.

Another anticipation of the full covenant would be the instructions regarding the Passover in Chapter 12. This material is deliberately recomposed and connected with the Exodus, presumably following a tradition attributing the original link to Moses. J. Pedersen proposed that the Exodus narrative as whole may once have been used as a Passover text. Here again, in any case, is another sequence of commands, positive and negative. The lamb which is slain is in this context a substitute for the first born son of each household, "without blemish, a male of the first year." The bitter herbs and the bread from which the element of fleshly life has been removed also register the idea of sacrifice, each in their own "language." The blood of the lamb, though, which would ordinarily be poured out to God in completion of the sacrificial act, is in this instance smeared on the houses instead, which would apparently make it an anointing within the third category to protect the inhabitants from the wrath otherwise to be poured out upon the Egyptians. Like the meat roasted in the fire and shared by the family, it constitutes a sign of the presence of the Lord, who in this way is with his people once again. Whenever elements within the second category are deliberatedly paired with elements within the third, covenant is implicit.

In history, private experience, and the details of cult, then, the essential exchange can be intimated or repeated. One master event is brought about in variety of idioms, "literal" or symbolic, narrative or legal. God reveals himself in the relation that may obtain between him and whoever comes before him. He is with his people precisely in demanding that they be with him in whatever way the situation permits. And just as we can read other neighboring episodes besides that of Sinai proper as individual or cultic repetitions of Sinai, so the festival of covenant renewal could have accomplished a similar repetition within the idiom of public ritual. The possibility of such a festival, secure a few years ago, is as we have said rather out of favor now. But the consensus is still almost willing to believe that the tribes first assembled in the promised land under Joshua would have had to meet regularly thereafter to ratify their allegiance to the God whose clients they collectively were. The fact that this feast would have had to be held at harvest time would explain, thinks Beyerlin, following other authorities, why a later repetition of this tribal gathering would have been called a feast of booths, for the representatives of the people would indeed have had to occupy *succoth* for the duration of the ceremonies. A re-reading of whatever at the time constituted the authorized text of the covenant; a renewal of the oath to keep the commandments therein required for fear of the curses threatened; and an appropriate set of sacrifices would have given Somebody something demonstrative to do within the second category. The continuing presence of the Lord within the third, practically evidenced by the earth on which the covenanters stood and by the sons who accompanied them, could have been made ritually manifest, Beyerlin supposes, by a cloud of incense rising over the altar to the accompaniment of a trumpet blast and the exceptional proclamation of the holy name. In all these ways the meaning of that name could have been enacted once again. The Lord *has been* manifest in the past as the history of the nation, such a liturgy would affirm; he *will* be manifest as the continuance of the promise; and *is now* manifest under a sacramental figure: the pronouncement of his name, which of itself pre-presents his presence.

2

Deuteronomy might initially be described as a prophetic repetition of what can be supposed to have been rehearsed liturgically upon the hills of Schechem or elsewhere. Its pre-edited core certainly recapitulates all the emphases associated with Sinai in the characteristic "E" style but with the help of "contemporary" rhetorical elaborations. In self-conscious accord with the formula for a treaty document, there is a historical introduction, a list of stipulations, an oath, and a set of blessings and curses. It is appropriate that the oldest name for the book is "Repetition of the *Torah*," for which the title *deuteronomion* is a Hellenistic repetition in its turn. It is characteristic too that its current Hebrew name should be *Devarim*, or "Words," for it is intensely literary. Among its sources, it has been conjectured, might have been not only portions of an older liturgy of renewal more or less verbatim but also homiletic material of the sort which might imaginably have been preached on those occasions. Moses is accordingly presented as almost a rabbi, like the scribes who would have supplied the materials and presumably included the inspired author.

The current scholarly inclination is to attribute to this text and the theology it codifies a dominant position in the development of covenantalism as an ideology. The second edition of D.J. McCarthy's *Treaty and*

Covenant, for instance, a magisterial survey by the dean of American covenant scholars, confirms previous arguments by Perlitt, Clements, and Nicholson that the influences culminating in Deuteronomy should be given credit for interpreting the relation between Israel and its Lord in explicitly covenantal terms. The treaty form at least, this new consensus affirms, should *not* be thought of as going back to Sinai, as Mendenhall argued. To adopt so thoroughly "scribal" a positon on the role played by a party of scribes is to place a more than Deuteronomic emphasis on the priority of literature over history. The chief difficulty with this position, I should imagine, is a presumption it harbors respecting the freedom of the party it hypothesizes. The "D" texts do not have the air of inventive theologizing. They bear all the marks of a "reactionary" revival of a faith well understood at the time to be the religion of the good old days. Such reform movements are not inclined to make up new theologoumena out of whole Assyrian cloth. On the contrary: an ancestral covenantality seems presupposed by what we see both the prophetic "D" and his disciple and successor the "Deuteronomistic historian" doing. The former's adoption of the treaty form as a mode of literary structure could than be accounted for as an appropriate articulation of the indispensable inheritance rather than as a perfectly new idea. We need in any case to recall that hypotheses about composers and their motives cannot be any more secure than hypotheses about the history behind their texts. Both are necessarily modern inferences, and are apt accordingly to incorporate modern presuppositions.

Not all scholars, to be sure, adopt the radical form of this position. John Bright among the Americans continues in *Covenant and Promise* to hold that the relation must have assumed a covenantal form from the beginning (pp. 35-43); and A.H.J. Gunneweg has reasserted the historical arguments of Noth against Perlitt in his *Understanding the OT* on the German side (p. 127). And an independent review of the earlier prophets might well serve to reinforce the more cautious view. Amos' prediction of judgement presumes covenantality, for instance, and Hosea mentions the covenant explicitly in 6:7 and 8:1, referring to it as already written in 8:12. These northern figures would thus be repeating the tradition within which they stand well before any "D" school of latter-day Judaea. What can be conceded to the new consensus is the need to remember that everything antecedent must be understood by way of some subsequent rendering. Textuality re-presents historicity — including so much of that as has already become textual. But we are not obliged to suppose that textuality as such begins with "D." Indeed if Exodus may be trusted and M.G. Kline is right, textuality would commence at Sinai, as we have already observed. In that case Deuteronomy could be understood as one stage in a persistent repetition rather than a single late "source."

We can probably be more sure of the first use of this book than of its place within the textual tradition it repeats. It calls for a severe renewal which should reach to the heart of David's son; which, we can learn from II Kings 23, it seems to have received. Rediscovered upon the accession of Josiah after the long reign of the wicked Manasses, Deuteronomy stimulated the most serious attempt at a thoroughly Sinaitic reformation the pre-exilic kingdoms were ever to know. That reformation did succeed in centralizing the rest of the cult, thus completing the Davidic revolution. But the death of Josiah in battle brought the rest of the program to a halt. Re-edited during the exile, Deuteronomy had been combined with the other texts of the Pentateuch by the time the moral meaning of the return could be confirmed under Ezra. Within the "Judaism" which should be dated from that moment it has accordingly remained the typical rendering of the covenant — as it has now become for the scholars we have mentioned as well. Josiah did not lose forever.

The covenantal style it embodies is unconditionally conditional in character. The Lord will (continue to) give the land to his people if and only if they obey his commandments. The basic negative command is still the same: do not sin; but with a special emphasis on the religious and therefore political lapses which had become the type of sin within a settled and urbanized nation. "Do not sin" now means most typically do not commit idolatry, public or private. The corresponding positive is not left obscure either. It is focussed on a series of imperatives: do, fear, obey, remember, hear, teach, all concentrated on the master command, keep. *Sh-m-r* is the principal verb throughout, governing all its semi-synonymous equivalents — including "love," which in this book never loses its obligatory character. The text is dominated by what Somebody is able to *say* should or should not be done. The book is all promise and threat, blessing and curse: the *last* word, in every sense. Moses speaks after Egypt and before Canaan: which is to say within the second category. Ahead, in the third, is the land; into which this speaker will *not* be permitted to enter. Because the land is the type of all possible gifts, it haunts summary and exhortation alike as that which is *not* present. It must still be conquered, it may be seen at a distance, it shall surely be taken away if the people fail to deserve it. This ab-sence within the text testifies constantly to the conditionality of the actual possession in which its presumed reader contrastingly rejoices. Are you, oh king, a better man than Moses, who could not come where you now sit in your vainglory? So the laws, negative and positive, are constantly presented as the means by which the religious entitlement of the nation may still be preserved: "do them, that you may live, and go on and possess the land that the Lord the God of y. ur fathers is giving to you"

76

(Dt. 4:1). Fear is linked to enjoyment, individual morality to national security, obedience to freedom: everything is demanded within the second category — so that
everything may go on being received within the third.

The *Shema,* or Dt. 6:4-5, is the traditional center of
this version of the covenant for good reason. Placed
after "D's" repetition of the Decalogue, which corresponds to the general stipulation of a treaty document,
and just before the detailed requirements which correspond to the "Book of the Covenant" in Exodus, these
verses concentrate the message of the book. Their purpose repeats the substance of the first two commandments in the Decalogue, obviously the most relevant if
the prevailing sin is idolatry. "Hear, Israel, the Lord
our God, the Lord is one" is repeated as if in emphatic
contradiction to the multitude of other gods, who are
finally no gods at all but all the same fearfully capable
of seducing kings and people nonetheless. Presumably
we may read a connection between this affirmation and
the practical measure of centralizing the cult: the Lord
is one — and therefore there should be no more than
one place in which to call upon his name. This freshly
proclaimed "attribute" of God would simultaneously
reinforce the complementary singularity commanded on
the other side of the relation. If God is one, so all the
more must *I* be. I cannot get away with inconsistency
and compromise, as We usually do; king or commoner,
I must now become Somebody indeed in the presence

of Somebody Else whose infinitude is inherently singular. Infinity and unity are then coordinate aspects of that "image" in terms of which man may be said to be created; that is, in terms of which I become myself before God.

What *this* first person can do is correspondingly absolutized in the next verse: "Thou shalt love the Lord thy God with all thy heart and with all thy life and with all thy might" (Dt. 6:5). Here the implicit positive corresponding to the negative of the Decalogue is made explicit at last. If love may be commanded, it must be the superlative of obedience, the concrete of fear, the specificity of faith. Such a love could run in true parallel with the principle of sacrifice within the cult, for any love that can be commanded must become sacrificial as soon as it is put into practice. It is much to the point, therefore, that this verse should be associated in the Jewish tradition with martyrdom.

The Lord is *one,* we learn, and thou shalt *love*; these *words* are to be upon thy heart and upon thy hand and between thy eyes and on thy doorposts. In Deuteronomy relation has become utterly verbal. So it is most properly the *word* which connects the second with the third categories: it is quite literally the key to the covenant, as bodies are within a cultic perspective. God *loves* those who *love* him. The relation generates a moral pun.

The word *shuv,* or "turn," is another instance: if

Israel will only *turn* back to God, God will turn her captivity and restore the land. On man's side this turn is not only from sin but towards God. The word expresses a positive as well as a negative, and so becomes parallel to the other master verbs like hearing and keeping and loving. The covenant is thereby defined as a *dabar* indeed, on both sides a doubly meaningful word of revelation. There is a subtler version in Dt. 26:17-18, "thou *hast caused* the Lord *to say* this day that he will be to you as God and that you will walk in his ways and keep his statutes and commandments and listen to his voice. And the Lord *has caused* thee *to say* this day that you will be to him as a people which is a treasure, according to his promise to you. . . ." I have caused the other to confirm his side of the covenant; he has caused me to confirm mine. We share the same language in mutual compulsion and reciprocal avowal. The *word* is causative for both of us grammatically as well as morally. The second and the third categories are still infinitely differentiated, for one is still flesh and the other is already Spirit — but at the same time they are wholly united by virtue of a relation which, like any other relation, can be expressed in a single word because in the nature of every possible case words do in fact mediate relation. Words are oaths, oaths are words, on both sides.

The logic of all these *logoi* is still thoroughly conditional. There is a neat miniature in Dt. 11:13-17, verses which have been incorporated into what is now the middle portion of the *Shema* as that has since been liturgically expanded. The instructions fall neatly into the familiar pattern: "*If* you will thoroughly hearken to my commandments which I am commanding you this day, to love the Lord your God, and to serve him with all your heart and with all your soul" *then* I (and not the Baals) "will give the rain of your land in its time, the former rain and the latter rain," so that "thou mayst gather thy grain and thy wine and thine oil. And I will give grass in thy field to thy cattle" so that "thou shalt eat and thou shalt be satisfied." It follows that if a drought should occur, it must be in punishment for sin: in this context, the sin of crediting the Baals instead of God. Therefore it is reasonable to put the corresponding warning into the mouth of Moses: "Take heed to yourselves lest your heart be deceived, and you turn aside and you serve other gods and bow down to them" For sin is punished: "the anger of the Lord will blaze against you and he will shut up the heavens and there will be no rain and the ground will not give its increase and you shall perish soon from off the good earth which the Lord is giving to you." Then the only resource is repentance: that is, a retroactive annulment of whatever was wilful in the sin. Punishment is necessarily collective; repentance is just as necessarily individual. Once punishment has brought about repentance, it should become possible to renew the relation in a refreshed obedience to the positive commandments — whereupon the

Lord will be free to renew his fulfillment of the promise, and the rain may fall again. If the rain does in fact fall, the punishment must have sufficed and the repentance must have been accepted. Such a moral structure makes covenantal sense of prosperity and disaster alike both before and after the fact.

Disaster in history is more serious than natural catastrophe both for the nation and the individual, but the same kind of argument can be made to apply. Sin must logically be followed by retribution. If and when disaster strikes, it can be rendered comprehensible as God's punishment — for whatever sins may be asserted to have occurred. As long as the suffering which follows is accepted as deserved, and so accompanied by repentance and a renewal of obedience, there is reason to hope that God will renew his gift too, and the land be restored. So it is never God's fault if evil befalls his people. Nothing prevents the eternal promise from being kept except man's sinfulness. The covenant can thus include human history ahead of time. Indeed it may be said to have invented the possibility, as far as the Hebrews were concerned. Every possible action or passion either on the individual or the collective scale could in effect be pre-defined in terms of this structure as potentially relevant to the absolute relation. For in principle nothing could happen which would not be either an act of obedience to or rebellion against some negative or a positive commandment. Thus Sinai would signify the whole moral world in advance. The covenant becomes a paradigm for history-in-general; which naturally makes it reasonable to compose histories in particular. Thus Deuteronomy "predicts" the "Deuteronomistic" books which follow it.

The most convenient context in which to appreciate the covenantal advantages of the "D" perspective would be war, as von Rad has shown. War is holy when it is commanded to conquer or defend the promised land. To take and keep possession of what has been divinely assigned is an act of obedience. When embarked upon at the direct command of the Lord it cannot help being successful. The chief instance of sin in this context would accordingly be fear, or mistrust of God's promise. Those who cannot help being afraid may as well be dismissed to go home with the men who have a new house, or vineyard, or a wife; they are too much caught up in the first category, apparently, to be fit for active service. If war brings the nations in arms against a city far off, peace is to be "proclaimed"; if it is accepted, and the city surrenders, the inhabitants become tributaries. If the enemy will not surrender, the city is to be besieged. As soon as it is conquered, the males are to be slain, but the women and children and cattle may be taken: these are gifts the Lord has provided. Such booty is in effect sacramental, as the waging of the war is a species of punishment. But if the cities are nearby, that is, within the land which the Lord has assigned to Israel, nothing alien is to be saved alive once the place has been conquered. Inhabitants and goods together are to be utterly destroyed. This is the *herem,* an institution with analogous applications in other contexts but with its center of reference in the first conquest of the land. The word is ambiguous in some contexts where it can name a devotional intention (as on Lev. 27 *passim* or Num. 18:14, 21:2, or 31:28) but the typical meaning in Deuteronomy seems clear: a *herem* is *not* a sacrifice, or positive act within the second category, but a negative. To *herem* is to impose upon outsiders in war that which corresponds to the punishment of death with respect to crimes committed within the national boundaries. Since the inhabitants of the alien cities are by definition guilty of idolatry as well as theft of land which no longer belongs to them, their destruction amounts to a large-scale retribution for sin — which should include annihilation of all the goods which would otherwise convey that sin to Israel by contagion.

The same attitude is maintained throughout the Deuteronomistic histories. The word *herem* is prominently used in a completely negative sense, for instance, in the story of Jericho and the sin of Achan in Joshua 7. The punishment of Benjamin in Judges 20 for its refusal to yield up the rapists and murderers of Gibeah is an internal *herem.* So too is the subsequent destruction of Jabesh-Gilead in Judges 21 for failing to send a contingent to the army which punished the Benjaminites. Because both these acts though are punishment and not holy war, the *herem* is incomplete: a remnant of Benjamin survives, to be married to the virgins of Jabesh-Gilead, so there may still be twelve tribes in Israel. Jehu's ruthless destruction of Ahab's family in II Kings 10 and his slaughter of the Baal-worshipers is understood by the narrator of these grim tales as a praiseworthy fulfilment of Elijah's prophecy, though the cruelty of the usurper is made very evident. Such conduct is still *herem* on the scale, as it were, of the individual, and so within the relation as obedience to the negative commandment, whatever the character of the person concerned in any other respect.

Deuteronomy too is concerned with internal foes of the covenant in the same style. The dreamer of dreams, the seducer to idolatry, the rebellious son, the maker of images must all be slain. A false witness against the virginity of a betrothed wife must be flogged and fined; an adulteress and her partner in sin must be stoned; if a woman is raped in the city and does not cry out, she must be considered guilty too and stoned with her assailant. All these negative commands are to be obeyed so that the people may go on being blessed in the land which the Lord has given. For if sin is not punished, and so collectively annulled in the same way that it is ideally annulled by the individual through repentance, the conditional right of the people as a whole to the gift is endangered. The evil must be put away from Israel

84

before any accomplishment of the positive commandments can become meaningful within the relation.

On the social scale, then, *do not sin* means punish sin whenever it appears, inside or outside of the nation. More often than not the complementary positives are not specified; but they are always present implicitly. Within the sexual context, for instance, the positive would be legitimate marriage. The various sexual crimes so violently repudiated are the sins which correspond to that positive action. To marry and beget children is therefore to do what may be done in this context within the relation. Thus private life too is connected with the national duty. For all morality is finally public when all actions become religiously relevant through their participation in the covenantal structure.

It has often been said in objection to the Deuteronomic version of the moral covenant that it converts the infinite relation into a "secularized" *quid pro quo*. The "if/then" relation between that is required within the second category and what is promised within the third has seemed a standing temptation to legalism. In that frame of mind I may come to think that by keeping the commandments externally I become entitled to an application of the promises to my case. But Deuteronomy contains within itself a corrective to this distortion. If the fundamental negative is *not* to sin and the fundamental positive *is* to love, then the risk of magic is obviated — at least in principle. For I can no more love God mechanically than I can repent mechanically. Such commands can only be obeyed subjectively if at all — and if subjectively, then to that extent without qualification; and if without qualification, then in an obedience which amounts to an articulation of faith. The positive "works of the Law" are ideally a specification of faith rather than its preventative.

A nearer danger seems to me to arise from the not/but form of these commandments. The patriarchal covenant with its comparatively informal cultic component in the second category to balance the promises in the third maintains without difficulty the fundamental difference between Man and God. A version in which the conditions are not only elaborate but typically legal or moral is bound to emphasize the difference between the negative and the positive commandments within the second category at the expense of the larger difference between the second category as a whole and the third. Instead of Man and God, the practical distinction becomes the difference between sin and righteousness, and so between the wicked and the just. The essential line would be drawn down the middle of the second category instead of between the second and the third. In this way the Law might imaginatively and practically though not in principle come to replace the covenant; which is in fact what some scholars suppose to have happened after the return from exile. It is this displacement of the fundamental difference that Paul and not only Paul is warning against. It is preeminently Deuteronomy that the NT conceives of itself as correcting — by drawing the line once more between the flesh and the Spirit.

3

Deuteronomy is a repetition of Sinai in terms of the meanings which that original could have for a certain pre- and post-exilic combination of circumstances. The Pentateuch as a whole can be understood as a larger and looser version of the same endeavor, as that could be accomplished in writing during the Exile and ratified ritually after the return. The question of who edited this final version of the essential *Torah* has been recently reopened by some Israeli scholars. Y. Kaufman and his student M. Weinfeld think the last redaction was worked through within the same filiation of doctrine and practice out of which Deuteronomy had emerged earlier. The more coventional hypothesis, which I have followed here, makes the last editing a work of the priestly school. Whoever did it, this task had to include a recapitulation of the various traditions associated with the cult, a bulky and elaborate inheritance without obvious connection to the covenant. It included as well a recomposition of the earlier narratives of "J" and "E," themselves already, we have assumed, combined by "JE" some time previous to the Exile. It included too — and here the question of which tendency, scribal or priestly, lay or courtly, had the upper hand is of some theological importance — the decision to include Deuteronomy itself in an up-dated and expanded version, and, somewhat nearer the close of the redactional process, a decision to exclude Joshua — though this book incorporates a significant rehearsal of the covenantal action in its final chapter and in any event describes the way in which the promises were kept and the land taken into possession: a last episode towards which the preceding narrative certainly looks forward. It has been suggested that Joshua was cut away because that book might have suggested embarrassing national ambitions to the Persians, whose good will was essential to the return.

As it turns out the combination of these five books rather than six becomes theologically meaningful as it stands. The commandments are offered and accepted, we have said, in the second category, where men can speak and act. That is where the Law applies: in the "wilderness." The ideal promised land is always *ahead*. And so any actual possession of that land has to be significant rather than ultimate, sacramental rather than absolutely eschatological. The "Deuteronomistic history," that is, the books from Judges through Second Kings which the final editing excluded along with Joshua, then becomes a separate cautionary tale or novelistic parable of one such indicative possession from beginning to end. That one such actualization of the sacramental possibility should have occurred could show that another was always possible in the future. Meanwhile the obligations imposed in the second category were all known and could be practiced as well as might

89

be. The future lay ahead; the present *was*, whether in Babylon or (in due course) Jerusalem.

Most of the redactional labor which went into the Pentateuch should presumably be imagined therefore as taking place during the Exile, though probably rather later than earlier in that period, when hopes could already have been rising that the return promised through the prophets might in fact be near. If we may imagine a single author for the last part of this work, as the curious finish and elaboration of the language makes it plausible to do, we seem to see a friend of Ezekiel and "Second Isaiah" who had read Jeremiah and hoped to see the old reform of Josiah's day carried out once more on a still grander scale — with the help of just such a re-collecting and anticipatory text as he could help put together; since that was all that could be done in Babylon. He could hope it would prove not a false tower but a true tabernacle for the faithful servants of the Lord.

"P," as I have been calling him, would have to be understood as reducing if not quite rejecting the special assurances associated with the royal covenant with David, perhaps because it had been rendered unreal by events, and as reaffirming Sinai as still absolutely relevant for the future as well as the past. The patriarchal narratives are accordingly rehearsed in such a way as to make them prefigure Sinai on the scale of the representative individual. Besides this anticipatory authority, these older versions of the relation also contribute, as we have seen, the note of eternity. Because these covenants were *l'olam,* they confirm that the relation cannot have been abrogated from God's side in spite of the failure of the people to keep the commandments specified at Sinai. A future is indirectly outlined, that is, in which a renewal of the covenant handed down from Moses might eventually be authorized by a re-fulfillment of the promise. The composite Pentateuchal text thus stands between an oath broken and an oath to be repeated. It remembers and hopes in the mode of a sacrificial imagination, testifying to traditional specifics which had been and might still be enforced to balance the promise as soon as that was once again fulfilled from God's side. The Pentateuch is as it were the covenant in literary suspension, the document of a relation that has *been* and *will be* confirmed.

It is released into action as soon as prophecies of the kind repeated in Daniel 9 allow the leaders to presume that God as well as Persian politics would permit a return. Whereupon it becomes possible again on the square before the water gate at the feast of Tabernacles, the old time of renewal, to listen to Ezra read out the "Book of the Law of Moses," and to swear once more to keep the commandments therein inscribed. When this "new" covenant is "cut" the archaic verb has become metaphoric: the term used in *amanah* rather than *berith,* and the event, as the chronicler depicts it in Nehemiah 10, seems oddly demythologized and "modern" — much more so, paradoxically, than the corresponding Christian story of the founding of the Church in Acts. It is certainly a major covenantal moment. In addition to the whole book of the Law, the special commitments subscribed to are reported to have included extra clauses applicable to the immediate situation, including especially a prohibition of foreign wives, the key to the matter according to the complementary account in Ezra 9-10. There a repudiation of alien women already married even to some of the leaders amounts to the chief negative commandment for the occasion: "And now let us cut a covenant with our God to send away all the wives and whatever is born of them, according to the counsel of the Lord and those who tremble before the commandment of our God" (Ezra 10:3). Who came first, Ezra or Nehemiah, is a long-vexed issue, but in either case the covenantal work of the two men dovetails neatly. The specific positive corresponding to the negative effected by a divorce of the non-Jewish wives is achieved when Nehemiah sets about rebuilding the walls of the city. When he makes his secret circuit to inspect the state of the fallen walls, that is already, religiously speaking, an act of building by anticipation. When he directs their reconstruction, that is religiously speaking a reconstitution of the holy place. And when he and Ezra and the people divide into two parties to perambulate the new walls with the singers and the priests, that is an act of worship: "And they sac-

rificed that day great sacrifices and rejoiced, for God rejoiced them with a great rejoicing, and also the women
and children rejoiced, so that the rejoicing of Jerusalem
was heard afar off" (Neh. 12:43). All these practical actions amount together to a fresh demonstration of faith
in response to the newly restored gift of the land. The
re-establishment of the city within its walls is in particular a work of artefacture equivalent within this repetition to the founding of the temple in the Solomonic pre-
cedent, and therefore to the construction of the tent in
the desert — or during the exile on the scroll. All these
are original acts within the second category, as had been
David's capture of the city in the first place. That God
should come once more to dwell there is as ever the
hoped-for response upon the farther side of the relation.

Thus the return acts out what is already remembered and hoped for within the Pentateuch, which
thereby becomes the program for a new set of ritual and
political actions. Redaction and reconstruction coincide,
as always. For "J" too, long before, had found occasion
for re-telling in written words the story of God's graces
and man's responses in the glories of David's kingdom
and his son's temple, which had then seemed to complete the sequence of divine deeds. The same is true of
whoever combined "J" and "E" sometimes after the
fall of the northern kingdom on the basis of a combined
story made up, it may have been, in hope of a re-unifi-
cation of the kingdoms. "D's" *Torah* formed, we have

93

seen, the literary occasion for the Josiah reformation. And when the people are assembled to stand in the rain and swear their original oath once more, the text read out has in effect been recast for just that purpose. In one of the Jewish apocryphal writings, commentaries repeat, it is said that all the books of the Law and the Prophets were destroyed in the fall of Jerusalem — and miraculously re-composed from memory by Ezra. There is at least a metaphoric sense in which this legened is historically true: Ezra presides over the whole process of religious renewal, whatever the extent of his actual responsibility for text or deed. And Ezra was both priest and scribe, who therefore united in one person, as least symbolically, both strands of the tradition. So he may even have been the authorial figure we are otherwise obliged to imagine or nickname alphabetically. But that has to remain a remote hypothesis.

C

You have received freely; freely give.
— *Mt. 10:8*

Scholars attracted to the covenant as a key to the OT have tended to sympathize most with that version of the possibility we have just been reviewing. They follow the Sinaitic line through actual narrative, inferred history, putative ceremony, and presumed redaction to a theology generalizing this progress, preferring "E" to "J" and "D" to "P" whenever conclusions are to be drawn. The covenant can seem accordingly a starkly moral or political conception. The royal version of the relation has then appeared peripheral if not decadent. And the cult, to which so much of the work behind our singular "P" and therefore the final version of the Pentateuch too has to be devoted, has seemed virtually outside the range of the covenantal idea altogether, a mere borrowing from paganism without essential link to the ethical relation. There can seem a degree of confessional influence in this bias, a reading back of certain "Protestant" or "Jewish" attitudes over against "Catholic" ones. And such attitudes can of course find ancestral confirmation, especially in the prophets, whose devotion to the "D" perspective can make them harsh critics of the sacrificial system.

But once the structure of the covenantal exchange

95

has been disengaged, it can be seen that the cult will fit into it as readily as the ethical stipulations and their accompanying promises. Indeed it will fill a space otherwise left open. The moral commandments, after all, are predominantly negative. The addressee should *not* do this or that, on pain of falling out of the covenant. The positive commandments in this idiom are for the most part general or rhetorical: love, keep, do. But the rules for the cult are predominantly positive. They give the addressee something specific to do to enact his side of the relation. And these specifics are wholly concrete. The cult repeats the connection established by the covenant in the most convincing terminology of all, the language of the body. Ritual is to religion as poetry is to the individual. It permits the substance of the first category to be incorporated within the language of the second — which in turn means that the third can become evident to the senses. For within the cult the promise can be kept sacramentally at any time, whether or not it is being confirmed historically. The cult can thus demonstrate the *whole* of the covenantal relation — in terms of ritual at least. In this way the imagination is given something to do on the scale of the collective.

What there is to do is some kind of sacrifice. The most general term for this is *corban,* a noun formed from the root *q-r-b,* meaning "to draw near." In the hiphil or causative mood, this means "to present." To perform a sacrifice is to present oneself to God *in the body*.

Chapters 1-7 in Leviticus tell in detail how this may be done according to the practices obtaining within the temple of Solomon, the authorized model for any future. The chief sacrifice is the *olah*, in which the victim was completely burned on the altar, or "went up," as the term suggests, in smoke to God. The victim had to be an unblemished male animal, bullock or sheep or goat, or a turtledove. To make the offering good one placed one's hand on the head of the creature chosen, evidently to signify that it symbolized one's self. The natural life of the first category is thus placed entirely at the disposal of a significant action within the second. The offerer slit the victim's throat, flayed it, and cut it up. The priest made the fire and poured out the blood before the altar. The pieces of the victim were then placed in the fire to be consumed. Thus the whole creature became an "odor of sweetness." The most important of these (or any) sacrifices was the *Tamid*, the lamb offered twice daily in the morning and in the evening as a perpetual holocaust before the Lord, who in Exodus promises in response to this sacrifice to "meet with you" at the door of the "tent," and sanctify the place with his presence (Ex. 29:38-46). The instructions for the *Tamid* are repeated in Numbers 28:1-8. This sacrifice is probably the "lamb of God" of Christian identification as much as, if not more than, the Passover lamb.

The second major species of sacrifice is the peace offering or communion sacrifice, the *zebah,* or *zebah sh'lamin.* In this the fat of the tail, the kidneys, the loins, and the liver were burned on the altar. Fat evidently counted as a solid equivalent of the blood; it too is reserved entirely for the Lord. Some of the flesh went to the priests; the rest was roasted and consumed by the offerers.

These two are the main types of sacrifice which can be offered from a neutral position; that is, by a just man. In the *olah* there is no provision within the rite to demonstrate an answer to the prayer acted out. In the *zebah,* on the other hand, an act of sacrifice within the second category is matched with a gift from God within the third in the form of roasted meat. To eat with God sacramentally is to consume his gifts. What I give to him is thus given back to me as coming from him.

There were besides sacrifices of grain, meal, cakes, and frankincense offered independently or attached to the animal sacrifices. The principle remains the same. Sometimes, as in the *zebah,* a portion of the sacrifice, flesh or meal, would be assigned to the priest. From the offerer's point of view this was still part of his sacrifice. From the priest's point of view it was a gift from God. The "covenant of salt" (that is, a covenant which must never be broken) in Numbers 18:19 and its context formalized these relations. In return for their services, the Levites are to receive the tithe which all Israel is to provide; in return for their services, the priests are to receive portions of the sacrifices — but neither are to receive any land. And the Levites are to give the priests a tithe of their tithes. For the offerer all these portions were in the second category; for the priest, in the third. But there is no change in the basic structure.

If we make the implied general command explicit, the negative half would be the same as before; do not sin — but in a characteristically bodily form, that is: do not become unclean. The positive command, corresponding to the general obligation to keep the Law in the moral version, would be: perform the sacrifices. In this context too there is a provision for the obvious secondary possibility; if one did become defiled, it was possible to offer expiatory sacrifices, the sin offering or *hattat,* and the sacrifice of reparation, or *asham.* Scholars have had difficulty telling these apart; there had apparently been some assimilation of method and purpose before the first texts were composed. Depending on the seriousness of the sin and the status of the offender, the victim could be a bullock, a ram, a goat, a lamb, a turtledove or pigeon, or even flour. In these sacrifices the blood was smeared on the horns of the altar instead of being poured out at its foot, and the flesh was either given entirely to the priests or taken out to be burned separately outside the sacrificial process.

These sacrifices for sin and the theology associated with them came to seem more important in post-exilic times, until all the species of sacrifice acquired an expiatory character. This assimilation of the general to the special and the cultic to the moral has in turn effected Christian thinking about the crucifixion of Jesus — through which the Church has had to make sense of the animal sacrifices of the old Law. But it would be wiser, it seems to me, to understand the expiatory sacrifices as secondary and base whatever interpretation one came to of the sacrificial process as such on the *olah* and the *zebah*. Together these primary species of sacrifice would then exemplify the "normative" possibility within the cultic context. In both, as we have seen, the flesh offered is consumed by fire, either in whole or in part. In both, too, the blood is poured out: the same act, it would appear, on the scale of the "soul" as opposed to the "body" of the creature concerned.

A commentator I cannot now track down has observed that it was not so much the blood which represented the life of the victim as the vapor of smoke off the blood freshly poured. This sounds right; then the smoke of the burning flesh would repeat the same idea. In either case a "sweet savor" would rise to the "nostrils" of the Lord. Both these expressions derive from the *r-u-ch* root. In other words, a sacrifice exposes that which was "breathed" into any living thing in the first place — and so into the man who offers it. The creature representatively destroyed is thus reduced to nothing *but* its life in the very act of losing it. All the rest is burned away. Sacrifice distills the world. It returns us silently to the moment of creation. The first category is utterly consumed in the second, in order that the third may be revealed — as the food one eats. By this means all the categories are finally reordered. For in passing the fullness of the first through the emptiness of the second, we are enabled to realize the ultimate significance of the first anew; that is, to realize that what we have been calling the first category, or Nature, is really the third, or Creation, as it were in incognito — and the third, we know, is already a sign of the fourth. Thus Man and God, Flesh and Spirit, are proleptically reconciled.

For if one animal from one flock or herd is sacrificed, the offerer in effect acknowledges that all things come from the hand of God. If the first fruits of a harvest are given up, the rest of it and the land from which it grows are implicitly confessed as belonging to the Lord, from whom these remaining goods are therefore freshly received. Thus the principle exhibited explicitly in the case of the *zebah,* that the third category should be represented within the act, may be seen to obtain implicitly for the *olah* as well. Sacrifice alters the mode of being of everything that is *not* included within the offering made as well as everything that is. To enjoy these "fruits" thereafter is in effect to receive them sacramentally, as one manifestly does the roasted meat of the *zebah.* It is this inherent complementarity between offering and gift which permits the different modes of sac-

101

rifice to be arranged within the covenantal structure, however pagan their source as individual practices. So the cult recovers the experience of the nations for the covenant with one of them. It predicts a universalism denied in the moral version, which indeed stands by denial: of the wicked, the alien, the uncanny. It therefore represents the whole of the flesh before God, instead of just half of it. The cult completes the covenant in the body.

We have seen in connection with the moral version of the relation how certain words acquire a meaning on either side of the covenantal structure, referring simultaneously to an obligation within the second category *and* to the corresponding blessing in the third. Within the cultic context the body of the victim is the principal unifying "word." But there are literal words too. Of these *q-d-sh* or "holy" is the most important: something can become holy because the Lord is already holy, who hallows those who hallow themselves and their offerings in relation to him. So hallowing is at once what man does and what God does, the offering (and thus the place where the offering is offered) and the gift. This doubleness reappears in the language used in Numbers 8 about the Levites. The Lord says, *I have taken* the Levites to serve in the sanctuary as a substitute for the first born, who are due to me as a matter of course. So far the Levite's service would be a species of sacrifice. But the Lord also says, *I have* at the same time *given*

102

the Levites to Aaron and his sons to assist them in carrying, erecting, and taking down the holy equipment. What God receives he also gives: the sacrifice and the gift is in God's eyes one and the same thing. Indeed the formula could also be reversed: what God gives he also receives. Man gives and God receives, in order that God may be realized as giving and man as receiving. *L-q-h* and *n-t-n* balance on opposite sites of what is thereby revealed as in the end a single act of intercourse.

The regulations for the sabbatical year, and even more for the jubilee, or sabbatic of sabbatics, exhibit the same bodily equilibrium. In the jubilee the land is given to the Lord — to whom it has always belonged in the first place. He gives it to the sons of Israel not absolutely but to enjoy the fruits of, as once to Adam in the garden. So the sacrifice of what might have been produced had the land been worked reveals the truth of the underlying situation. The land and all its fruits, wild as well as cultivated, is always a sacramental, not a real estate. Which is another reason why, once the land has in fact been taken away and the people driven into exile, the prophets among them need not despair. They have lost nothing that really belonged to them. They can even hope to receive the same land back; perhaps after as many sabbaths had passed as had previously been neglected.

In principle the cult is thus more profound than the Law if in practice it may seem more superficial. This

103

ambivalence cannot be resolved, but it need not appear scandalous. The profundity lies in the power of the cult to generate a universal sign of which the meaning is God. The particular lamb or bullock is in spirit and in truth all sheep and cattle; and so in the end it is Nature as a whole. Therefore it includes myself, as soon as I present that. Out of all this God makes the sign of *him*self. God is thus the signified of which the signifier is everything else whatever — as soon as that is realized not just as one body or some collection of bodies but as *the* body. Words exist by differentiation from each other, and so in multiplicity, like the Law; but every body is presently the body — or so the cult "says."

Sin in the body is uncleanliness: morbidity, *in*sanity, *im*purity. The root idea here is probably the integrity of the natural body, which is lost by death, decay, sickness, the breach of its boundaries or the distortion of its structures. The negative commandment which applies in this context is therefore purification by exclusion, quarantine or *herem*. The complementary positive is the best that can be done in a pure or integral state; of which sacrifice is the type. There are advantages which correspond to the risks of so "regressive" a vocabulary. Moral language, for instance, is obliged to remain general even at its most severe. It is classes of action which can be forbidden or commanded ahead of time. The cultic idiom on the other hand is utterly concrete. It is always some actual creature which must be killed and

104

burned — and sometimes eaten. The mortal world can be sur-vived and the kingdom of God come — to just this extent. From a distance to be sure it may seem that sacrifice is only imaginary. The creature I kill, after all, is *not* myself, nor is the flesh of any body the same as its soul. I can therefore seem doubly removed from my own action. This alienation may stand behind the prophetic distrust of the cult. But it should be remembered that within the act of sacrifice, metaphoricity is in fact consumed along with every other species of difference. What is enacted makes the soul one again with its body, and all bodies one with each other. The whole deed does occur — whether or not the individual concerned goes along. What counts within a cultic action is life and death and life restored; not the consciousness of the offerer, which may or may not accompany what takes place. For once the body is allowed in, it tends to mean whatever it says. In this respect sacrifice resembles other actions which involve the actual flesh: eating, copulation, warfare.

Meanwhile the Law protects itself by insisting that only inadvertent sins can be done away with by acts of sacrifice, which makes good ethical sense: deliberate sin ought to be dealt with in the same context within which it has been committed, that is, by punishment or repentance or both. Punishment is the simpler case: the sin "with hand on high" must be followed, the commandment says, by excommunication: the perpetrator must be cut off from the people by death or exile. The addition of repentance though permits a recombination of the moral with the cultic. For in repentance, as we observed, I retroactively annul whatever was deliberate in my previous action. Thereby I convert my sin into an inadvertent error — of the sort that may be legitimately purged away in a cultic demonstration.

This mode of resolving potential conflict may be seen as well in the ritual for the Day of Atonement itself, the most important occasion for the performance of expiatory sacrifice. The Levitican account combines pre-exilic elements with what was to become the post-exile practice. On *Yom Kippur* the high priest offered a bullock for his own sins and those of his house during the previous year. Then he chose by lot one of two goats to offer for the sins of the people at large. The blood of the bullock and the goat was smeared upon the golden cover of the ark or *kapporeth* in the holy of holies instead of being smeared on the horns of the main altar as usual. The carcasses of the two animals were burned outside the camp. The sins of Israel were then confessed over the head of the second goat, which was driven off into the wilderness. The two halves of this half "modern," half archaic ritual thus intensify respectively the positive and negative commandments. The blood of the victims is brought that much more closely before God, whose throne is imagined as rising directly above the *kapporeth*. And the sins, placed upon

106

the scapegoat, are driven as far away as possible. In effect the two goats divide a single intention: sin is absolutely denied and excluded, *and* the most complete sacrifice possible is made, at one and the same time.

It is understood moreover that the ritual of the Day of Atonement could expiate deliberate as well as inadvertent sin, unlike the usual sacrifices of the kind. But the same rule continues to apply. For voluntary sin could be expiated by the rituals of the Day only when these were accompanied by fasting and repentance — which in effect enact a repudiation of sin on the scale of the individual in bodily and moral terms respectively. *Then* forgiveness may be hoped for, as the mode in which the Lord will be with his people in spite of their failings, and so with each individual among them.

2

Once the moral and the cultic dimensions of the covenantal relation are reconciled it becomes easier to comprehend other features of the tradition: the food laws for instance. Some food is eaten sacramentally; that is, within the third category. To consume the roasted flesh of a communion sacrifice is to experience the fulfillment of the promise in the mode of bodily nourishment. But ordinary food is prohibited or allowed within the second category. Unclean foods are subject to a negative commandment. Clean foods are subject to a positive command. This makes eating the permitted foods an act in parallel with the act of sacrifice. The idea that eating can be "sacrificial" as well as sacramental seems very Jewish: one may remember the *un*leavened break at Passover, or the *bitter* herbs. There can be then an obedient as well as a festive consumption. The food laws thus paradoxically associate this kind of eating with fasting, its physical opposite. An apparently self-serving action is thus re-defined religiously as a mode of worship. A more recent example of this kind of reasoning is the traditional Catholic practice of eating fish on Fridays. The basic commandment in that context was, do *not* eat meat. To eat fish then stood in for the complementary positive, which would otherwise be to fast altogether. The rules applied to Adam in the garden provide another example, quite in the "P" style: thou shalt *not* eat of the tree of knowledge, but thou *shalt* eat of every other tree — including (apparently) the tree of life. This was *kashrut* for him.

And there are other contexts within the "P" work susceptible to a covenantal interpretation in sacrificial terms. One of the most prominent is artefacture. The first major block of priestly material in Exodus is devoted to an elaborate description of the cultic equipment. This is put in Moses' mouth as a series of positive instructions. To put together the tabernacle and its furnishings is to carry out what amounts to a sacrifice in the mode of making things for God. The doubling of the description enforced by the arrangement of the Sinai narrative before and after the episode of the golden calf allows for a repetition of this idea in two different keys. The initial set of instructions is couched in the second person singular *wav*-consecutive perfect; that is, the imperfect: *thou shalt make.* Then comes the sin of the people, after which the covenant, so freshly made and broken, is once more reconstituted. This time around the work is actually done: the ark, the rings, the staves, the ark-cover, the cherubim, the candlestick, the tabernacle with its complicated structure of curtains and boards, the altar, the priests' garments, and the rest. It is made to seem like hard, careful work, for the text is remorselessly repetitive and detailed. This time the verbs are in the *wav*-consecutive imperfect: that is, the perfect: *he* or *they do* in fact *make* whatever-it-is. For the most

109

part this work is done by "him," the ideal singular artisan, though sometimes he is named Bezabel or Ithmar.
The third person then represents whoever among the
people is wise of heart and stirred to do the work will-
ingly. In something more than a grammatical sense,
then, the work is indeed all the deed of one person; as
the result, however many and various its pieces, is essentially singular. This ideal "he" is then rhetorically the
same person as the "thou" who receives the orders in
the first place; "thou" dramatically is "he" narratively.
And both are therefore representative of *myself,* as soon
as either is in relation to Somebody Else to the infinite
degree and so accomplishing whatever is worthy and
just in that relation. Such work is a true *avodah:* that is,
a sacrifice. For the work of the artisans is repeated in the
work of the priests for whom the equipment is intended,
as the work of the priests culminates in that of Aaron,
who bears the names of the twelve tribes upon his
shoulders "for a memorial" (Ex. 28:12) as he performs
his duties. To perform as priest is to enact the intention
embodied in all these variously beautiful things in one
implicitly singular deed accomplished by the nation as a
whole in the person of its ideal representative.

And within the narrative as we have it this complex
sacrifice bears fruit. First the parts of the tabernacle are
ordered; then, after the golden calf episode, they are
made; lastly they are placed. And finally, after "Moses
completed the work" (Ex. 40:33), "the cloud covered

the tent of meeting, and the glory of the Lord filled the tabernacle" (Ex. 40:34) — which is to say, an *avodah* in the second category is matched by a sacramental fulfillment of the promise in the third.

Whoever reàds slowly through the long list of instructions which precedes this climax, and it is slow reading, may find him or herself especially impressed by the repetition of the phrase describing the colors appointed for the curtains to be used around the holy places and for the liturgical garments. *T'kelat v'argamon toleat shni v'shesh mash'zar ma'asseh chosev* the words go, over and over again: "blue, deep blue; purple; worm-crimson; and fine linen twisted, the work of the weaver," Such language is too rarely translated literally enough. The dyes, from shellfish and worms, must, one imagines, have generated deep, strong colors, the colors of creation indeed; like a room full of Rothko paintings, a modern reader may think. In the sanctuary these hangings were additionally woven to show cherubim. Such work, actual or imagined, inherited or hoped for, would magnificently represent the possibility of sacrifice in the mode of artefacture; and so the place of the imagination in the religious life. For the repetition of the words repeats the work almost in the style of a hymn, though the instructions are literally in the direst and most technical prose. Pedantry is poetry. To do such things for the Lord, in woven cloth or written words, is to sing with one's hands. It is to make a new body out of the body's interaction with other bodies, and to give that body up: which is in fact what occurs in animal sacrifice — or, we might also recollect, in the original sacrifice of Isaac, which, some later authorities were to agree, stood behind the animal sacrifices to render them efficacious.

The section on the sanctuary presumably represents priestly memories of the tabernacle of David's time, before Solomon could build the first stone temple. Incorporated within this complex image of that complicated erection may also be still older traditions reaching back into the desert period. So memory represents anticipation, as in the parallel scheme offered in Ezekiel, roughly contemporary with this rendering. This text is as always in transition between past and future. The composition of the tabernacle is especially prominent, we might guess, in part also because it represents in the order of ritual the act of putting together the Pentateuch as a whole in the order of narration. Literature replaces liturgy, as well as recollects and predicts it. For written composition is "P's" peculiar art, and like that of those fathers whose names he repeats, a service amounting to a sacrifice in the mode of artefacture. Indeed he calls the skill of the artisan a kind of wisdom; in which case wisdom too might be understood as a kind of skill — and the other words eventually assembled under that head still another species of sacrifice in the mode of artefacture. The wise man could then be understood as putting together wise sayings, hymns, and stories, fictional or historical, in the same spirit in which the artisans of the sanctuary fabricated their works of liturgical art. If so, we would have another way in which to reconcile the priestly with the scribal traditions, which the wisdom books exemplify.

History as well as art can also be interpreted in cultic as well as in the more familiar ethical terms. The regulations for the release of slaves at the Jubilee, for instance, show how the Exodus event too could be understood within the "P" perspective as an action corresponding to sacrifice within the cult. All slaves are to "go out" from their bondage in the year of Jubilee, says Lev. 25:54-55; "For I caused the sons of Israel to come out from their bondage in Egypt, and now they are all servants of mine, and no longer slaves of men." The Jubilee thus repeats the Exodus on the scale of the contemporary enslaved individual. Slavery to other Hebrews is a repetition of the bondage the nation as a whole once suffered under foreigners. The institution could not be done away with altogether. But at least the master could be ordered not to lord it over his slaves with rigor. That makes a minimum version of the negative commandment. And the corresponding positive allows the slave to "go out" when the holy year comes round. If this act of manumission is to be ranked as a positive deed, it too must count as a species of sacrifice. And if it is placed in parallel with the Exodus of the

whole people from Egypt, that event too is made imaginatively equivalent to a cultic act. The slavery of the nation was incontestably a sin. The negative commandment in that context would be the order Pharoah repeatedly disobeyed. The positive commandment was to
leave — so that the people might present themselves before God. Thus the sons of Israel could become servants of the Lord instead of slaves of men. The complementary third category event along this line would still
be the occupation of the land. For "P" as for "D" this
possession is not absolute but sacramental. The story of
the distribution by lot in Numbers 26 confirms as
much. The census which precedes this distribution is
therefore still another equivalent to sacrifice — which
would help explain the religious aura that continued to
hang about this procedure.

The land is a blessing, as the punishment of the rebellious generation is a curse. All blessings are religiously speaking the same blessing, as all curses are the
same curse. The blessing, whenever it takes effect, is the
promise indicatively fulfilled. It therefore obtains within
the third category. The curse correspondingly takes effect within the second category. It represents an abandonment to the negative which is the essence of that category in every context. Thus it is possible for Leviticus
26 to understand the Exile as a consequence of the
curse. If there were no covenant, all history would occur entirely within the second category, and the curse

would be absolute. For those who stand within the covenant, though, a curse can take the form of a punishment; that is, it can have limits. The nation is given over to sin and the punishment for sin, but not forever. *L'olam* applies only to the promise. Eventually the sin may be cancelled by suffering and repentance. Then the covenant can be reconstituted — and the sacrifices renewed. At the close of Leviticus, then, the "P" work makes contact with and repeats the arguments characteristic of "D."

The most important appropriation of history within the "P" perspective though is not the Exodus or the fall of the kingdoms but the cosmic history of mankind as a whole. It is "P" who deliberately places the story of creation at the beginning of the assemblage of traditions he has taken in hand to put in order. In the first chapter of Genesis God speaks out his "breath" in words which generate things. *Y'hi or,* he says, "let there be light"; and there *is* light: *v'y'hi or.* Such a sequence could obtain only within the third category. In the sphere of the flesh, Everybody knows, the thing comes first and the word second. The first category is sheer existence, not creation. And if one tries to make sense of existence, one arrives at some myth of origins — or at the idea of evolution, the modern equivalent, religiously speaking, of the Babylonian stories "P" is reacting against.

Which means, paradoxically, that the creation story which now stands at the head of the Pentateuch must be understood as presupposing sacrifice rather than as setting the scene for it. Creation comes later rather than earlier theologically as well in editorial sequence. There is an important sense in which the beginning of Genesis comes *after* the "end of the world" threatened by the prophets or re-imagined in the apocalypses. For the story Genesis tells can only be true in the Spirit, which always comes after the flesh has been concluded. Something of the principle implicit in this choice of position must have been understood by John as he composed the introduction to his gospel. For to him incarnation is a repetition of creation. Both are third category events; and both presuppose the accomplishment of a sacrifice which in chronological order comes later. For this perspective the "pre-existent" Christ is a post-crucified Christ: we begin the Bible, as it were, posthumously, in the true kingdom of God.

D

Behold a man, Shoot is his name, and from his place he shall shoot, and build the temple of the Lord; and he will build the temple of the Lord; and he will bear the glory, and shall sit and rule on his throne . . .
— Zech. 6:12-13

It is possible, then, to bring the cult and the practices and traditions which cohere around it into the covenantal structure once this has been outlined in such a way as to leave room for other sorts of content besides the moral. So the "P" work need not represent a contradiction to or even an alternative to the "D" approach, different as they evidently are. There can be more difficulty with the other major version of the covenant besides the covenant of Sinai, that is, the promise to David.

Nathan's prophecy in II Sam. 7 is the key text here. Through Nathan the Lord reminds David that he has been picked to lead Israel from following the sheep, and that "I have been with thee" in battle, where all David's enemies have been defeated. In the future the Lord promises to make him a "great name" and to establish Israel securely in its own land. Then comes the central prophecy: "the Lord makes clear to thee that the Lord will make for thee a house." Once David dies, "I shall set up thy seed after thee, which shall proceed from thy inwards, and I shall establish his kingdom. He it is that shall build a house for my name, and I will establish the throne of his kingdom forever" (II Sam. 7:12-13). In Jewish exegesis this "seed" is assumed to have been Solomon, who did indeed build a temple, as David was forbidden to do. But through all of the monarchical period and for long after the promise was held to apply as well to the Davidic dynasty as a whole. It may be, as T.N.D. Mettinger holds in his recent *King and Messiah,* that this difference reflects different versions of Nathan's prophecy. In any event the anonymous historian has combined any possible sources to extend the scope of the promise. In that form it persisted through many changes until, some anecdotes indicate, well after the time of Jesus. "Forever" is a powerful word.

But that dangerous *ad olam* is not the only difficulty the prophecy entails. For immediately after promising a perpetual dynasty, the Lord tells David through the mouth of Nathan that the promise just made will have no conditions. "In case of his sinning, I will chasten him with the rod of men, and with the stripes of the children of men. But my mercy shall not depart from him" (II Sam. 7:14-15) — as *had* happened to Saul. Neither in this initial rendering nor in I Chron. 17:1-15, which repeats it, is any stipulation made. It is a promise in what M. Weinfeld has called the "royal grant" style with a vengeance. But if there are absolutely no conditions, could the promise so established be fairly named covenantal at all?

118

Some other renderings of what is none the less called the covenant with David confirm the book of Samuel in rehearsing its unconditional character. In the blessing of Jacob at the close of Genesis the verse "The sceptre shall not depart from Judah" (Gen. 49:10) would apparently represent the Davidist "J's" understanding that this promise was unconditional. Psalm 89 is a more prominent instance of the same kind. So is Psalm 2, in which the famous affirmation that "thou are my son, and I this day have begotten thee" is unmatched by any complementary request. Psalm 72 does include an expectation that the king will do justice to the poor and needy, but this is not construed as obligatory. It is simply one more manifestation of his God-given glory. Psalm 110 is even less qualified in its praise of the monarch. To be sure Psalm 132 includes some stanzas which make the royal covenant conditional. F.M. Cross in his *Canaanite Myth and Hebrew Epic* (pp. 232-233) has accordingly dated these stanzas earlier than the other renderings, so as to make it consistent with Sinai from the start! In his view Solomon is the source of the subversive unconditional version. But this seems on the face of it implausible: it is clearly David who is the religious innovator, not his son.

Elsewhere in the "Deuteronomistic history" we can see additional evidence of a need to recast the royal promise into conditional terms. Ancient scribes could be as scandalized by amorality as modern scholars. Thus the

119

"last words" of David in II Sam. 23 seems to require "righteousness" of a ruler who expects to enjoy the benefits of the "everlasting covenant." In I Kgs. 2:3-4 David is made to rehearse the covenant in explicitly conditional language as he presents the kingdom to his son Solomon in old age; but the lines in question are probably introduced by the Deuteronomistic redactor to enforce just this point. I Kgs. 2:33 promises David continued peace for himself and his house because he is guiltless of the attack on Joab, which would imply a conditional understanding of the relation. When Solomon prays in the temple he has built in I Kgs. 8:25 he repeats the promises as if they were conditional: the Lord has said that "there shall not be cut off from thee a man from before my face sitting on the throne of Israel if only the sons of Israel keep their way, to walk before my face in the manner in which thou hast walked before my face." This certainly conditional in form, if morally still somewhat ambiguous. I Kgs. 6:12 is similar. I Kgs. 9:4-5 is a degree stronger: the Lord tells Solomon that *if* he walks before him as David did, that is, so as to do all that is commanded and to keep the statutes and ordinances, *then* his throne will be established forever as promised.

The ambiguity persists through the following generations. In II Kgs. 8:19 the narrator says that the Lord would not destroy Judah in spite of the wickedness of Jehoram because of the promise to David, which im-

120

plies an unconditional understanding. But when Jehoida the priest makes a covenant between Jehoash the child king and the people on one side and the Lord on the other, it is firmly conditional: the people commit themselves to be the Lord's, which involves execution of the usurper queen Athaliah and eradication of Baalism as well as an oath to the rightful monarch, while the king for his part promises to do justice. *Then,* the implication runs, the Lord will once again be with them both. In II Kgs. 21:7-8 the Lord repeats the promise in a completely conditional sense; but these are the days of Manasseh and the conditions are defied. We should presumably not understand the northern kingdom as constituted on the basis of a royal covenant as well as Judah, but in any case the prophecy that Ahijah repeats to Jeroboah in I Kgs. 11:38 is thoroughly conditional: *if* the new king of the new kingdom will keep the statutes and the commandments, the Lord will be with him, too, and build a sure house for him, as he did for David.

On the whole the effect of these repetitions and revisions is to normalize the royal promise in terms of Sinai by (re-) introducing the missing condition. And this is of course what one would expect of histories written or revised under Deuteronomic influence. Then the "statutes and ordinances" fill up the space apparently left open within the second category. But a more profound and perhaps original candidate for the same position is already suggested by the primary story in II Sam. 7 and the chapters following. There we are told that David must *not* build a "house" for the Lord, but that his son should. The implicit obligation presumed by the new gift would then be the construction of a temple. If so, the principle of reciprocity is restored, and with it an appropriate content for a full covenantal exchange, without either calling upon or subverting the ethical demands of the Law. A new dynastic promise to the king would be matched by a new cultic obligation imposed on his successor and their descendants. The two "houses" would then balance, a common word mediating between the two halves of the covenant in the familiar way. Such an understanding would appear confirmed by the course of events: David did in fact shift the cult center to his new royal city, and Solomon did in fact change the old tent for a new temple. And the construction of the "house" (the word is stressed) in I Kings 6 and 7, with many details of measurement and luxury quite in the "P" style, makes Solomon another repetition of those craftsmen who put together the tabernacle in the wilderness. Now he too "builds, makes, carves, and overlays," his royal command effectuating yet one more sacrifice in the mode of artefacture.

If the implicit condition, then, is the relocation of the covenant center and the building of a proper temple, this "new" covenant would in fact parallel the "old" on its cultic side — once that had been assimilated to the general structure. For the construction and maintenance of a permanent sanctuary would then become a completion in the new monarchical circumstances of the old positive commandment to worship the Lord according to his directions in the complementary modes of artefacture and sacrifice. This double positive would then in turn correspond to a logically antecedent negative, to shun idolatry — the very sin of which the kings of David's line were so often to be accused. If so, the Davidic covenant could be read off in full in the usual way: do *not* follow after strange gods *but* worship the Lord in his holy "house" AND I will then maintain your "house" forever; that is, for as long as this implicit condition is carried out. In which case the fact that the temple and the dynasty disappear together could become theologically significant as well as historically decisive. For when a second temple is rebuilt after the exile, the liturgy is conducted under priestly rather than royal auspices. The idea of sacrifice is separated altogether from the idea of a dynasty. The covenant with David could then be understood as coming in with the monarchy and a cult presided over by the king and going out with both — until the ideal future, when both might be ultimately restored.

There is an interesting prolongation of the "house" theme through the rest of the story of David, where it appears negatively in the various sins he commits and the punishments to which these are subject. His covenant does not require private virtue of this *messiah*, nor does he display it on his own. He destroys Uriah's "house," stealing his officer's wife Bathsheba and sending the deceived husband into battle to his death. Thus David becomes guilty simultaneously of rebellion against God, adultery, and murder. As king he cannot be brought before any human court. Nor can he lose the benefits of a promise which apparently has been unconditional with respect to such matters at least as far as he is concerned. But he is punished all the same; ironically, by a repetition of the same sins within his own "house" — and under conditions which make it impossible for him to punish them. David's son Ammon rapes his half-sister Tamar, and cannot be taken up for his crime by his father, though two years later David's second son Absolam kills his half-brother in an act of private vengeance. David cannot bring himself to punish this crime either. Instead he allows himself to be tricked into recalling Absolam to court. A sexual crime and a murder thus repeat the adultery with Bathsheba and the death of Uriah. Whereupon Absolam revolts against his father, as his father had revolted against God. All this is most subtly worked out in the characteristic "secular" style of the Deuteronomistic historian: events of themselves illustrate the moral changes in the relation between David and the Lord, as they are eventually to do for the nation as a whole. If history *is* theology, as this author can afford to believe, then all crime is eventually punished if not by explicit human justice, as the Law demands, then by further crime, domestic or international, which will in due course reveal the implicit justice of God. God enforces his Law, even when men fail. So the moral balance too is eventually kept, even when nobody stands by to point it out in so many editorial words.

2

Within the text as we have it, then, there are ways to accommodate the Davidic covenant to the general structure both cultically and morally. Other explanations are possible if one looks behind the story to its possible historical background. An impressive part of that background is evidently the patriarchal covenant. R.E. Clements has argued that the promissory character of the relation with David should be understood as a deliberate repetition of the same element in the covenant with Abraham. There would have been, he believes, a historical link between the patriarch and the king by way of Hebron, where Abraham, we are told, built an altar (Gen. 13:18). There, thinks Clements, Abraham and his tribe would have made a covenant with El Shaddai, the god of the locality, exchanging permission to occupy the neighborhood for religious loyalty. The memory of this arrangement could have been handed down as the legend of that cult center, to become eventually the ancestral story of the "house of Judah" as a whole. David's association with Hebron and with the other sub-tribes of what may have been a southern confederacy within a larger amphyctyony is already attested. His own covenant could then have been consciously modelled on the older story. The promise of the Lord would have been unconditional for him because it had been uncond' ional for the Patriarch. As

Abraham was promised the land about Hebron, so David would have been promised an empire over greater Israel. The "J" writer, re-composing the story of the patriarchs from a deliberately Davidic perspective, would then have retold the older story in such a way as to emphasize the likeness between what for him have been a prophecy and its fulfillment.

But one need not rely entirely on such "traditio-historical" inferences to locate a connection between the Davidic revolution and Abraham. By capturing the Jebusite city and shifting the cult center there David established the ark in physical coincidence with the tradition that upon the same ridge Abraham had offered Isaac to God. Geographical association would of itself have connected his covenant with that of the patriarch, for propinquity, in religious affairs, is synonymy. By way of Abraham Sinai could in effect be shifted to Moriah, as Moses could be repeated in David himself. With Jerusalem as the new capital, a city is at last accepted as an image for religious centricity: monarchy and urbanism come in together, along with a cult elaborate enough to require a permanent temple. These are major changes — and they all occur together. No wonder if they required a new version of the covenant to articulate them — as well as, in the next generation, a new text to celebrate or lament the history thus providentially renewed.

Once one has come to terms with unconditionality, one is free to confront monarchy, the other major element within the Davidic revolution. The prophecy of Nathan ratifies kingship as religiously relevant in spite of its non-Mosaic "modernity." The difficulty at the time and since would have been to settle what *kind* of royalty could be assimilated into the structure of the covenant. For the court party the king had to be as sacramental as prophecy or the charismatic "judges" the king was to replace. A "J" reference in the Pentateuch accepts this requirement: in Numbers 24:17 Balaam prophesies "I see him, but not now; I behold him, but not nigh; there shall step forth a star out of Jacob, and a screptre shall rise out of Israel," who shall lead the people to victory over Moab and Edom. Thus a "messianic" king, actual or potential, is a blessing to be hoped for, the chief public way in which the Lord may be expected to accompany his people. Whenever a true king appeared, then, his authority would be essentially spiritual, however powerful or weak he might seem in the flesh.

In this crucial respect he would differ from the kings of the nations, as well as from all warlords, usurpers, rebels, or even elected kings within Israel, who must manifest themselves entirely within the second category. Some may seem "legitimate," others very much the reverse; but their authority is in any case no more than human. If, like modern kings, it is authorized by custom or descent, it derives its legitimacy from the first category. If it is self-made, like that of other modern leaders, it occurs exclusively within the second category, the active possibilities of which it typifies. The contrasting favorable and unfavorable attitudes towards kingship in I Samuel 8 and 9 would then represent a clash between opposing definitions of the role as well as between the theocratic and royal parties of the day. When Samuel does at length anoint Saul, following the direct instructions of the Lord, he makes sure that Saul will be to that extent a king within the third category — as well as a war leader within the second. Saul is the first *messiah,* blessed (for as long as he keeps it) by the Spirit. Such a royalty derives its legitimacy directly from the will of God — as even David at his most desperate and ambitious is depicted as recognizing.

The fact that a king in Israel should be a third category pneumenon is obviously determinative for later messianism, which can be interpreted as the survival of the possibility after the actuality has ceased to be probable. The presence of this possibiltiy could then have given presumptive legitimacy to the conclusion passed on in the New Testament that Jesus was a king; as well as to the apparently opposite conclusion, just as strongly enforced, that he was *not* a king. Jesus, we may securely infer, was no worldly monarch or pretender in his own eyes (though his Roman enemies then and some theologians since have interpreted him as one). But the Davidic (or Saulic) tradition would have made it at least theoretically possible for him to be a king within the third category — without being a king within the second category at all. In that case the *titulum* over the cross, another secure item within the tradition, need not be only sarcastic.

But if the Davidic monarch derives his authority from his sacramental identity, his normal function is entirely within the second category — like the Law, which in this respect as in others he acts to specify in the concrete. His moral task in this world is to combat external enemies and to see to it that the statutes and ordinances are enforced internally. Thus he implements both the negative and the positive commandments, drawing the line in the "not/but." It is for the "wisdom" to do this properly that Solomon prays in I Kings 3:4-15, and we read there that this was granted him. Thus the good king "justifies" the gift he has received and guarantees that the nation will continue to deserve the communal priveleges that correspond to the virtue he enforces. So Psalm 72, which concludes the first or Davidic "book" of psalms, prays that the Lord may "give thy judgements to the king, and thy righteousness to the son of the king, that he may judge thy people in justice, and thy poor with judgement." The negative of this identity is the wicked king, who is inconsistent with his own principle; though even the worst actions cannot cancel his divine appointment. The king is thus in his own person another common "word" with meaning on both sides of the relation. This double understanding informs

Deuteronomy 17, which might be understood as the answer of the moralistic tradition to the more extravagant pretensions of the court party. It is admitted there that the king is a sacrament provided he is indeed chosen by the Lord. But the various duties anxiously outlined are scrupulously within the second category. The king must *not* be a foreigner, or multiply horses, or wives, or silver and gold. Instead he is to make a copy of the Law and read it and keep it, so that he will not be lifted up or turned aside. Then he may expect that his days will be prolonged. Otherwise he will deserve to be cast down like the rest of the nation he has led into sin. The king has a "divine right" to *be* king, then, but only that; the rest of his conduct is entirely up to him, and will be estimated in the same terms as that of his subjects. From a Deuteronomic point of view, monarchy is a very minimal sacrament.

3

In another kind of book, prophecy would have to bulk far larger than it does here. But in such a review as we are making of the major covenantal moments the indispensable comment can be reduced almost to the scale of an appendix. For prophecy, in spite of its variety and prominence, is structurally very simple. It fits with far less difficulty than either the cult or the monarchy into the standard moral version of the covenantal equilibrium. For the prophet, early or late, is no rival to the Law but a witness to its authority as this may apply in some specific national emergency. His spoken word, like the king's deed, is in the concrete what the written word is in general terms. So he *applies* the covenant — either as judgement within the second category or promise within the third.

This is as true narratively for the legendary prophets as it is argumentatively for the literary prophets later on. In the Deuteronomistic stories, the prophet acts out the whole of the covenantal stipulation so that the promise may be fulfilled, either in immediate representation or in future hope. So when Elijah repeats the words of the Lord, that "the jar of meal shall not be spent, neither shall the cruise of oil fail" (I Kgs. 17:14), that promise is sure to come true in the widow's house "according to the word of the Lord" (I Kgs. 17:16). When he prays that the soul of the widow's child should come back, it does (I Kgs. 17:21-22). In the contest with the priests of Baal, Elijah prays that God will demonstrate the difference between the false and the true God — and a fire from heaven descends to consume the bullock, the wet wood, the stones of the altar, the dust from the ground, and the water in the ditch (I Kgs. 18:36-38). When he tells Ahab he may feast for the rain is coming and the drought is past, it rains (I Kgs. 18:41-45). In all these cases Elijah acts within the second category both to rebuke the king and to slay all false prophets, that is, to enforce the negative commandment in a specific situation, and then to predict what God will do, that is, to satisfy the positive commandment in the form of an exceptionally effectual prayer. Thus he personally acts out the whole of that obedience from which the nation as a whole and its monarch in particular have fallen away — which in turn makes it possible for God to keep his side of the covenantal promise with an equivalent concreteness to this representative of Israel as it ought to be.

The prophet is juxtaposed against the king in the second category as a man of words in contrast to the man of deeds. In principle, deeds should count for more than words. But if the deeds are *not* done, words alone may still be decisive. If kings were true, prophets would not be needed. The story of Elisha and Joash in II Kgs. 13 can illustrate this reciprocity within the category. Joash the king of Israel visits Elisha on his deathbed. The prophet tells the king to take a bow and arrow and

133

open the window to the east. Then he lays his own hands upon the king's hands, and tells him to shoot the arrow out of the window. This gesture acts out the war against Aram the prophet is asking for and the king is to execute. Similarly the prophet tells the king to smite the earth with his sword. This the king does but only three times: which means, Elisha tells Joash, that he will win against Aram but only thrice: he will not quite annihilate the enemy, as he should have done had he struck the ground more often. Thus the prophet's words become the king's symbolic deeds, which in turn prefigure the king's actual deeds — which should accomplish negative justice both within and without the nation. Words and deeds together specify the commandments under the covenant. History and prophecy between them are the Law *spelled out.*

The words of Elijah all take place within the second category. The miracles in the third category occur upon his prayer, but they are accomplished by God. Elisha though is dowered with a "double share" of his "father's" spirit. He is accordingly represented as able to accomplish miracles within the third category on his own initiative. He extends the widow's oil, assures a son to a barren woman, cleanses a pot of poisonous food by casting meal into it, and multiplies food for a crowd. In all these episodes he behaves more like Jesus than Elijah. When Naaman the leper appears, Elisha tells him to wash seven times in the Jordan. This is a positive

134

commandment as far as the king is concerned. *Then,* says Elisha, his flesh will come back to him and he will be clean. Is this promise a prediction that God will be good, on the model of Elijah's prayers, or is it an act of his own will and power? The story is ambiguous. He makes the promise so that a foreign potentate may realize there is a prophet in Israel, which suggests personal power. But later he accepts no reward, which implies that the cure is not his own deed. In such cases it is possible to say that a prophet may also act within the third category as well as speak within the second.

With the literary and therefore less legendary prophets there is no such ambiguity. Their words function entirely within the second category in the "normal" way, though like the kings their authorization is originally charismatic. The prophetic message is not complex in principle, however complicated in detail. The book of Isaiah, for instance, notoriously bristles with difficulties of all kinds. The problems of authorship and date are knotty; the different oracles are confusing and perhaps confused — and the amateur Hebraist finds the vocabulary dauntingly large. But the underlying structure is remarkably simple. The prophet speaks in the name of the holy one of Israel to condemn the sins of the people; to predict punishment for these sins by means of a foreign power; and then to prophecy punishment of the punisher for *his* sin in attacking Israel. Thus all the oracles of judgement repeat the negative commandments of the Law. The complementary positive would be represented by a renewed allegiance as long as that is still possible. If though the blow has already fallen so that hope cannot be sustained, the prophet or his spiritual heir is also authorized to predict a restoration of a chastened remnant under an ideal king who *will* be faithful. This hope of salvation represents Somebody's idea of what Somebody Else to the infinite degree might yet do to fulfill the promise from the farther side. It amounts to a constant member in the third category corresponding to the multiple judgements mobilized within the second.

There is a typical miniature of this familiar prophetic dialectic in a story which appears toward the close of Jeremiah. In chapter 34 we read that during the siege of Jerusalem the king Zedekiah made a covenant with the princes and the people that they should release their slaves. This is apparently intended as a deliberate renewal of a sufficiently representative element of the total covenant, adopted in the hope of persuading the Lord that the people's hearts had changed, so that the siege might be lifted and the nation saved even at that last moment. But then an invasion from Egypt forces Nebuchadnezzar to withdraw from the siege; and the leaders of the people, thinking all would be well again, take their slaves back. Whereupon the word of the Lord comes to Jeremiah that the king of Babylon will return and the city fall after all. In punishment for their sin,

136

the bodies of the slave owners will remain unburied. The episode rehearses the basic covenantal motifs in brief epitome, from the self-consciously archaic ritual of cutting a lamb in two halves to the moral conclusions drawn by the prophet. Not only had the people sinned in general and for many generations against the original covenant, they had also sinned all over again against the particular covenant they had just made. That covenant to be sure was between men, not directly with God; but God, we learn from this and similar episodes, invariably interprets covenants established between men as if they were made with him. And the prophet is the voice of that judgement.

Isaiah and Jeremiah and the other prophets officially so called are explicitly inspired in the third category to re-specify the commandments within the second for the contingencies of their day. As such they are gifts of God for the instruction of men — and both within a Sinaitic understanding of the covenantal relation. But the greatest prophet of this kind may not be Somebody the tradition could call by that or any other name. Deuteronomy repeats Moses word by word. We do not know who could have found himself authorized to take such a liberty *in writing*. (It is hard to believe it could have been a "school," however learned or wise.) But we do have one clue in the text. I am struck by the suggestion made by H.J. Kraus in his *Worship in Israel* that the famous "eschatalogical" promise of a prophet "like"

137

Moses in Dt. 18:15 should be understood in the first place as fulfilled by the very words we read (pp. 105-112). "D" is so very "like" Moses as virtually to disappear into him. The other prophets re-specify what is already generalized in the Law in their own words. "D" repeats the Law verbatim, as nearly as he can. But he too functions as we have seen, within the same covenantal situation as his fellows. He too must have understood himself as inspired, to undertake such a work. So his authority derives from the third category. Yet all his work is in the second, there to recommend yet once more the positive and negative commandments as these have been handed down. That is what there is to do there within this version of the covenant, whoever one is.

PART III

Reconciling the Covenants

*For no one of us lives to himself, and no one dies to himself;
for if we live, we live to the Lord, and if we die, to the Lord
we die. Therefore whether we live or whether we die, we are
the Lord's.*
— Rom. 14:7-8

"It is impossible," writes D.J. McCarthy towards
the close of his standard review of the topic, "to bring
all the interpretations of the various covenants together
under one definition . . . There are problems in the relation of the promise to Abraham with the covenant with
him. There are problems in the relation of the Abrahamic covenant with the Davidic. Most of all, there are
problems in the relation of the Sinaitic and the Davidic
covenants" (*OT Covenant,* p. 85). There are problems
indeed, as we have seen; but it should be some encour-
agement to realize that the last and most serious is already being addressed at various points along the real
or hypothetical development of the OT itself, long before Christianity (or Christian scholarship, that much
later after the fact) was obliged to come to term with it.

David already had to, and his royal descendants after him. Whoever combined the Sinai stories of "J" and "E" would presumably have had to think of himself as working out a textual reconciliation between the old traditions of Moses and the new claims of David. We have already seen how the Deuetronomic tradition handled the problem. Later still, the Chronicler shows David assigning Solomon the task of building the temple — and enjoining on his son the obligation of maintaining the commandments and ordinances as a condition for the security of his sovereignty (I Chron. 28:6-8). And several Psalms reflect the same effort of com-position.

Modern students have simultaneously identified and repeated these earlier efforts at reconciliation within the generalizing idiom of a "neutral" scholarship. John Bright's standard *History of Israel,* for instance, argues that Isaiah reconciled the Sinaitic and the Davidic versions (to the second of which, as a passionate Zionist, that prophet was committed) by interpreting the Assyrian attack as punishment for the breach of the former and reaffirming the latter as offering a promise for the future (pp. 278-279). J.L. McKenzie, moving farther along this line, argues in his tartly summary *Theology of the OT* that the permanence promised in the covenant with David had better be understood as essentially a repetition of the permanence already attributed to the Sinaitic covenant. If David's dynasty is promised an eternal reign, that extravagance amounts to a repetition within the new circumstances of the original extravagance, that the covenant with Israel would remain as constant as the will of the God who had initiated it (p. 25). To adopt this mode of reconciliation though would be to pass over the suggestion, intermittent in the OT and repeated by later scholars, that with the fall of Jerusalem the Sinai covenant was abrogated — which would leave only the promises to rely on. M.G. Kline has it seems to me arrived at a clearer rendering of the difference in such a way as to make a theoretical re-compostion easier. A "law" covenant is sworn, he observes in his *By Oath Consigned,* by men; a "promise" covenant by God. One is defined, that is, as a deed within the second category, the other as a complementary gift within the third. In that case neither need get in each other's theological way.

A practical reconciliation would in any case have been imposed by the presence of the king. When according to I Kgs. 8 Solomon and the Levites install the ark of the covenant in the holy of holies of the newly built temple they collaborate to act out a coincidence of Sinai and David. We are told by a narrative in which priestly tradition is confirmed by Deuteronomistic redaction that this common offering was accepted: the Lord appeared, it is said, as a cloud in the temple as once in the wilderness, for "the glory of the Lord filled the house of the Lord" (I Kgs. 8:11). Solomon's speech on this occasion presents him as virtually a new Moses quite in the Deuteronomic mode, praying in advance for the forgiveness Israel will need through all the generations to follow. Much later the Hezekiahan and Josiahan efforts at reform obviously repeat Sinai with a vengeance. The recovery and enforcement of Deuteronomy itself certainly amount to an implicit rejection of any confidence founded upon an amoral understanding of the promise to David. But the reform centralized the cult in David's city. And it was the king, we read, who was most affected by the reading of the Law and who promulgated the new instructions on his own authority as well as that of the book. Thus Josiah could stand in the place of Moses and Joshua (themselves, after all, implicitly "royal" figures) in this renewal of their covenant. If "David" could enforce Sinai, there need be no practical incompatibility between the two versions, whatever the intellectual difficulties.

We have observed that prophecy operates within a conditional understanding of the relation. This is certainly true for the oracles of judgement which make up the bulk of the prophetic inheritance. The relevance of the alternative formulation is felt chiefly in connection with the hopes for the future as these are expressed in the oracles of salvation. Jeremiah, for instance, is passionately "Deuteronomic;" and in severe conflict with the royal and priestly authorities of his day. But like Isaiah he too can confirm that after the necessary punishment a remnant will be restored — and a righteous shoot raised up to David. The extravagant promise is still to be kept, that is, but only after the moral debt has been cancelled. The covenant with David cannot be broken, says Jeremiah 33, any more than the covenant with Noah, which guarantees the day and the night: creation is confirmation for them both. The catastrophe must be put in terms of Sinai, but once judgement has been effected, the corresponding forgiveness can be represented by the unconditional promise.

So it would be both naive and unnecessary to see the conditional and unconditional versions as vying for the same moral space within the second category. Seen in that way, the Sinaitic must of course be preferred, as it always has been by the deuteronomistically minded of every age. If though it should become desirable to reconcile the two formally by enlarging one to take in the other, it would seem as imperative to follow "P" rather than "D" and think of the Mosaic version as included within the Davidic (or Abrahamic) rather than the other way around. Then the intelligible justice of God in the second category can be matched with his mysterious mercy in the third. Another way to put such an ideal combination would be to say with J. Jocz that the relation should be understood as conditional on Man's side and unconditional on God's. One consequence of any such re-structuring though is inconvenient: the attempt to accomodate both covenants together either practically or intellectually has the inadvertent effect of making them both seem more or less conditional. The Davidic covenant is the escape valve of the Sinaitic — until it is addressed on its own right, whereupon it turns back into an exchange like the other. There is no other way to *understand* it.

2

To seek out ways in which the different versions of what we are now on the verge of having to call the "old" covenant are already combined within the OT or might be reconciled theoretically is implicitly to begin upon a reconciliation of the OT as a whole with the New Testament, which offers a "new" covenant different from both previous versions, though evidently closer to one than the other. The key text for such an enterprise is of course Jeremiah 31:31, which is the connecting link between the OT and NT in something of the way that the Eucharist is the connecting link between the NT and the Church. The passage is worth quoting in full:

"Behold, the days are coming, says the Lord, when I will cut with the house of Israel and with the house of Judah a new covenant; not like the covenant which I cut with their fathers in the day I took them by the hand to bring them out of the land of Egypt; for they broke my covenant, though it was I who was lord over them, says the Lord. But this is the covenant which I will cut with the house of Israel after those days, says the Lord; I will give my law in their inward parts, and on their hearts I will write it; and I will be to them as their God, and they shall be to me as a people; and they shall not teach any more each man his neighbor and each man his brother so as to say, know the Lord, for all of them will know me, from the least of them to the greatest of them, says the Lord, for I will be forgiving towards their iniquity, and with respect to their sin I will remember no more." (Jer. 31:31-34).

This is the only passage in the OT *explicitly* invoking a new covenant. It is accordingly, as J. Coppens points out in an interesting article, the source for the corresponding references in the Qumran literature as well as the NT. It has not been easy to determine what Jeremiah meant by a Law which would be found in the inner parts of the house of Israel, or written upon their hearts. It has even been doubted that the pericope was Jeremiahan at all. The difficulty has been to settle whether this new covenant was to be a repetition of Sinai, only that much more thoroughly introjected, or something really novel. The Qumran sectaries understood the "new" covenant by which they found themselves bound in the first sense, as had Ezra before them; and the editors of the Soncino edition of Jeremiah, I discover, in more recent times. This is the "Jewish" solution, which presupposes that the fall of the kingdom represented a failure to keep the Law but not necessarily an abrogation of a relation in which the Law could figure as the authorized second category element. Christianity has of course understood the prophecy in the alternative sense, which presupposes that failure to

146

keep the Law has in effect dissolved any version of the covenant in which it could figure, so that a relation founded on another principle is required — and has obtained. Jeremiah 31:31-34 will not of itself resolve the difference.

Ezekiel's references to a covenant still to come are also susceptible to different readings, though because he is writing after the fall and during the exile his perspective is a degree more futural. This does not mean though that the "everlasting" covenant to which he looks forward need be imagined as unconditional. When the Lord says in Ezekiel 36:26-27 that he will give his restored people a new heart and a new spirit, it seems clear from the context that this spirit, though "*my* Spirit," is not thought of as doing away with any need for the statutes and ordinances but as prompting a redeemed Israel to obey them with new fervor.

But Ezekiel's "new" covenant is not just the old repeated either. His application of Hosea's marriage metaphor in chapter 16 indicates the difference. Israel is an unfaithful wife — though did not the Lord find her as a babe exposed in her blood? And did he not foster her, and when she had grown to beauty, did he not adorn and marry her? Yet she had been faithless with many lovers. The Lord must punish her for her adulteries, as a man is obliged to divorce his wife for adultery, for infidelity nullifies the marriage contract, and a husband must avoid complicity in his wife's sin. If the metaphor

147

is applied to the nation, the implication would be that the original covenant was indeed annulled by the betrayals of the human partner. But *un*like a human husband, the Lord is able to establish a new marriage with his divorced people. I will "remember" the old covenant, he says, and establish an "eternal" covenant to replace it (Ezek. 16:60).

The same emphasis on a new and extravagant blessing appears in the famous vision of the valley of dry bones. The bones are dead and dry to begin with. Their old life is utterly gone. When they are brought back to life by the word of God transmitted through his prophet, their flesh is altogether new, and the breath breathed into them is new as well. Once the allegory is applied, it becomes expressly resurrectional: "Behold, I will open your graves, and bring you up from your graves, my people" (Ezek. 37:12), says the Lord, "and I will put my spirit into you, and you shall live, and I will place you in your own land" (Ezek. 37:14). The breath animating the new bodies will be the Spirit of the Lord himself. We do not hear of the Law in this context; within the allegory, there is nothing to represent it. We seem wholly within the third category.

There is just a hint of what the apparently missing second category element could be in the references to shepherds in chapter 34. First God himself will become the good shepherd, and seek out his sheep, and feed them. Presently it is "my :rvant David" who will be

148

the "one" shepherd, and feed the sheep, and "I will cut with them a covenant of peace" (Ezek. 34:24). Evil beasts will cease, showers of blessings fall, and the people be safe in their land once more. The element within the second category which corresponds to these gifts is not a condition but a matter of fact, twice repeated: "they shall know" that I am the Lord, their God who is with them. That knowledge would then be a version of faith within this context; but not such a faith as would exclude the Law. To know the Lord is to know what is to be done in his service, which the Law can specify. But this need not be mentioned explicitly. The context stresses the gift, and "knowledge" in general as a response to the gift.

Futurity tends to be "Davidic" in its effects in all contexts. For any covenant not yet instituted is bound to appear to the prophet who envisions it in terms of what God will do rather than what man should do in response. The third category is in the nature of the case essentially *ahead.* Second Isaiah is as futural as Ezekiel. The Lord promises a "covenant of peace" (Is. 54:9-10), like that which he swore once with Noah. No condition is attached, unless it is the reader's faith that this will come true. In the following chapter (Is. 55:3) the promised covenant is called "everlasting," always a key word, and "of the sure mercies of David." In third Isaiah this covenant has become a promise that "my spirit which is upon thee," that is, the prophet, "and my words which I have placed within thy mouth shall not depart from thy mouth or from the mouth of thy seed or from the mouth of the seed of thy seed . . . from henceforth and forever" (Is. 59:21). God's side of a new covenant in the Davidic style, that is, would not be another dynasty but the presence of his Spirit within the community. This promise is placed directly after the prophecy of a "redeemer" who "will come to Zion and to those who turn from transgression in Jacob" (Is. 59:20). The same prophecy is continued in Is. 61:8-9 "I will cut an everlasting covenant with them," says the Lord of the returning Israel as a whole, "and known among the nations shall be their seed, and their offering in the midst of the peoples. . . ."

Such prophecies of salvation take the highest possible line. They could, a cynic might observe, afford to. As long as the third category is indefinitely futural, its content may be as cosmic as one pleases. Some of the hyperbolic language in the later prophecies may even have been prompted by the insufficiencies of the actual return. So little of the glory predicted was in fact apparently fulfilled. The actual new covenant, sworn and enforced under Ezra, could not help but seem very much like the old. Prophecy could accommodate itself to these facts: Haggai's rebukes to the people are wholly in the conditional mode. The people have suffered because they have not completed the temple; let them do so, to release the rest of the promises. But an alternative was to look forward further still. What was incomplete about the restoration was left over for supplementary visions which could afford to become more extravagant in proportion to their unrealizability. The same phenomenon was to occur within Christianity in connection with the delay of the Parousia. Something had happened in both contexts to represent the third category — but not everything that had been predicted. The rest had still to be anticipated in language which in the nature of the case could not help becoming increasingly fantastic.

It should be impressive in this connection to observe that what Jesus announces and enacts is precisely the kingdom of God in the midst of this world. There is nothing fantastic or "other-worldly" about what he is represented as doing. He is shown rather as all but filling up the prolonged post-exilic deficiency in the third category — which would restore that half of the covenantal equilibrium. He can accordingly invite the corresponding Abrahamic complement of faith instead of observance of the Law because faith is all that is needed to acknowledge a third category state of affairs which is actually present. What the gospel which reports this presence replaces, then, is not the Law (which is either taken for granted *or* ignored) but the apocalyptic hope on the scale of the community and the posthumous hope on the scale of the individual. It says: heaven has indeed begun here and now.

In that case what would correspond to the gospel in

151

terms of that repetition of the Mosaic version which denies it would still have to be the land. This was the one element in the third category which *did* obtain from Ezra to Hadrian — and in hope and some degree of practice thereafter too. There has never quite been a time when some Jews were not living in *Eretz Israel*. Modern Zionism has recovered this possibility on such a scale as to permit the speculation that in the current state of Israel we might have what should amount to still a third version of the "old" covenant — counting Moses and Ezra as the previous two. For the land is the constant type of the third category in any version of the relation in which Somebody is still the Jewish people. The corresponding second category element would in such a version be not the Law or the Cult but the Nation. Service to the nation in peace and war would then be the religious equivalent to observance of the Law — and enjoyment of the land the covenantal answer, as always. So the contemporary Israeli could feel himself altogether a Jew in good standing without necessarily observing the Law any more than private sentiment or public policy might require. In which case the theologian could interpret Zionism religiously without having to understand the current state of Israel as itself a third category pneumenon (which would have to disturb Christians and does disturb Orthodox Jews) or simply defining it as a secular project altogether (which could not do justice to either the motives felt or the achievements accomplished). But as far as I know no contemporary Nathan has appeared to articulate this possibility, even as a speculation — much less with authority.

BOOK TWO
The New Testament

In evangelio est Dei regnum Christus ipse
— Marcion

PART IV
Covenant in the New Testament

The collection of texts declarative of what God had done in Jesus of Nazareth was presently to be called a new *diatheke,* as if that were what the revelation these texts variously proclaim should be thought of as inaugurating. And the celebration of the Eucharist, which would seem to have constituted the community's self-understanding from the earliest days, makes reference in *its* central text to a "new covenant" therein rehearsed in ritual terms. There are besides a scattering of other references within the NT which testify to the currency of the idea in the minds of the first generation. Some of the OT texts referring to an anticipated covenant were clearly significant to the early Christians, and allusions to these may be picked up here and there. All the same, scholars and theologians alike have sometimes experienced a certain difficulty in realizing the Christian revolution in covenantal terms. The revival of interest in covenant as a master term for the interpretation of scripture has in modern times been limited to Old Testament scholarship. Covenant has not even seemed a satisfactory way of connecting "Judaism" with "Christianity," much less of explaining Christianity to itself.

Nevertheless the NT references exist, whether or not they can be made use of theologically. They include most prominently Hebrews, especially 7:22 and its context, and 8:6 through 9:28; Galatians chapters 3 and 4; II Corinthians chapter 3; and the words over the cup in all four of the Eucharistic passages in Paul and the synoptics.

According to the author of Hebrews, the most elaborately developed of these, a "greater" covenant now obtains than the one within which the Law and the sacrifices it called for were effectual (7:22). The change involves a shift from a sequence of mortal officiants to a single immortal priest; from a daily and yearly cycle of variously differentiated animal sacrifices to a single complete sacrifice without metaphor; from an outward and earthly to an inward and heavenly "tent." In all these respects Jesus Christ becomes the cultic mediator of a "better" covenant (8:6) which therefore replaces the old. Jeremiah 31:31-34 is naturally quoted in support. Hebrews understands what has happened as a concentration of all the rituals of the year in a perfected

156

Day of Atonement, in which an absolutely representative high priest passes through into the heavenly holy of holies on a tide, as it were, of his own blood. "We have therefore, brothers, freedom to go into the holy place in the blood of Jesus, which has renewed for us a fresh and living way through the veil: that is his body . . ." (10:19).

The language employed in this recapitulative distillation of the old "P" work provides an explicit link between the new Christian dispensation and the previous cult, an important connection, for the author of Hebrews is virtually alone among NT writers in his high regard for this side of the tradition. With the help of cultic language Jesus can be defined as at one and the same time an absolutely efficacious sacrifice for sin and the constituting sacrifice of a covenant. He thus epitomizes all those creatures sacrificed by Moses to provide the blood sprinkled on the people to confirm the first covenant. But explicitness on one side involves a certain obscurity on the other. Jesus is the ideal sacrifice which establishes the final covenant; but it is not explored in any other language what the covenant itself consists of. That is taken for granted. The constant emphasis on faith (meaning, in this context, fidelity to a commitment already made) would appear to indicate one such component. The promise of heavenly life is apparently another. But these are very loosely associated with an argument which stays firmly in cultic language throughout. And cultic language, in the OT or the NT, cannot explain itself. Meanwhile the new covenant is of course the superlative to the original's comparative. But celebration is not explanation.

In Galatians 3 and 4, the second major locus for covenantal language in the NT, Paul understands the promise to Abraham as a covenant founded upon the faith of the partriarch, a promise representatively fulfilled in the birth of Isaac. It is *this* covenant, he believes, that is now reconstituted in Christ, thus bracketing the intermediate covenant of Moses. This is more helpful, since it confirms the filiation to which this new covenant belongs, and with the help of the rest of Paul's argument in this letter and in Romans it can in fact provide a major clue to a thoroughly covenantal interpretation of the Christian revolution. But the rhetorical context, without that background, is *not* useful; we learn only that the two covenants may be contrastingly allegorized as Hagar and Sarah — which is insulting to adherents of the old without being very illuminating for members of the New.

There is also a brief allusion to the key text from Jeremiah in Romans 11:27 and a more interesting reference in II Cor. 3:2-3. In that letter Paul defines the church at Corinth as itself a letter not just of recommendation for himself but from Christ: a letter written not with ink or on tablets of stone but upon the human heart. He goes on to contrast the "ministry" of death

158

mediated by Moses with the ministry of the Spirit mediated by Jesus. The scriptures over which a veil remains for Jewish unbelievers are themselves called the "old covenant" (3:14). The chief point of interest here is the identification of the interiorized Law promised by Jeremiah with the gift of the Spirit. Such an interpretation might indeed be fitted into a covenantal structure — but only if this were already well established. It will not of itself define one. We learn at most that for Paul as for the author of Hebrews the language of covenant was familiar but not as such central to the working out of his theology.

Paul also witnesses to the persistence of covenantal language within the inheritance out of which the NT texts developed in his repetition of the essential Eucharistic *paradosis* in I Cor. 11:23-26. "This cup of the new covenant in my blood" is the formula he repeats as authoritative for his congregation because it was so delivered to him — presumably, it has been supposed, at Antioch, the center for the Gentile mission. The ritual practice of that community is apparently also reflected in the language to be found in the corresponding verse of Luke's narrative of the Last Supper (22:20). The word over the wine in the other narrative gospels, Mark 14:24 and Matthew 26:28, represent a slightly different version of the common tradition which apparently did not use the adjective "new" in the corresponding formula. It is clear though from the close agreement of all

159

four witnesses that the liturgical traditions of the early Church were confident that Jesus meant to associate this ritual innovation with the establishment of a covenant, and that (if the word "new" may be depended on) he too would have had Jeremiah in mind.

J. Coppens believes that these Eucharistic texts, descending as they do within the core of the tradition from Jesus himself at a crucial moment in his central deed, may safely be taken as representing the true source for all the scattered references to covenant in the NT and therefore ever since within the history of Christianity.[3]

---

3. The same Joseph Coppens to whom I referred in connection with the verses from Jeremiah completed that essay with two further studies in *CBQ* 25 (1963): "The Eucharist: Sacrament and Sacrifice of the New Covenant, Foundation of the Church," 161-204 and "The Church, the New Covenant of God with His People," 13-25. I have followed his argument here.

There should be another comprehensive footnote at this point, to take in major secondary texts that have influenced this portion of the argument. In fact it is difficult to specify any, not because standard and recent books on the NT in general or on Paul and Mark in particular haven't been consulted but because, as I observed, the covenant has not been a master idea within NT studies in modern times. Some parenthetical comments though might be in order. The analysis of Paul into three "gospels" is very much my own, but J.A.T. Robinson's classic *The Body* (London, 1952) set the terms for my account of the third of these. It may be observed that E.P. Sanders' recent and massive *Paul and Palestinian Judaism* (Philadelphia, 1977) promotes a similar apprehension of the Pauline center. As for Mark, it will be seen that I lean towards a "high" idea of Mark's own contribution to the tradition he recomposes, a tendency just now going out of fashion again. Quentin Quesnell's *The Mind of Mark* (Rome, 1969) has been an important stimulus. It will be perceived by "insiders," though, that I am unconvinced by the arguments of that school of "redaction-critics" which descends from Willi Marxsen and his *Mark the Evangelist* (Nashville, 1969). His American "sons" would include Norman Perrin, W.H. Kelber, and T.J. Weeden. One almost wants, in the Markan style, to warn readers against the *pseudomarkoi* generated by these enthusiasts, who have claimed to know their author's motives with a confidence which comically resembles the old notion that Jesus' mind could be readily entered. I have found especially unpleasant the "provocative" thesis of T.J. Weeden that Mark is an eccentric parousialist who does not believe in the Church and hates the disciples. His *Mark — Tradition in Conflict*

In that case it would have been Jesus who first interpreted the change effected through him as amounting to
the establishment of a new covenant. By themselves,
though, these liturgical texts, like the other NT references, would indicate only that a certain conventionali-
zation of the idea had set in very early in the development of the new tradition. The Eucharistic references
are verbally as perfunctory as the others. This rhetorical
state of affairs would seem to confirm an impression
that in all these cases we are dealing with an inheritance
from "the Lord" himself, something it therefore behoov-
ed every author to accept and repeat whether or not it
seemed meaningful. The authors of the NT appear to
assume they were indeed in a new covenant, but (with
the partial exception of Paul and the author of Hebrews) they seem to have believed this more because
Jesus had once told them or their informants so than
because they felt any need to work out the theological
consequences for themselves.

The paranetic style which most of these references
share would substantiate the taken-for-grantedness of
the idea. All the comparisons between the old and the
new fall into the less/more or not/but pattern, intended

(Philadelphia, 1971; second edition, 1979) has unaccountably over-influenced E. Schillebeeckx' enormous *Jesus* (New York, 1979), in which the various problems are rehearsed in
the light of recent German discussion.

Local debts are acknowledged as I go, as usual. The quotation shortly to come from D.R.
Hillers, for instance, may be found in *Covenant: The History of a Biblical Idea* (Baltimore,
1969), p.188.

161

primarily to deprecate the former and celebrate the latter, so that the first may be dismissed as irrelevant or at most identified as a type now fulfilled. This "supersessionary" attitude, naturally attractive to Gentiles, would of itself make it difficult to take the idea of covenant seriously, for to understand both the old and the new *as covenants* would be to realize the likeness between them, not the difference. All the references allude to Jeremiah 31:31-34 — as if that explained itself. This casualness of reference has encouraged skepticism among some students of the problem: it has been possible to conclude, in the neat formula with which D.R. Hillers rounds out his useful history of the covenantal idea, that "the Essenes had a covenant, but it was not new; the Christians had something new, but it was not a covenant."

An approach at the surface level of the NT evidence, then, is apt to prove frustrating. Without assistance from other perspective one is reduced to guessing at Jesus' own intention — always a seductive possibility, but always dubious too. It would be more helpful to step back again into the point of view from which it might be possible to detect structures within larger argumentative sequences or narrative units. If the change effected through Jesus is to be understood as a covenantal "moment" corresponding to and repeating the parallel moments of the OT, then the equilibria illustrative of that possibility should manifest themselves with a certain simplicity and regularity. If the gospel really does announce a new covenant, that truth should not have to remain a minor dead letter. But to test this possibility one would have to examine large blocks of material. Sufficiently representative texts or combinations of texts would have to prove readable as a whole in a covenantal sense.

It seems fair to assume that Paul and Mark would provide sufficiently typical instances to test this hypothesis. Let us see what happens, accordingly.

PART V
Paul

And I sought from them a man, who might hedge up the hedge, and stand in the breach before my face on behalf of the land, so that I should not destroy it, but I did not find one.
— Ezekiel 22:30

The gospel, the first generation of Christians agreed (usually without thinking), proclaims a new covenant. Paul *does* think: passionately, occasionally, discontinuously. In what he writes (that has survived) we do not find the covenant mentioned as if it were a central element in his thinking, though as we have observed he can contrast the "old" and the "new" to the rhetorical advantage of the latter in the usual style. And he knows that the new covenant is in some sense a recovery of the patriarchal version of the old. What we find instead, of course, is the gospel itself; and in more than one version. In fact if we step back from the irregular testimony on the letters in order to formulate a theology for Paul as a whole (always a difficult, always a necessary task) it is possible to find three distinct versions of this gospel —

164

and therefore three distinct contexts within which a covenantal structure might or might not be detectable as the articulation of what is proclaimed.

The first and apparently most prominent of these would be what might be called the gospel according to justice. This is the kerygma which since the Reformation at least has seemed peculiarly the "gospel according to Paul," if only because of the powerful line of interpreters descending from Luther and Calvin through Barth and Bultmann. E.K. Sanders has recently challenged the hegemony of this view — and A.M. Hunter some time ago showed that whatever the degree of its importance to Paul personally, there is in fact no reason to suppose that the gospel according to justice was anything but the common declaration of the early Church. This gospel may be found especially in Galatians and Romans.

There is also what might be called a gospel according to wisdom, which would stand towards the gospel according to justice as Hellenism towards Judaism. This gospel may be found in the first four chapters of I Corinthians. It may be comparatively original with Paul, as a "philosopher" in his own right and a leader in the mission to the Gentiles.

Finally there is a gospel according to the body. This can seem the most profound of all; and at once the closest to Jesus and most peculiar to Paul himself. It is certainly the hardest to disentangle *as* gospel — and

165

therefore as a way in which to articulate a version of the covenant. The chief evidence which invites its formulation is scattered through the late chapters of I Corinthians, though bits and pieces appear elsewhere. The gospels according to justice and wisdom represent the "Deuteronomic" side of Paul. The gospel according to the body would represent the less obvious "Levitican" side. As with the corresponding dimensions of the OT, the question arises, should the gospel according to the body be considered in competition with or subordinate to the gospel according to justice or wisdom; or as embracing both of these in a more comprehensive synthesis? Paul did not need to address himself to this question — but his reader should. To raise it now though would be premature. Let us begin with the obvious first case, the gospel according to justice.

2

This gospel may be found at its most programmatic
in the first three chapters of Romans. Some re-ordering
is required to outline the stages of the argument, but
less than is sometimes necessary for Paul. The revelation of God's justice uncovered in Jesus may be realized
as logical, Paul argues, as soon as the condition it meets
is admitted. That condition has two aspects, factual and
moral.

The factual precondition of the gospel according to
justice is the universal sinfulness in which mankind
finds itself as soon as it acknowledges its situation before God. All men, according to Paul, are already *un-
just* in God's court. To the enforcement of this initial
proposition the first two chapters of Romans are devoted. The evidence is divided there into three sections:
the sins of Gentiles, the sins shared by Gentiles and
Jews, and the sins peculiar to Jews. Gentiles sin by refusing to interpret nature as evidence of the Creator.
They do not, that is, realize the third category in that
context. Instead they fall into idolatry, or worship of the
first category; and from idolatry into sexual vice, and
thence into every other form of depravity. Gentiles and
Jews together are guilty of hypocrisy, the sin of attempting to conceal one's sinfulness from others and so from
oneself, or worse still, of judging others for sins of which
one is oneself guilty. It is the privilege of Jews alone to

sin by "boasting"; that is, by presuming on their possession of or positive obedience to the Law. If this boast
were well founded, it would still be sinful, in Paul's
eyes, for it would reveal only an impossible confidence
that the will seeking its own moral advantage could
conquer sin in the eyes of God. In practice though Paul
seems to assume that boasting is only a cover for hypocrisy. "You who boast in the Law, through the breaking
of the Law do you dishonor God?" (Rom. 2:23) evidently presumes a positive answer. The conclusion is
clear: "Jews and Greeks too, all are under sin" (Rom.
3:9).

This matter of fact, as Paul believes it to be, provides one aspect of the state of affairs presumed by the
gospel according to justice. The other is the assumption
that all men are free to choose and so may reasonably
be held responsible for their sinfulness in God's eyes.
They can all realize the difference between good and
evil (though in fact they do nothing but evil); the Jews
by way of the Law, which was, Paul believes, given
them for that purpose, and the Gentiles by way of conscience, which should in principle be equally reliable.
They can all know by one or the other means that God,
as scripture says, "will give back to each according to
his works" (Rom. 2:6). They can know therefore that if
there *were* any who did well, these would receive eternal life, and therefore too that the wicked should expect a
correspondingly absolute annihilation. And they should

168

know that any apparent delay in the convocation of God's court is not due to God's weakness, much less his complicity with sin. It is only meant to lead men to repentance — if they should be capable of that.

This combination of the fact that all men do sin with the moral presupposition that all men are responsible and so deserve condemnation creates the problem for which the revelation of God's justice announced in the gospel is according to Paul the only possible solution. For doing the positive works of the Law will no longer, in this view, provide such a means. That cannot make a man just again, once he has sinned, and he has. All it can do is add hypocrisy to his other vices, whatever they may already be. Conscience, the equivalent of the Law in the Gentile, can do no more. Neither has the power to cancel sin once it has occurred. All either can do is expose his moral identity to the sinner.

What is required, then, is some means to do away with the nothingness which hangs over every head without compromising God's absolute justice, in the light of which sin must always remain sin. The gospel according to justice is a proclamation that such a means has in fact been revealed. The key lines are Romans 3:21-26. Here they are in the RSV translation:

"But now the righteousness of God has been manifested apart from law, although the law and the prophets bear witness to it, the righteousness of God through

169

faith in Jesus Christ for all who believe. For there is no distinction; since all have sinned and fall short of the glory of God, they are justified by his grace as a gift, through the redemption which is in Christ Jesus, whom God put forward as an expiation by his blood, to be received by faith. This was to show God's righteousness, because in his divine forebearance he had passed over former sin; it was to prove at the present time that he himself is righteous and that he justifies him who has faith in Jesus."

It has often been observed since Luther at least that Romans is the master text within the NT. If so, it would have to follow that the first three chapters present the major argument of Romans; and that this sentence is the climax to that argument. In which case it would concentrate the meaning of the whole NT — with respect to the gospel according to justice at least. Not inappropriately perhaps, the sentence is excruciatingly difficult either to translate or paraphrase. The Greek is highly compressed and the usual Pauline parentheses abound. But the main line of thought clearly runs through the idea of justice (or "righteousness," in this translation). God's *dikaiosune* is now at last revealed in what has occurred in Jesus. God has "put forward" Somebody as a legal substitute for all those sinners who are ready to receive him as their moral representative. If they consent to accept him as the one who will suffer in their stead,

170

they become just in God's eyes. By this means God's justice is preserved inviolate, for an absolute judgement is still made against sin — but in the person of Jesus instead of those immediately guilty. God's love is thereby freed to recognize the newly justified — *re*-justified would express the conception more exactly — as subjects in good standing of his kingdom. Thus too it is possible to say that such sinners are thereby "redeemed," or bought back from the power of Sin, regarded anthropomorphically as a foreign slavemaster. The entire procedure comes into effect by the announcement of the opportunity and assent to it by those who are willing to seize this chance. Their consent becomes their faith: "faith," in context, meaning acceptance of Jesus as one's representative for the purpose at hand. Faith is agreement that Jesus should exercise a power of attorney in God's court. We are then cosigners with Jesus — and our mark is essentially the same as his.

I have put this summary of what is usually called the doctrine of the atonement, that is, the argument explaining the roles of Jesus and the believer within the gospel according to justice, as much as possible into the language appropriate to such a gospel, the language of the Law. For it is within that language alone that it could be reasonable to speak of moral representation at all, and so of a substitutionary atonement. Paul, it seems to me, does in fact presume just such a straightforward version of the relation between Jesus and the believer. One of the difficulties in reading this passage from Romans or any other of the same import derives from the fact that mixed with the legal language proper to a gospel in terms of justice are elements from what is really another language, the language of the cult. In these verses, for instance, Paul calls Jesus "an expiation" that is, an *ilasterion* or expiatory sacrifice, and more especially an expiatory sacrifice of the kind offered on Yom Kippur, when the high priest is commanded to atone for the sins of himself and the people by entering the holy of holies and smearing the blood of the creatures sacrificed upon the *kapporeth* or cover of the ark, the Hebrew term for which is translated in the LXX as *ilasterion*. There need be no confusion in Paul's mind or those of his generation, since the expiatory sacrifices of the cult had long since been subsumed into a legal framework. But it is desirable in the interests of clarity to differentiate the two ways of thinking while attempting to repeat what should be understood as taking place in what we call the atonement. There is an aspect to what happens which makes perfect sense in terms of the gospel according to justice taken by itself. And that is the aspect which is uppermost in Paul's thinking in this context. He is the "D" of the new covenant — on just this one of his sides.

Clearly a distinct species of faith is crucial to this rendering of the gospel according to justice, as obedience is for Deuteronomy; so much so indeed that "justi-fication by faith" has played a powerful role within the subsequent tradition virtually in abstraction from its parent argument; which has meant in turn that the no-tion of faith employed here has become dominant in re-ligious contexts at some distance from the problem of justice. But *pistis* has several senses in Paul himself, not all of which are relevant to the gospel according to jus-tice. In parenetic contexts the word usually connotes something closer to faith*fulness,* that is, perseverance in the Christian life. Elsewhere it may mean simply an un-qualified trust in God's direction of the world. This is the sense illustrated by the story of Abraham, who was counted righteous, Paul reminds his reader, because he believed that the promises God had made to him would be carried out. But Abraham's faith also had a specific content: the unlikely birth of Isaac. In the context of the gospel, the equivalent object of faith would be the risen Christ. The Christian has faith in the resurrection of Jesus as Abraham had faith in the birth of Isaac. This resurrection is manifest to him or her in various gifts of the Spirit, through which God's promise can now be kept, and man's faith answered. To have faith in gen-eral would then be to receive whatever is given as evi-dence that a divine promise made sometime in the past is now being kept in the present and so to trust that other gifts of the same kind will be continued in the fu-ture. Faith in the broad sense is therefore an acknowledging response to something in the third category.

When one thinks of faith in connection with Paul, though, one usually has in mind the special meaning the word acquires within the context of the gospel according to justice. And within that context, faith would mean moral consent to what the earthly Jesus suffered as well as a grateful reception of what the heavenly Christ transmits. More exactly it means acceptance of the death of Jesus as sufficient for the nullification of sin, and so of oneself as among those whom that annulment benefits. Legally, faith is consent; morally, it is identification; religiously, it is the equivalent of (an expiatory) sacrifice in me.

Justification, then, would be by faith on the part of the believer only. It is still very much a "work" on the part of Jesus, whose passion thus becomes the epitome of all the other positive works required under the Law, and especially of the sacrifices for sin considered as the type of these. *Because* God has permitted Jesus to do so much, no more than faith in what has been done through him need be asked of anybody else. It is thus the combination of Jesus and his "nation," that is, of Jesus and *myself*, which effectuates what is required by God's justice in order to achieve the rejustification of all.

Faith would extend beyond its role within the act of justification as the various ethical repetitions of the idea alter in tonality from identification to imitation. In the initial deed of justification I have faith in the deed of Jesus. I believe in its application to myself. Later on, I begin to take part myself in the same deed, which is thus revealed as a universal as well as an individual possibility. My service in faith can now become the equivalent in my context of his service in his. I too may "crucify" the flesh, says Paul — after whatever fashion the situation I am in requires. Then I too may become an instance of God's justifying action, and others in their turn may come to have faith through me. The end of Galatians and the whole of Phillipians will illustrate at large: Paul moves through a variety of contexts in each of which an ethic invited by the Spirit as opposed to the ethic determined by the Law is repeatedly demonstrated. Throughout these local arguments the paradigm is still the fidelity typified by Jesus. To have faith in him, then, is sooner or later to imitate him in a "faith working through love," as Galatians 5:6 puts it: that is, love becomes a species of faith within an on-going process of sanctification.

But to notice manifestations of faith which may occur after the fact of justification is to go beyond the range of the gospel according to justice as such. Within that horizon, the chief profit to be drawn from the realization that faith in the believer corresponds to the act of Jesus is the formal chance this provides to reconstitute a covenantal structure in a genuinely new style. For the gospel according to justice may readily be re-assembled in such a way as to demonstrate that a covenant is indeed instituted thereby. On man's side is nothing but faith: faith divided into the initial faith of Jesus, who obeyed the will of God that he should become an *ilasterion* for the sins of the people, and the subsequent faith of the believer in just this determination, who thereby declares himself one of those for whom it has become true. This is the double act referred to in Romans 3:22, where the justice of God is described, again in the RSV translation, as coming "through faith in Jesus Christ for all who believe," a clumsy redundancy which should be both more freely and more accurately translated as "through the faith to be found in Jesus Christ, and so for all who are able to have faith in him." These two aspects of faith are yoked together, then, on the human side of the covenantal relation. As a cooperating pair they accomplish all that can be done within the second category according to the new covenant.

Once this double fidelity has taken effect, God is free as it were to come forward from his side. He has already (as far as the believer is concerned) manifested his acceptance of what Jesus contributed by means of the resurrection, in which he has kept his promise to be with the one who obeyed his will along that line. Along the other line, that is, in answer to the faith of the believer, God will manifest his acceptance in the forgiveness through which his mercy is made evident. That forgiveness will then *be* the resurrection as far as the believer is concerned. It will amount to the way in which the Lord is with him or her — within the context of justice.

The fundamental structure, then, of the gospel according to justice is still thoroughly covenantal — and the provision on God's side still what it always was in any previous version. That God *will be with* his people after one mode or another is after all the whole of the promise under any form of the relation: God does not change. What has changed is what man must do. Instead of many works of the Law to be collectively accomplished by a single nation there is now no more than one work and one man — but also a mode of participation in that work and identification with that man which suffices to render this version of the relation accessible in principle to all. Faith can thus be the likeness between Jesus and each individual Gentile *or* Jew; a spiritual rhyme, as it were, which might in principle link the exceptional individual to the whole world.

We may sum up our results so far by distributing the principal elements of the gospel according to justice into the categories in such a way as to display the reciprocities which re-establish a covenantal pattern:

Second category	Third category
Justice	
Wrath	Mercy
crucifixion	resurrection
faith	forgiveness

The justice of God divides into his wrath within the second category, where it sweeps away all sin, otherwise the undisputed possessor of that ground, and his mercy in the third category, where the gifts of the Spirit are provided. The passion of Jesus absorbs the wrath — for those who consent to that dealing on their behalf. This double action constitutes man's side of the relation. It is matched on God's side by the corresponding double gift: the resurrection (for Jesus) and forgiveness, or perhaps more accurately forgiven-ness (for the justified sinner). These together amount to the way in which God's presence manifests itself sacramentally — within the context of justice.

The first set of elements on the chart above are attributes of God. The third set are experiences of men. The middle set are respectively the humiliation and exaltation of Jesus Christ — who in this as in other respects is therefore intermediary between the two principals in the covenantal relation, as Moses had been before. All modes of expressing the gospel, it is invariably worth recalling, have to be propositions concerning the identity of Jesus. So in this context: Jesus Christ *is* the justice of God. This means that he is at once the wrath of God and the mercy of God, the two aspects or phases of God's justice. The wrath of God is directed against sin; the mercy of God is enjoyed by the just. Jesus *is* the wrath of God though not by wielding it, as another king might have done in deeds or another prophet in words,

178

but by absorbing it. As a result of this passion (as opposed to an action, which strictly speaking Jesus does *not* accomplish) God's justice becomes identical with his mercy — for those who accept this means.

I have said that within the covenant God does not change. But it would be possible to understand the gospel according to justice as registering not only a change in the status of Man but a change in the image of God. Within the condition of sin, God must seem punitive; we feel this wrath through Law or Conscience, and cannot imagine him otherwise. That is what his justice will seem to amount to: absolute punishment by an implacable judge. But if sin has been done away with through the patience of Somebody suffering in the place of sinners, then another God is revealed, a God of mercy instead of wrath. And that God is revealed as the true God all along, the God realized in the Spirit rather than according to the flesh. The atoning act could then be understood as involving three agents, all acting together: the sinner, the expiator, and the God of wrath. *All* these are in effect consumed together. Some theories of the atonement allow for the absorption of the first two only; which would leave a punitive God still free to occupy the heavens, there to be worshipped by the orthodox or hated by the rebellious. Either reaction would be evidence that the moral vision which the theory of the atonement is intended to explicate had not yet been comprehended in full. So certain kinds of Calvinism or

179

anti-Calvinism would be incompletely Christian.

Paul though does not make that mistake. For him the God of judgement is nailed to the cross along with the Law which expresses him — at least for those who will share in Jesus' passion. For Jesus may be understood as concentrating within an exemplary and accessible present the whole of what would otherwise have to be feared in the mode of apocalyptic expectation. He has brought the worst of the absolute future upon himself *already*. Thus he may be said indeed to "take the kingdom by violence" — by receiving it into his own bosom. The last judgement is therefore complete right now for those who can share in this anticipation of it. Nothing more need happen to them in the second category (faith is that nothingness appropriated). Everything is in principle already in the third, just as it stands. The new covenant places one on God's side — to just this extent.

B

The rejoicers in that which is not a thing, the sayers, is it not in our strength we take to ourselves horns?
— Amos 6:13

The gospel according to wisdom need not prompt as full an explication as the gospel according to justice. Its chief interest lies in the demonstration that the essential message can in fact be repeated in terms of the value which could be thought of as holding a position within the religious culture of the nations corresponding to the position occupied by justice in Israel. For it is Greek, not Jewish, wisdom that Paul has in mind. This gospel is to be found entirely within the first four chapters of I Corinthians. It is introduced rather casually at the close of Paul's opening plea against faction within the local church in a sentence on his own vocation. I did not baptize many, he says (which might have made him the focus of a party) "for Christ did not send me to baptize but to preach the gospel, and not with the wisdom of the word, lest the cross of Christ be emptied out" (I Cor. 1:17). The term *sophia* instantly generates its opposite to fill out a typical Pauline comparison: "For the word of the cross, to those who are perishing, is folly; but to us who are being saved, it is the power of God" (I Cor. 1:18). A confirmatory quotation from scripture is followed by a paragraph ringing changes on the polarity that has just been set up:

181

"Where is the wise man? where the scribe? Where the disputer of this age? Has not God made foolish the wisdom of this world? For now since, in the wisdom of God, the world did not know God through wisdom, it pleased God through the folly of the preaching to save those who believe. For Jews ask for signs and Greeks seek for wisdom, but we preach Christ crucified, for Jews a stumbling block and for Gentiles a folly, but for those who are called, Jews and Greeks alike, Christ is the power of God and the wisdom of God. For the folly of God is wiser than men, and the weakness of God is stronger than men" (I Cor. 1:20-25).

Flesh and Spirit are contrasted here in terms of both wisdom and folly: there is a wisdom of men and a wisdom of God, and a folly according to men and a folly according to God. Identifying which of each is meant as one reads though sometimes means amplifying as one goes: the last verse quoted, for instance, must mean "the folly of God is wiser than *the wisdom* of men, and the weakness of God is stronger than *the power of* men." Once the different kinds of wisdom and folly have been sorted out, it is not hard to recast the assertions made in such a way as to disclose their equivalence to the corresponding gospel according to justice. In that context, we are told, Jesus Christ is *not* the justice of men *but* the justice of God; which though has been brought about by a means which from the per-

182

spective of men looks very much like *in*justice. So now Jesus Christ is *not* the wisdom of men but the wisdom of God; and in the same way, God's wisdom seems sheer folly from the point of view of men's wisdom, while from God's perspective, men's wisdom is in fact folly; just as men's attempts at justice are, absolutely considered, no better than so much *in*justice. So it is not difficult to put these pairs of contrasts into the standard covenantal structure, distributing the elements into the second and third categories as required:

Jesus Christ

is

not the wisdom
of men   which is really
                                     folly

but what seems
folly   which is really
                                     the wisdom of God

Men's folly *is* God's wisdom, just as God's wrath *is* his mercy — to those who have eyes to see. What is folly to men is the crucifixion; but the resurrection demonstrates the wisdom of God. These polarities *are* the gospel insofar as they demonstrate the action accomplished through Jesus Christ in one more context where what is proclaimed may be repeated in the soul of the believer. In this context too faith is required: in the form of a willingness to accept something so very *un*wise, *il*logi-

183

cal, and *un*literary as the cross as the way to the true wisdom of God instead of the prudent, rational, and attractive recommendations of the "wise man" or the learning of the "scribe."

The wisdom of this world which must be rejected then plays the same role in this context as the Law in the gospel according to justice. Paul presumably has in mind every species of religious "philosophy" which might offer by secret doctrine or esoteric practice to unite the soul to God. Efforts of this sort, Paul insists, cannot make a man truly wise any more than doing the works of the Law can make him just. God's means are the opposite of those which the best men would otherwise choose for themselves. True wisdom, this act of God has revealed, is arrived at not by an elevation of the soul but through the degradation of a body. What men estimate as noblest and best in themselves is in fact, viewed from God's side, precisely as good as nothing at all; and only the most unqualified appropriation of just that nothingness can release the real wisdom of God.

The folly of the cross must be repeated in the faith of sinners. So the low social status of the Corinthians occurs to Paul as exemplifying their share in the necessary folly — if it is accepted as such. For God "chose the low born and the despised in the world" (I Cor. 1:28) to exhibit what *he* deemed noble in the face of those who claimed a higher status. And the *un*sophistication of Paul himself, who came to Corinth determined (after

184

an attempt to speak "philosophically" in Athens?) not to "know anything among you except Jesus Christ, and him crucified" (2:2) is a still more intimate repetition of the same principle. He was with them "in weakness and in fear and in much trembling" (2:3), he says, nor was his language at all eloquent. But his words none the less conveyed the power and knowledge of God. As Paul develops these applications of the pattern, we see him repeating the original wisdom/folly contrast in terms of other equivalent differentiations between knowledge and ignorance, power and weakness, high and low social status, eloquence and simplicity of speech, each pair with its own polarity of human and divine meanings. And these subsidiary contrasts could also be arranged in the same way within the standard covenantal structure.

If the wisdom of men is the wisdom of the soul, the wisdom of God is the wisdom of the Spirit. It is through a reception of the gifts of the Spirit within the community of Christ that one realizes this true wisdom, the wisdom released by way of the folly of Jesus. So it becomes possible for Paul to say that for the "mature" Christian at least — the one who has learned to appropriate that folly as his or her own — there is after all a Christian *gnosis* which it is possible to impart. We Christians too, he says, have a "wisdom in secret, hidden" (2:7), which "God has revealed to us through the Spirit" (2:10). Among such esoteric truths would be, apparently, vari-

185

ous features of the *parousia* with which Christian prophecy had already supplied the churches. Paul repeats and expands on some of these in chapter 15 of I Corinthians as he had previously in his letters to the Thessalonians. The course of events from the "first fruits" to the full harvest, or from the third to the fourth category, could only be known in the Spirit, which "searches into everything, even the depths of God" (2:11). But he also apparently has in mind such instances of "meat" as too many of the Corinthians themselves were choking on. Such formula as " 'All things are lawful for me' " (I Cor. 6:12; 10:23) or " 'Food for the guts, and the guts for food' " (I Cor. 6:13) would be examples. The most general of these is the verse, " 'The earth is the Lord's, and the fullness of it' " (I Cor. 10:26), which could apply to other contexts besides eating meat sacrificed to idols, for it formulates the principle of the third category as such, where everything has become creation once again, and so an unconditional *mysterion* of God's presence. "For all things are yours" within the covenantal relation, as Paul has already said, "whether Paul or Apollos or Cephas, or the world or life or death, present or to come, all are yours" — but only in the Spirit; that is, in proportion as "you are of Christ; and Christ is of God" (I Cor. 3:21-23).

Paul's special instances of the wisdom of God range from the immediate to the universal, since he would apparently rank among truths realizable in the Spirit the

186

right of an apostle to carnal support in return for his spiritual provision as well as the primacy of *agape* among the *charismata* or the importance of unity as a sign of the Church. In principle every "revelation or knowledge or prophecy or teaching" (I Cor. 14:6) that is recognizable *in* the Spirit as *of* the Spirit may be accounted an instance of the wisdom of God. In a general sense, then, all of Paul's apostolic instruction might reasonably come under that head, though the reader most appreciates the special character of what he apparently has in mind at high moments. One of these would presumably be the sudden insight into the dialectic of salvation which concludes his effort to work through the problem of an unconverted Israel in chapter 11 of Romans. God's wisdom in this context is formulated, apparently on the spur of the moment, in a breakthrough which Luther was later to call the "great text" of the whole epistle: "For God has locked up all in disobedience, that he may have mercy on all" (Rom. 11:32). Paul is apparently so overwhelmed by this intuition that he falls into a doxology of thanksgiving then and there.

But precisely because the members of the Church (or Israel in the third category) may share in and even formulate the wisdom of God, it is imperative that all concerned realize the acute difference between this wisdom and the merely human wisdom which is perpetually attempting to masquerade as spiritual. The power to detect this crucial difference is itself a gift; which Paul himself is frequently obliged to exercise. His test is always practical. Faction is one proof that the Corinthians are still for the most part in the flesh rather than totally in the Spirit as they pretend. Psychic conceit and the moral carelessness and failure of charity which naturally go with it are still more serious evidence of the same confusion. The cure for such pretensions is constantly the same: the cross once more. "Let no one deceive himself. If anyone thinks he is wise among you in this age, let him become a fool, that he may become wise" (I Cor. 3:18). One enters into the pneumatic privileges of the new covenant by rehearsing the passion which constitutes it within the context in question — which is always one's own. This means becoming a servant over and over again, as Paul and Apollos have been in their turn, planting and watering as God's occasion requires, but claiming nothing for themselves. The apostles have indeed become "spectacles to the world" (I Cor. 4:9), like criminals in the arena — or Jesus on the cross. Let the thought of *that* folly shame those who have boasted themselves too "strong" to be hindered by what they enthusiastically understand as petty legalisms. Let them rather become imitators of Paul, as he is of Jesus. Then and only then will the wisdom of God be purified of human parodies, and appear as the gift it truly is.

C

*Always bearing the death of Jesus in the body, so that also the
life of Jesus may shine in our body.*
— II Cor. 4:10

I have mentioned three Pauline gospels. The first
is the gospel according to justice — which one usually thinks of as *the* gospel, especially in connection
with Paul. The second is the gospel according to wisdom; which might have attracted more attention
than it has. And the third, at which we have now arrived, is the gospel according to the body.

The starting point for any discussion of Paul's
body language has to be J.A.T. Robinson's *The
Body*. A passage in the preface of that book sums up
its argument:

One could say without exaggeration that the concept of the body forms the keystone of Paul's theology. In its closely interconnected meanings, the word
soma knits together all his great themes. It is from
the body of sin and death that we are delivered; it is
through the body of Christ on the Cross that we are
saved; it is into His body the Church that we are incorporated; it is by His body in the Eucharist that
this community is sustained; it is in our body that its
new life has to be manifested; it is to a resurrection
of this body to the likeness of His glorious body that

we are destined . . . . To trace the subtle links and interaction between the different senses of this word *soma* is to grasp the thread that leads through the maze of Pauline thought. (p. 9)

It is easier though to accept Robinson's generalizations than some of the particulars of his case. One difficulty is the old problem of distinguishing between *sarx* and *soma,* or "flesh" and "body." The Hebrew *basar* can include both senses, but the Greek and the English both distinguish them, and usually to some purpose in Paul's case. But his usage is ambiguous. "Flesh" *can* mean "body," and "body," "flesh." It is true that "flesh" tends to become the pejorative term and "body" the honorific. So it is not altogether implausible for Robinson to conclude that "while *sarx* stands for man in the solidarity of creation, in his distance from God, *soma* stands for man, in the solidarity of creation, as made for God" (p. 31). But we should not I think allow ourselves to be carried away by Paul's merely rhetorical practice when that obscures the shape of his thought. Paul's "letter" is the flesh of his message, not the Spirit of it. It seems to me accordingly that it would be best to re-define *sarx* as we may suppose Paul would have done if he had been as single-minded as theology would prefer: that is, as meaning the stuff out of which things are made, good or bad. *Soma* could then be reserved to mean the unit of being in question, whether

190

that was sinful or gracious. In which case *soma* might often be translated in modern terminology as "identity." The body of something would be what it *is*; the flesh, what it is made of.

Such a lexical disambiguation would seem already adumbrated by Robinson's own chief example, the continuity between the body on the cross and the body of the Church. For though in any Christian theology these must be the same *body,* it is equally obvious that their flesh is utterly different. The flesh of the body which hung on the cross has disappeared; the flesh we might now live in as Christians has to be the flesh of the risen body. Both sameness and difference are equally significant. One needs a complementary differentiation of terms to confirm as much.

Robinson also blurs the distinction between the resurrected or gracious state of things, which, as the third category, may now obtain for members of the new covenant and the glorious state of things, or fourth category, which is still absolutely ahead. The difference between the ecclesial and the eschatological modes of being though is just as great for Paul as the difference between the individual Jesus and the risen Christ — though all three are still bodily. Nor does Robinson discuss the Eucharist in detail, though he notes that some have thought Paul's body language as a whole must have been generated out of that context. Nor — more strikingly still — does he take up the sexual body except in

191

passing, prominent as any reader of Paul must feel that is. He sticks closely throughout to the communal body. So there is more to say.

The first task, once one has discriminated the necessary vocabulary, is to organize the different contexts in which body language appears. Of these three clearly predominate: sex, food, and community. There is besides the problem of the glorified body; which upon inspection though turns out I believe to constitute a sub-heading under the idea of the communal body. An even greater difficulty than the ambiguity of the words employed or the variety of separate issues is the apparent omission of any specifically kerygmatic formula in somatic terms. I shall be obliged to claim that there is in fact a "gospel according to the body" without being able to start with any obvious passage in which a "body" gospel appears. What we seem to have instead is a set of descriptions of the state of affairs preceding the essential act of God, that is, the state of sin, and the state of affairs subsequent to that act, that is, the state of grace. The condition of sin previous or antipathetic to the gospel is that in which we find ourselves before entering into the new covenant, as the state of grace following upon the reception of the gospel is the fulfillment of the promise in our case. The gospel proclaims the ways in which it is possible to move from one to the other, which is to say, from the second category to the third. But because body language is on the face of it better adapted to describe states of being than to define an action, the gospel and so the way in which the transition from a sinful to a gracious state can be accomplished is apparently left out of Paul's body talk. This appearance is in fact deceptive: there is, I believe, a way in which the gospel too can be worked out in terms of the body, so that the message consigned to this language can be arranged in parallel to the gospels according to justice and wisdom. But first one needs to examine the material which Paul does in fact provide, and arrange that in a convenient order.

Body language is most in use from the fifth chapter of Ist Corinthians through the fifteenth. It commences, that is to say, just as wisdom language is coming to an end. The first context within which it appears is the sexual; and within that context the initial instances are examples of sin. The first of these would be the case of a man living with his father's wife in chapter five. A second case of *porneia,* or sin in the sexual body, appears at the end of chapter six. This example is put suppositionally, though it presumably reflects actual conditions within the Corinthian community. The body language is dense from the beginning: "the body is not for *porneia,*" he says, "but for the Lord, and the Lord for the body . . . ."

Do you not know that your bodies are members of Christ? Shall I therefore make the members of Christ members of a whore? Let it not be so! Or do you not know that he who is joined together with a whore is one body? (For it is written, 'The two shall be in one flesh.') But he who is joined together with the Lord is one spirit. Flee *porneia.* All other sins a man does are outside the body; but the doer of pornic deeds sins against his own body. Do you not know that your body is a temple of the Holy Spirit within you, which you have from God? You are not your own; you were bought for a price. So glorify God in your body. (6:14; 15-20).

This is a rich passage; a good deal of Paul's total doctrine of the body is latent in it. Porneia, or sex under the dominion of sin, is exemplified by the dual body enacted when a man copulates with a prostitute. In condemning this conjunction Paul evokes as its opposite the body under the dominion of grace. In the passage this is primarily that body of which the "members" or flesh consists of the individuals composing the Church in Corinth and the soul or directive element is Christ himself; that is, according to the usual Pauline identification, the Spirit. The opposite of a pornic body, then, is in this instance not a gracious sexual body (he has not yet arrived at that possibility) but a gracious communal body. Paul is crossing vocabularies as it were on the diagonal to establish his immediate contrast. But the final

194

verse may also suggest that the same ratio could be thought of as obtaining with respect to individual Christians. If each of these as well as the communal body can be "a temple of the Holy Spirit," it too must consist of flesh (not the "physical" flesh only but the human soul as well) and spirit (which is to say, the Spirit). That Paul believes this gracious possibility does in fact obtain we know from other instances, of which the best known would be the famous formula, "not I, but Christ in me."

A body then may be individual, or dual (as in any sexual context), or communal. In each case the whole body (*soma*) will consist of a fleshly element (*sarx*) and a "spiritual" element (*psyche; pneuma; nous*). That much is Hellenistic common sense, which Paul adopts without questioning. Under the regime of grace, this spiritual element within any somatic composition is the Spirit indeed. The body in that case will a "spiritual body"; that is, a body of which the flesh is the flesh and the soul is the Spirit. Paul uses this expression only of the communal version, or Church body. But the principle of composition would apply to the individual and dual versions as well. If in a spiritual body of whatever kind, the soul is the Spirit, then the flesh would include whatever else made up a part of that body. In a communal body, for instance, the flesh would presumably include not only the whole persons of the "incorporated" individuals but also such things as the buildings they met in, their common property, and so forth. In any version, a spiritual body is what we can call in a later terminology a sacrament: that is, any Spirit/flesh combination. All third category *pneumena* are thus spiritual bodies in this sense.

A pattern of this kind may be detected behind everything Paul says about bodies, gracious or sinful. Part of the difficulty of working it out, as we noticed, comes from his casualness in the use of words. The chief ambiguity in this passage hovers as usual over the relation between the words "flesh" and "body." By "body" he should ideally intend the combination of flesh and soul we have just been outlining. But sometimes, as in these verses, he means only the fleshly element by itself. So we would have to read verse 15a of this passage, for instance, as meaning "do you not know that your bodies *of flesh* are members of Christ's *spiritual body?*"

If a gracious or spiritual body is a body of which the flesh is the flesh (of whatever kind) and the soul is the Spirit, its antithesis, the sinful body, would have to be a body of which the flesh is the flesh and the soul is one of the "powers" of this world. So in this case: to unite with a prostitute, especially if she is a temple prostitute, is to enact a dual body of which the flesh is a man and a woman and the soul is Aphrodite herself. So a pornic body would be the moral opposite of a Christic body; for a Christian to form part of such a body is in effect (though perhaps not in conscious intention) to apostasize. For to take the members of Christ, among which the sexual member is preeminently one, and to unite oneself with a woman who has devoted herself, body *and* soul, to the service of the Great Goddess is to act out an undoing of the redemption, and so to choose all over again the very bondage from which participation in the passion of Jesus should have made one free. Porneia is religiously speaking self-contradiction for the believer. "The doer of pornic deeds sins against his own body" (I Cor. 6:18). It is, we may realize, because porneia in such a context is religiously competitive that Paul adduces a communal opposite for a sexual sin; he is thinking immediately of the religious significance of the act.

The gracious equivalent of a pornic body within the sexual order is made evident in Chapter 7, which follows immediately and appropriately with a series of instructions on marriage. These begin right away with some secondary matters which have been bothering the Corinthians; the core of Paul's doctrine on the subject, which determines all his detailed recommendations, is to be found further on in the chapter: "A wife is bound to her husband for the same time that he lives" (I Cor. 7:39). Paul has this axiom by way of ecclesial tradition from the Lord himself, as we can tell by the confirmatory reference in I Thess. 4:2-8 and by consulting the corresponding instruction in the narrative gospels. The relevant verses in Mark employ very similar language, though with *sarx* where Paul would use *soma*:

> . . . from the beginning of creation male and female
> He made them. For this a man shall leave behind his
> father and mother and cleave to his wife, and the two
> shall be one flesh, so that no more are they two, but one
> flesh. What God has joined together, let man not divide
> (Mk. 10:6-9).

For the early Church, that is, Jesus had himself
while still in this life determined that in the Kingdom
marriage constituted a single spiritual body, of which
the man and the woman were the flesh, and the soul
was the creative power of God: a body of which the act
of intercourse would then be a "ritual" demonstration.
It has frequently been observed that providing for a gracious sexual possibility in this way is extraordinary; in
Judaism marriage takes place within the second category as an act of obedience, not in the third as a manifestation of grace, and in the "higher" forms of paganism, the religious life means leaving marriage behind as
well as fornication. But Paul is obliged (somewhat
against his own ascetic tendencies, apparently) to affirm
a married couple as the type of a spiritual body within
the sexual context.

From this center derive various instructions which
fill Chapter 7. Because a married pair form one body in
the Spirit it follows that even if one of them is still an

198

unbeliever, the flesh they share is imbued with the Spirit; the unbelieving spouse is "hallowed" through bodily contact with the partner, in the same way that the children of a Christian union are hallowed even before baptism. Grace, as a student once put it, is a venereal "disease". Because the union is established by God as a repetition of his original creation, it participates in that eternity. If the pair must part for circumstantial reasons, that cannot undo their marriage in the eyes of God. In the same way, within the mutual body, neither partner rules over his or her own flesh any more. It is a common possession with God; so neither partner can withdraw from sexual contact without the consent of the other. These are all practical and derivative decisions which adjust the initial word of the Lord to immediate contingencies, in the usual rabbinic style. They do not alter the principle which governs them all. Paul's "oral law" follows the primary *Torah* of the Lord, as one would expect.

Marriage though is not the only gracious possibility within the context of sex. Celibacy is the other, which Paul himself prefers, ranking it higher among the gifts of the Spirit. Accordingly he recommends celibacy to widows and those among the unmarried who can bear it. His criterion here is service to the communal body. The unmarried are in principle free to care about the affairs of the Lord directly, while the married cannot help but become absorbed in the merely fleshly affairs of the family unit. The celibate opportunity might for this reason be ranked among the ecclesial possibilities as well as among the sexual.

We have then two kinds of bodily existence within the sexual context, *porneia* of all kinds under sin in the second category and marriage and celibacy under grace in the third. To place these in order is to be reminded that there should also be a first and a fourth category possibility along the same line. Within the sexual context, the first category possibility would be innocence: a condition which, one gathers from Romans 7, would in Paul's view be limited to childhood, at any rate among human beings. The sexuality of animals would also presumably fall under this head; and therefore the difference between male and female taken simply as a natural fact. There is evidently though no *erotic* innocense for Paul: once the sexual life has begun, it must be either pornic or Christic according to him. The fourth category is also not hard to fill out — in this case with nothing. For in heaven, Paul would agree, there can be no marriage or giving in marriage. Our glorified bodies, though still in some sense bodily, are no longer sexual, for the flesh in that state of being is wholly consumed by the Spirit. Marriage, like celibacy, is a gracious but not yet a glorious estate.

We can now put the various bodily possibilities within the sexual context into a chart:

1st Category	2nd Category	3rd Category	4th Category
Innocence	Porneia	Marriage/ Celibacy	[ ]

With the Spirit/flesh structure of any third category body in mind, we can incidently work out corresponding structures for the other three species of body. Innocence presumes a body of which the soul as well as the flesh is entirely fleshly (or in modern language, involuntary or unconscious). A pornic body would be the reverse of a gracious body: flesh would dominate spirit. A glorified body, we have just observed, would be a body of which the soul is the Spirit, as before; but the flesh would be all Spirit too. This gives us a progression from the most to the least carnal state of affairs:

$\dfrac{\text{flesh}}{\text{flesh}}$	$\dfrac{\text{flesh}}{\text{spirit}}$	$\dfrac{\text{spirit}}{\text{flesh}}$	$\dfrac{\text{spirit}}{\text{spirit}}$

It may be observed that the very structure of a sacramental or Spirit/flesh body presumes that hierarchy is compatible with grace. So Paul is able to rank celibacy ahead of marriage, as in principle more eschatological. So too he is able to assert male dominance and female subordination. Women, he says, should wear a veil in church — apparently to express an acceptance of subordination. They should keep silence in church too — a

201

rule which may represent a testy change of mind from the more liberal position implied in I Cor. 11:5, which contemplates women prophesying. Paul has no word of the Lord on this matter. He can indeed appeal to the traditions of the chruches, but apparently in some insecurity of mind, judging by his tone. (The "traditions of men," he well knows, are as such of no authority in spiritual matters.) His real authority for the views he holds with such vehemence is evidently nature; which, he says, teaches everyone that long hair is a good thing on a woman and a bad thing on a man. In other words, sexual hierarchy is for Paul a first category state of affairs. As such it is morally innocent; and may therefore be incorporated into a third category body, as the fleshly illustration of a spiritual truth. As God is to Christ, so Christ is to man; and therefore man to woman (I Cor. 11:3). Male/female is as it were a fleshly anticipation of, and so potentially a demonstration of, Spirit/flesh. For Paul to assert this need not mean that his views in I Corinthians are in contradiction to the statement in Galatians 3:28 that in Christ there is no male or female. The context there makes clear he means that in the Spirit as such there can by definition be no fleshly distinctions of any kind. In the fourth category there will no longer be any sexual hierarchy — nor is there now, in the purely spiritual dimension of the state of grace. But within the *fleshly* dimension of that condition there may be — provided that sexual hier-

202

archy, like any other kind, is understood as a visible repetition of the fundamental subordination of flesh to Spirit. Our chart may thus acquire another set of members:

male	female	male	[ ]
female	male	female	[ ]

"Female/male" would express neatly enough what occurs in the conjunction of a Christian and a temple prostitute, for that embrace obviously subordinates the man in question to the female principle. The same, Paul would no doubt affirm, occurs implicitly in every other case of *porneia*. In marriage, on the other hand (and *a fortiori* in celibacy), the man is dominant; as, in Paul's view, he ought to be. *Innocent* nature can thus rhyme with grace; the first category *is* the third, as soon as the Spirit is counted in.

A contemporary theologian who wished to argue against Paul on this issue might therefore be advised to go back to Paul's initial assumption and deny that. It would be necessary, if his case were to be overthrown on grounds that Paul himself would have to recognize, to show that sexual hierarchy is neither natural nor innocent; that it does not, therefore, belong in the first category but in the second, where it could be defined as a manifestation of *in*justice; which is to say, of sin. Once that had been established as common sense, it would follow that sexual hierarchy could not possibly form part of any gracious condition. For the matter of any sacrament must be innocent. But most of our contemporaries who feel as strongly as Paul on the other side of this issue seem unlikely to entertain so much patience for the ground of their opponent's argument.

2

With the question of hierarchy we come to the end of Paul's theory of the sexual body. There is still no explicit proclamation of the gospel in sexual terms. We are given sin and grace: the condition from which our participation in the event declared should have rescued us, and the third category state we should realize we have entered into as a result — but not the covenanting act itself. This central omission continues true with respect to the second major bodily context, the matter of food. It is easiest to follow Paul's thinking in this context if we begin with the gracious instance, which in this case is the Eucharist. The Eucharist is to food what marriage, or rather the sexual act within marriage, is to sex. It re-presents the spiritual body of Christ as the hallowed bread and wine. As food these would of course be first category phenomena. Within the Eucharistic act, they become, taken together, the flesh of a sacramental body of which the soul is the Spirit: that is, Christ himself. Taken separately, the bread and the wine offer a re-demonstration of the basic third category contrast, the bread representing the flesh and the wine the blood (that is, the soul or "life") of this spiritual body. The difference between the bread and the wine would then parallel the sacramental value of the difference between the female and the male in the sexual context.

The structure of these distinctions is obscured by the

language of the text handed down, for in all the versions, including the one which Paul repeats, Jesus is presented as saying "this is my body" rather than "this is my flesh." And in the version which Paul quotes, he also says "this cup is the new covenant in my blood" rather than simply "this is my blood." There is good reason to suppose, as I shall be repeating in a later chapter, that the simpler alternatives would in fact have been what Jesus is likely to have said at the last supper. In any case, Paul's own theory of the Eucharistic body, as that is implied by the polemical context within which he quotes these ritual phrases, is certainly consistent with a straightforwardly reproductive version of the formulae. For him the body that the Corinthians are in danger of profaning is absolutely a spiritual body — is in fact *the* spiritual body in the alimentary mode, just as a married couple is the spiritual body in the dual, and the Church in the mode of community.

There will be more to say later about the covenantal significance of the Eucharist as such. For the present we need only observe that Paul's discussion of this rite suffices not only to locate it as the principal representative of the gracious possibility within the alimentary context but to indicate some of the other members in that context. Innocence, or the first category, would be represented along this line by the non-ritual eating which he recommends for the hungry before they attend the rite. Sin would be represented in the first place by the chaotic greed of which the Corinthians have unfortunately been guilty at their *agape*. And, as with sex, there is a blank in the fourth category: one does not eat or drink in heaven.

The issue of meat offered to idols addressed in chapters 8 through 10 would also belong in this context. A mature Christian knows idols have no real existence. That truth is part of the wisdom of God. All food, then, is really innocent, whether or not it has been offered to an idol. So it may be eaten by anybody at any time. Food is always licit in principle — as sex, in Paul's view, cannot be. As such, then, it belongs to the first category. But there is also sinful eating. The most prominent case of the kind would be eating meat that had been offered to an idol *as* offered to an idol. Such an act would amount to an anti-Eucharist, the alimentary equivalent of copulating with a prostitute. Even if the participant (in either of these cases) thought himself free of any internal commitment, none the less his bodily participation would involve him willy nilly in the worship of strange gods. Let the Christian therefore avoid even the appearance of such a thing: "I do not want you to be sharers with demons" (I Cor. 10:20).

And there are besides subtler cases of sinful eating. The one that attracts most of Paul's attention is eating meat which has been sacrificed to an idol under social circumstances that might scandalize either unbelievers or believers imperfectly secure in their knowledge that all food was licit in principle. This might happen at a dinner party where a Christian could find his attention called to the fact that the meat served once formed part of a pagan sacrifice. In such a case he would not be taking part in an act of false worship, as he might in a temple, but the results could be as unfortunate if an outsider concluded that Christians were not serious or a weak brother was led to think that sharing even at one remove in the food of demons did not matter. It would be better in such a case not to exercise one's theoretical right to eat in order to avoid injuring the potential or actual faith of others.

Another related error would be manifested in any boastful confidence that participation in the Eucharist would of itself suffice to inoculate against the danger of sin in this or any other context. This is not so, he reminds his addressees, any more than sharing in the manna in the desert (the equivalent of the Eucharist in that set of circumstances) guaranteed the Hebrews against falling into vice — as events proved. Any one of these possibilities, then, like disrespectful behavior at the ritual, can represent modes of sin within the context of food. They would all be manifestations of the "old leaven" which should be burned up, as at Passover, so that all may sit down to eat the "unleavened bread of sincerity and truth" (I Cor. 5:6-8).

We now have enough information to fill out another line on our chart of the gospel according to the body:

208

1st Category	2nd Category	3rd Category	4th Category
eating to satisfy hunger	disorder idolatory scandal	Eucharist manna	[ ]

3

The third major context after sex and food within which body language is used to define a variety of sinful or gracious states is community. The principal instance of a gracious body in this context is, of course, the Church: or Israel after the Spirit. This pneumenon constitutes the spiritual body *par excellence,* of which the flesh is the flesh of the different "members" who make it up and the soul is as always the Spirit. Participation in this body is the central privilege of the new covenant, and therefore the eventual if not initial focus of Paul's thought. Paul's ideas regarding the internal order of this very "corporate" body are elaborated chiefly in chapter 12 of I Corinthians. Just as a natural body consists of many members, the familiar analogy goes, all cooperative as parts of one organism though different in kind and dignity, so the third category community contains many individuals whose share in the common Spirit is reflected as various *charismata.* In this context, as in the sexual, Paul is at ease with hierarchy: the "gifts" can be ranked, from tongues at the bottom to apostleship at the top. The presence of the Spirit which makes all these pneumena gifts from God indeed is reflected through them all as love; which is, as it were, the blood of the body of Christ: *agape* is to the gifts as the gifts are to those who receive and exhibit them. A free, unconditional, and potentially universal love has to be eternal, like its source; it cannot pass away, as other gifts may from individuals or communities, for it is the eschatological principle in them all.

If the Church is the communal version of the gracious possibility, a sinful equivalent would be the sect or faction, against the formation of which Paul warns the Corinthians at the beginning of his letter. Parties divide instead of unifying; and disunity is for him always evidence that carnal interests are at work. Paul's immediate instances are all internal; there is no demoniac collectivity or totalitarian anti-Church on the horizon at the time of writing. He does not take up the problem of Israel after the flesh in I Corinthians, but if he had, we can see from what he says elsewhere that the Jewish nation could never have represented for him the possibility of ostentatious sin on the scale of the community. Old Israel is for him rather an instance of sin as it were to the second power: that is, a manifestation in terms of community of the intention registered in a human use of the Law; which is to say, the hope of conquering sin by force of will. In Romans 11, where he does address the problem, body language is not in use. Instead Paul envisions a dialectical process by which to see the *un*converted body of his people as in transition; no longer under the gross dominion to sin, as some other deliberately wicked nation might be, but on the way in spite of their own resistance to the fullness of the kingdom. If through their refusal to believe, the Gentiles are being (representatively) brought into the Israel of grace, that resistance has as it were indirectly played a part analogous to that of the passion on the scale of whole nations. It may be God's plan to bring the rest of the world into the third category first, before including the remainder of the Jews; if so, their eventual inclusion might coincide with the completion of the eschatological process. We are invited, that is, to realize Israel after the flesh as so much of Israel after the Spirit as has not yet found itself to be itself.

Along this line, then, the second category would include such evidently sinful pseudo-bodies as internal factions within the Church and proleptically gracious but still fleshly collectivities like the unbelieving Jews. The first category, or natural community, would be represented by the family (or better, the household) on a small scale and by the typical Gentile nation on the large scale. If the Church is collectively the "first fruits" of the kingdom of God, the fourth category would be the full harvest, for which Paul has a variety of images scattered through the letters. His discussion of the state of things which is to obtain at the general resurrection is as much of this as is ever put into body language. We can therefore arrange what he has to say about the glorified body in chapter 15 of I Corinthians along the same line as the other modes of collective existence.

Christ has been raised, he says; which establishes the

third category for good in every context. At his coming again all shall be raised who are not altogether done away with, thereby inaugurating the fourth category, in which everything that is *not* the Spirit has been annihilated *by* the Spirit, when God will become "all in all" (I Cor. 15:28). Even then bodiliness will not cease, however hard it may be to imagine. Paul evokes two analogies to help, both necessarily drawn from nature. Celestial bodies, he observes, differ from terrestrial bodies, and celestial bodies differ among themselves. Terrestrial bodies have distinctive glories, and so do celestial bodies. As their bodies differ, so do their respective glories. The glory of the sun is different from the glory of the moon, as the sun itself is different from the moon. Sunlight is plainly not moonlight. Yet light of whichever kind is bodily after its fashion, just as the parent bodies are. Similarly, he concludes, with respect to the case at hand: men will have their glory too, as the sun and the moon and the stars already have. But as celestial bodies are superior to terrestrial bodies in having glories at all, so men are superior to celestial bodies. The glory to which they are entitled will be spiritual, not natural. When it finally does shine forth, their glory will be as characteristic of them as sunlight is proper to the sun, or moonlight to the moon. And so that glory too will still be bodily, after its fashion (I Cor. 15:39-41).

This is one analogy; with which, apparently, Paul is none too pleased, for his presentation of it is very truncated compared to any paraphrase one may work out. His second analogy is more traditional and easier to explicate. The body of flesh, he says, is like a seed; the glorious body will be like the plant which grows from that seed once it has been sown in the ground. As a wheat seed produces a wheat plant, so a hallowed body, sown in death, will "produce" after its kind, however unlike our present mode of being that conditon will be. This analogy, like the first, drawn its matter from the first category. As prophetic parables of the eventual state of affairs, both therefore occur within the third category, where they function as sacramental signs of their own meaning — which must be the fourth. Both analogies therefore presuppose an inner continuity between created or re-created flesh and creating Spirit, and so between a gracious and any glorious state of affairs. The body is as it were the "name" of this continuity; participation in it is infinite in principle.

We are now in a position to make a full chart for all the conditions entrusted to body language throughout I Corinthians and so by extension for Paul's thinking as a whole:

	1st Category	2nd Category	3rd Category	4th Category
sex	innocence	*porneia*	marriage-celibacy	[ ]
food	ordinary eating	idolatry, etc.	Eucharist	[ ]
community	household nation	faction	Church	general resurrection

tongues . . . apostleship

We are also in a position, with the help of such a chart, to appreciate anew an all-important aspect of the new covenant which is especially entrusted to the gospel according to the body. This is the impressive fact that within this version of the relation Israel herself is shifted "bodily" from the second to the third category. Within all the other versions of the covenant, ancient or modern, that apply to the single nation this collective identity demonstrates itself both morally and liturgically within the second category. *This* world is where the Law can be obeyed and the Nation served. The primary element within the third category, according to all these variants of the old covenant, is the land and its fruits. Within that category too may be found authorization for the exceptional prophet or king. But the collective is *not* to be found there. That possibility is reserved for the days of the Messiah. Within the version of the relation which is enacted in Jesus *as* this Messiah, then, it not unnaturally follows that the religiously significant community is reconstituted as a third category pneumenon. "Israel after the flesh" is replaced by "Israel after the Spirit."

This all-important shift explains Paul's views on the position of the Jews. They are not in his eyes really sinners for good and all but as it were victims of a delayed consciousness. From a Christian perspective they would be so much of the communal body as has not yet passed through the second category to occupy the rest of its proper identity within the third. In Jesus that collectivity *has* passed through — on the scale of the exceptional individual. On the scale of the ordinary individual, the same passage can be made in faith. But it has not yet been accomplished on the scale of the nation. The passion is to that extent still incomplete; and so therefore is the resurrection. When both are completed, Paul thinks, the End will indeed have come.

4

We have observed more than once that though so much is entrusted to body language, the gospel itself is apparently not. Paul seems to give us the before and after but not the moment of transition. One reason, we suggested, might be that a gospel announces an action; and body imagery, in the nature of the case, is better adapted to express states of being. If the body of flesh is where one starts and the spiritual body is where (for the time being) one ends, the evangelic event would have to be an *un*bodying — which is difficult to represent *as* a body.

There are all the same reflections of the kerygma in body language to be found scattered through the letters. One is already implied by the image used to define the glorified body. If the seed is the body of flesh, and the new plant the spiritual body, then the means by which the one is transformed into the other is (humanly speaking) the act of sowing. "What thou sowest will not come to life unless it dies" (I Cor. 15:36). The link between this inevitable adjunct of the seed image and the passion was evidently already traditional within the Church as Paul repeats it. There are still closer repetitions of the same idea in those verses where Paul focuses on the ethical consequences of the gospel. In Colossians 1:21-22, for instance, he (if that letter is genuine) reminds his addressees that "being estranged and hos-

217

tile in mind in evil deeds, he has now reconciled you in the body of his flesh through death, so as to present you holy and unblemished and blameless before him . . . ." The clearest instance would be the verses in Romans tracing the spiritual career of the typical self. We know, he says, "that the old man in us was co-crucified, so that the body of sin might be destroyed, and sin might no longer enslave us" (Rom. 6:6). The "body of sin" is the Old Man, of whose body we are all members in the flesh. When Jesus dies, Adam is executed — a sentence which had *not* been carried out in the garden. To rise with Christ is then to become a member of *his* spiritual body instead. The gospel announces an exchange of bodies; which is to say, of identities: not Adam but Christ "in me." The peroration of this sequence is most emphatic: "Wretched man that I am! Who will rescue me from the body of this death?" (Rom. 7:24) — a rhetorical question for which an answer must be supplied between verses 24 and 25: God, he alone, through my (bodily) identification with Jesus Christ, *he* has delivered me: for which reason I now can say: "Thanks be to God through Jesus Christ our Lord!" (Rom. 7:25). Body language can be employed too not just of the original redemptive moment but for the continual repetition of that moment within the career of the Christian. So in II Corinthians Paul can describe how the apostles are "afflicted in all, but not destroyed; always carrying in the body the dying of Jesus, so that the life of Jesus may also be shown in our bodies" (II Cor. 4:8-10). Nothing could be more emphatic than the kerygmatic structure of this last verse: to suffer the trials of the missionary is to rehearse the crucifixion in one's own body, so that the life of the risen body may be revealed in the body of the community. As with Paul, so too for his addressees: to accept the gospel as that which has been proved true in Jesus is to re-enact the paradigm on behalf of others in a repetition which has to be as bodily as the original to count as faith. So we are asked to "crucify the flesh" (Gal. 5:24), to "sow to the Spirit" (Gal. 6:8), and to "present our bodies as a living sacrifice, holy to God and acceptable, our reasonable worship" (Rom. 12:1).

With the help of such hints, it should be possible to work out an evangelic proposition of the same not/but pattern which can be seen to obtain for justice and wisdom. In those contexts Christ is *not* the justice or the wisdom of man *but* the justice and the wisdom of God. In this context it should be correspondingly possible to infer that Christ (*this* Christ) would be the body of God; a strange but not entirely implausible thought — provided we remember that God is altogether spiritual. If Christ *is* the Spirit, then, it would follow that he is *not* — what? The specious alternative to the *Spirit* of God must be the *soul* of man. In which case Christ (*this* Christ) is *not* a genius, or a hero, or any other mythical representative of that soul. He is simply the Spirit. Then

219

a gospel according to the body would have to say that the soul of man, however ambitious, could *not* rescue this world or anyone in it from the inevitable fate of the flesh. Gnosticism, ancient or modern, could not do it; asceticism, external or internal, could not do it; "therapy" could not do it; above all the will could not do it. All these would be pseudo-spiritualities which do not in fact involve the Spirit.

This Christ *is* the Spirit, then. But such a truth could only obtain within the third category, which it defines. How then could such a Messiah appear within the second category, should he ever enter it? *Not* as the proud soul, as men had hoped (and would go on thinking), but as so much disembodying flesh: the figure on the cross. We may fill out the kerygmatic pattern within the covenantal structure accordingly:

Jesus Christ

is

not the soul of man	which comes to nothing in the end
but his dying flesh	Through which the spiritual body *may* show

Thus the gospel too can be formulated in body language. And once the possibility has been clarified, the presence of this gospel according to the body may be detected within the presentation of the same message in other terms. For to preach the gospel at all is sooner or later to preach it in body language, implicitly or explicitly. Bodiliness is subsumed, for instance, within the gospel according to justice, for the moral efficacy of the atonement depends upon a process of identification, which has to be bodily. The expiatory process relies on this exchange of identity between the representative and the community he represents, a reciprocity which makes sense only in bodily terms. For the community and the individual are morally equivalent only to the extent that they are somatically interchangeable. It is this pre-verbal identity that once sustained the older idea that a community might be held responsible for the sins of its members, or that a man could be guilty of his forefather's act — or that a city might be saved if one just man could be found therein. This primitive sub-strate offers, as it were, the matter out of which the legal argument in the gospel according to justice derives its elementary plausibility. There is a similar underground connection between the gospel according to wisdom and the principle of bodiliness, for wisdom, especially in the Greek view, is normally a way to escape from the body of flesh. The gospel preached in that language must therefore stress the folly of the cross, on which hung the dying flesh of at least one body of just this sort. As usual the gospel directs us the *other* way.

And once the gospel has been re-apprehended in bodily terms, it becomes possible to connect it *un*metaphorically with sacrifice, and so by way of sacrifice to return once more to the covenant. We may notice in this connection that the passion of Jesus could readily be defined as an instance of all the species of sacrifice for which provision is made under the Law. It is an *olah,* for the original flesh of the body offered is completely consumed, if not on the cross, then at least in the tomb. It is also, by way of Jesus' anticipatory ingenuity, a *zevah sh'lamin,* or communion sacrifice, for the believers assembled to enact the Eucharistic repetition are thereby enabled to consume the new flesh of the very body which has already been immolated. And it is also an expiatory sacrifice, a *hattat* or *asham,* which atones for sin. The doctrine of the atonement makes much of these last. But the two former species are really more demonstrative of the intention involved. They need not be theologized by an addition to the effect that Jesus died "for our sins," true as that may also be, for they already define that death itself. The flesh of Jesus did vanish; the Eucharist was established. To that extent one could be sure he is an *olah,* and sure too he is a *zevah sh'lamin.* "All," says Paul, "fall short of the glory of God" (Rom. 3:23). This condition is not necessarily a sin. It is simply the normal predicament even of the just man. And the just man, we have observed, is free to carry out the two higher forms of sacrifice. Let him, the implication would seem to run, get on with them.

We do not need moral language, then, to arrive at the central meaning of sacrifice under either dispensation. We need only an appreciation of what is at stake; which we arrive at in those moments when any body speaks. What it *says* is: death, death, death. To live in a body of flesh is to realize with every out-breath, evacuation, or orgasm that we do not live forever. The first category is already lapsing away into the second in the act of being realized. Culture resists this by prolonging the life of the primary body in symbolic "bodies" of one kind or another (there is no *real* body in the second category). Sacrifice though appropriates this fatality as a choice. It passes through what must otherwise threaten from a specious distance. Each act of sacrifice, then, reverberates paradigmatically; and a complete act of sacrifice would accordingly reverberate absolutely. The gospel according to the body permits us to realize a Jesus who would represent us not only morally but ontologically. He passes through our necessary terror. So he takes upon himself the task which in the nature of the case *I* am constantly avoiding, or I would not be who I am, whatever that is. For he deliberately surrenders the fiction I am continually asserting against the encroaching dark. To have done so amounts to unqualified faith

223

in him. It becomes faith in me too as soon as I identify with his surrender of everything I still hold on to, knowing only that holding on will do no good in the long run. And that which I hold on to *is* my body, immediate or symbolic. So faith too becomes bodily as soon as it becomes actual.

PART VI
Mark

But a profit to the land in all
Is a king to the field beservanted.
— Eccles. 5:8

Paul will represent the argumentative gospel *par excel-lence;* if his message can be fitted into a covenantal structure of faith and blessing then the general point is half gained: the new covenant will be recovered as not only new but authentically a covenant — and to that extent not absolutely new either, but a universalization of the old for a potentially indefinite "moment" of eschatological crisis. But the New Testament includes specimens of narrative as well as argument. To complete our case it is necessary to examine a sufficiently representative instance in that genre. If an entire narrative gospel could be read as rehearsing the structure of the new covenant in as many contexts as there are pericopes, we should have finished the other half of the job too if not exhaustively at least indicatively. And the choice of example cannot be hard: Mark, the original "gospel," offers the obvious test case. Let us re-read it, then, with this purpose in mind.

One's first impressions upon beginning Mark's story are discouraging. For no covenantal form seems detectable within the episodes of the early ministry with which this narrative commences. The sudden appearance of Jesus as the agent of the Spirit in Galilee seems on the contrary to annihilate all such structures of expectation. We are instead invited to see the Spirit loose once more in the world of the flesh, and acting there with extraordinary freedom but without any readily understandable link to human behavior, positive or negative. The various cures and exorcisms occur with disconcerting randomness. There are no obvious answers to the questions, why here, why now, why this individual rather than another. And in this atmosphere of disheveled accidentality it seems impossible for anyone within the situations described to realize the events which occur as divine manifestations. Both the beneficiaries of the power Jesus wields and those who remain suspicious invariably interpret what happens in fleshly rather than spiritual terms. The people suppose Jesus a wonder-working rabbi — of the sort to which some modern scholars, ironically, have once again found it easy to reduce him. The local intelligentsia think he must be casting out devils with the help of the chief of devils. Neither party recognizes him as the presence of the Spirit in any way that could be read as calling for a new relation to God. All this can be disconcerting not just for those concerned within the stories but to the covenantally minded student, who is not getting the help from his author he would like.

The first impression, then, is of incomprehensible power. The Spirit of the Lord — and that, at least as believing readers, is what we already know this must be — not only enters the world unpredictably but sweeps as if from nowhere all the way into the shore of our bodily existence. The second category is scoured clean as if by some great wave which washes away whatever suffering and sin happen to obtain quite without regard for individual merit or the authority of the Law. Only sheer human being is left undisturbed — to be converted, one may try to see, into the flesh of a new creation. But who has eyes? The gifts received are so absolutely gratuitous that the very possiblity of grace is lost in the flood of beneficence. At most some victims may have to ask for help, but even that is not regularly necessary. Good is simply done for them, freely and randomly. There happened, we are told, to be a man possessed by an unclean spirit in the synagogue at Capernaum, which happened to make a noise; so Jesus, interrupted in his teaching (about which we are not told) simply orders the bad spirit to come out. The miracle itself could conceivably be understood as a negative commandment doing away with evil. But the positive commandment which should correspond is entirely missing. Nothing is asked of the victim before or after. Going home to Simon's house from the synagogue, the party finds Simon's mother-in-law ill with a fever. So Jesus helps her up. The fever has left; and she begins to wait on them. Are we to understand her service as religious, or simply as taking up ordinary life where it was left off? It looks as if anything more than that would be forcing the text. By evening people have brought in all the sick and possessed in the town. They crowd around the door and Jesus cures and exorcizes them, casually, as they happen to arrive.

All this occurs on what Mark represents as the first day's work — on a Sabbath. The next morning Jesus goes off to pray, as if to indicate that he too has been disturbed at the breakdown of distinctions. When Simon and the others follow to report that there are more looking for him, he replies that the party should now go on to other towns; for he came, he says, to preach the Kingdom — which is not, one gathers, entirely a matter of curing illnesses. But how, in such an environment, is the difference to be made?

In any case Jesus' conduct is not shown to alter in the days which follow. He continues to go about Galilee preaching in synagogues and casting out devils. A leper is cured in much the same way as before, and though Jesus orders him to show himself to the priest, presumably so as to demonstrate that this most exceptional cure is indeed the work of God alone, the point does not get across: the man "proclaims" the "word" of his cure promiscuously, and soon Jesus is unable to enter any of the towns because of the press of people.

And so it goes: the free gifts of the Spirit prompt the crowd to interpret the results as good luck. For them the Spirit *is* the Flesh, only more of it. Instead of gratitude and awe, these random benefits stimulate enthusiasm, cupidity, superstition and suspicion. All this can seem intensely "realistic"; one may well feel inclined to attribute this aspect of the story to the most trustworthy tradition as much as to any redactional intention to exhibit a *theios aner*. For the episodes do not show a Jesus who can control the way in which his gifts are received. He cannot teach the crowd to make better sense of what is happening. It looks as if he were at a loss.

Nor does he have any better luck with those who might have been expected to know better. Chapter 2 begins a series of conflict stories with the scribes and Pharisees. These people represent differentiation, and so at least the possibility of covenant. It is therefore not unreasonable for them to ask if these extraordinary cures are legitimate as well as effective. The test is just as obviously to ask whether they are consistent with the Law. God would presumably not contradict himself. A cure on the Sabbath which could as easily be put off until the next day would surely be illicit; the man who would do such a work must be an exploiter of whatever

229

powers he may dispose of. Such an argument is impeccable provided the doer of the deed is Somebody like other good and bad human agents. Thus the intelligentsia also interpret the actions of Jesus in a fleshly sense, like the crowd in its more elementary way.

What the scribes leave out is a possibility so impossible there seems no reason to take it into account at all, much less presume it as the basis for an interpretation of what is going on. If Jesus is acting as the agent of Somebody Else to the infinite degree, then of course it would follow that he is master of the Sabbath, or of any other law, since he transmits the same *dynamis* which constituted the Law in the first place. *Such* a "Son of Man" would indeed be able to forgive sins, for example, as easily as he could restore a victim's legs. The two would be different aspects of a single recreative deed accomplished by the same will that creates life and reveals forgiveness to begin with. The interweaving of a physical cure with moral forgiveness, which has led some commentators to see the cure of the paralytic in 2:1-12 as the conflation of two separate stories, could even, one might think, have been intended by Jesus as well as by Mark or the tradition immediately behind him. For the inter-translatability of the two idioms would serve of itself to represent the deed as an instance of the third category — once that possibility had been entertained as possible at all. Which it is, of course, only for the already believing reader. Within the situation depicted the friends of the paralytic possess no more than an animal "faith" of the sort that would lead them to seek a cure in the conviction that Jesus could effect it. The scribes do *not* respond with any more adult equivalent, since for them the deed done is firmly within the second category as a "blasphemy." One presumably reads that they are not swept away in the wonder of the crowd at the miracle, either.

The like conclusion could be shown to hold for the conflict over table fellowship with sinners, or the regulations for fasting, or gleaning in the fields, or curing a crippled hand. The climax to these conflict stories comes when a party of scribes who have come down from Jerusalem attribute all the cures to the power of Beelzebub. Such an attribution seems the equivalent on the level of explanation to the state of possession from which some members of the crowd suffer on the level of accident. Like the crowd, the scribes deny that the Spirit could possibly have done what they see done. The crowd's denial is unconscious. That of the learned is no worse as long as they merely accuse Jesus of being a sinner for breaking the Law. This would be only a misunderstanding. The denial becomes culpable as soon as they attribute the actions done to Satan. For that is to assign the power of doing good to an evil principle — which is in effect to abolish God. This would be the blasphemy against the Holy Spirit which cannot be forgiven — since after all it is precisely the Holy Spirit who

231

forgives. The scribes thus deliberately repudiate the possibility that the others have simply failed to recognize. Mark seems to provide an ironic coda to this last rejection by placing at just this point the story of Jesus' mother and his brothers. They have come to take charge of him, convinced he is out of his mind. Now they are standing outside. From the purest good will, they too are virtually guilty, though without knowing it, of the same error which in the scribes at least has already become explicit sin. They assume he is possessed himself. The counter-stroke is very characteristic: "Who are my mother and my brothers?" (Mk. 3:33). Not his relatives after the flesh, we are told, but those about him — provided they accomplish the will of God. But then what *is* the will of God?

The members of the crowd cannot know. They only know that their bodies have been touched. But once they have been cured, they carry on as before. If they do anything at all, it is apt to be mistaken; they spread the news, for instance, which is not what Jesus wants; or they bring their friends and relations, which he does not want either. Certainly there is no moral change either achieved or expected. Nothing is *said* to them, even, most of the time; an omission that bothers Matthew, who introduces great blocks of teaching from another tradition, to make up this difference. Nor are the Pharisees and scribes offered any positive command. They should *not* ascribe the cures to Satan. But they are not

232

given anything else to do instead. It does not appear that there *is* anything to do.

Except for the disciples, who now constitute a third group with a role to play beside the crowd and the scribes. They appear at the very beginning of the second chapter, when Simon and Andrew and James and John are called, and a little later when Levi is called. For these people at least there *is* a positive command, though a very simple one: "Follow me," says Jesus, and instantly, as such things happen in Mark, they do. Here too is the note of randomness. We do not hear why these men in particular were chosen. The fishermen are ignorant; Levi, as a tax-collector, is a sinner. Apparently this "Joshua" is choosing virtually anybody at all to represent the twelve tribes of the new Israel. The formulation of this command is to be sure covenantal in structure: "Follow me, and I will make you fishers of men" (Mk. 1:17). The second clause occupies the usual position of a divine promise. But the first clause is strikingly unspecific; or rather, it is specific in an unhelpful way. Anyone may literally enough obey a command to come after another person and live with them. By itself though obedience to such an order would be merely human. In order to become covenantal indeed, "following" would have to become metaphoric as well as literal. And as naive readers of Mark's narrative, we do not know yet any better than the disciples themselves what the word (or the action) could mean.

Which brings us to the end of this section of the story, as Mark has organized it; we must suppose on purpose, and not just because he thought it had once happened that way in history. The Spirit returns into the world, and the effect, to start with at least, is that the works of that Spirit are interpreted in terms of the flesh. The Spirit is in effect denied *because* it is present. And this occurs because nothing is supplied to define the second category, which is all that distinguishes the first from the third: the flesh, that is, *from* the Spirit. If the first part of Mark were our only evidence, we should have to abandon hope of reading a narrative gospel covenantally altogether.

2

The chapter devoted to the parables does supply a little more help, though not so much perhaps as one might like. Mark sees to it that all the parables are told on one eschatological "Day," like the first set of cures. Here then is another turn of the spiral, from deeds without words to words without deeds. And the words are as indirect as the deeds were ambiguous. There is evidently an inner cohesion to the parables assembled; all, it has been observed, repeat more or less the theme of the first, that of the Sower and the Seed. This parable has given exegetes a hard time from the beginning: the interpretation repeated by the evangelist has not seemed a satisfactory solution to most moderns however applicable it may have been to the church from which Mark presumably inherited it. But whatever else the parable might mean, it seems clear that the reader should understand it as applying to an action that takes place within the third category; that is, an action of the same kind as those we have just seen Jesus doing. The parable would then be making an imaginative comment on the cures and exorcisms and controversies. In which case we could assume that Jesus himself is the Sower, at least in the first instance, and not the seed or the harvester, as Carrington and Quesnell on the one hand and Dodd on the other have argued. For the previous episodes have indeed shown Jesus "sowing the seed"; that is, revealing the Spirit in various actions: which is to say, parabolically. If that is so, the parable would in effect be saying that it was the task of *this* Christ to go on doing just such actions, whether the recipients make sense out of them or not. The seed falls on good and bad ground alike. God, not man, not even the Son of Man, will bring about the eventual harvest in his own good time.

If the seed is being sown in the third category, it follows that the corresponding harvest must be the fourth; the end of the world, when the Kingdom, already brought "near" in the deeds and words of Jesus, will have finally "come" altogether. A parable connects what is happening now within the third category to what will happen eventually within the fourth. Such an absolute reference is sure to be parabolic indeed, since the fourth category cannot be spoken of at all except in the third; which in turn must employ the first as its vehicle. The final fulfillment of the promises must be wholly spiritual, and so not even parabolically a "harvest." But *in parable* it is possible to refer to that otherwise unimaginable consummation as a harvest. Parables are eschatological art.

The elements of the other parables may be similarly arranged. The lamp under a tub or bed would be the light of the Spirit as that now shines; that is, obscurely and through cracks. But in the end God will put it on a lampstand to illuminate the whole house. Once again the basic contrast is between the state of affairs obtaining since Jesus' advent and a condition thereafter to be anticipated. *Then* there will be nothing hidden now that will not be fully disclosed. The parabolic as such will be wound up, disappearing along with the rest of this fleshly world. We may understand the difference between the amount measured and the amount given, or between that which a man has and that which he will yet receive, in the same way. The series ends with two more "seed" parables, still in the same pattern. In the first the seed grows slowly of its own accord, and only when the crop is ready will the farmer begin to harvest. In the other, a mustard seed grows up into a large tree.

If though the parables themselves must be understood as occurring within the third category, where they present a spiritual meaning in terms of some fleshly matter, and if that meaning *is* the fourth category, we still have no obvious point of contact with the covenant, which should connect the third category not with the fourth but with the second. The parables explain what Jesus is doing — parabolically. They might even be read historically as interpreting Jesus to himself, I suspect more confidently than is usually done. It is agreed after all that the parables are original, whatever may be the case with the explanations appended. And if their field of reference is as we have just supposed, they could conceivably tell us something about Jesus' own sense of his mission. But they do not contain within themselves any

237

instructions for *other* human beings. It is no use commanding people to be good ground.

The fact though that the parables exist at all is some help. For there *is* something that can be done with a parable, even if not inside it. It can be understood. "Listen," says Jesus after telling the first and most important: "Anyone who has ears to hear!" The shift from mute action to indirect language does make some difference. For those in the story who *do* understand the parables are thereby changed. They are no longer just members of the crowd, who can appreciate only the literal sense. They become (incomplete) disciples, who can realize at least that there is a metaphor to translate, even if they do not know how. Something *is* required in the negative, then: one should *not* fail to understand what is being done, or the language in which that gift is indirectly described. If and when anyone *does* understand, he or she becomes a disciple indeed — intellectually at least. We can then "follow" in something better than a physical sense. The "mystery" is concealed "so that," as 4:12 cruelly puts it, those outside may stay there: for to understand is already to that extent to "be converted and be forgiven." Mark's own idea of this possibility may be better represented by 4:34, which presumes that Jesus spoke in parables but always in the hope of being understood. Such a supposition would be supported by 2:3 and 6:2, as Eduard Schweizer has observed, as well as by the opening of chapter 4, which shows Jesus teaching freely from a boat.

In any event, a parable is offered: and understanding it is (just) possible. And this combination *will* fall into a covenantal structure. In which case we could leap ahead to define understanding as a species of faith. For it is precisely the function of faith to interpret the spiritual signified of any fleshly signifier in any context. The seed is to the ground, we can realize, as the Spirit generally is to the flesh universally; or as Jesus is to his hearers; or Mark to his reader. The structure of any parable is itself parabolic, and preaches the gospel formally, as its content prophesies an absolute future which the gospel opens out.

So the chapter is parabolic for the gospel as a whole. Nor need we understand Mark's understanding as peculiar to himself. In representing a Jesus whose deeds and words cannot help but be enigmatic, he may simply be reproducing the style of his master. For actions within the third category would *have* to remain ambiguous. Revelations of the Spirit *in* the Flesh could not very well be otherwise. Mark's stress on Jesus' effort to keep his deeds of power hidden — the famous "Messianic secret" — may only be his way of formulating the inevitable. After all, does the Jesus of any version of the tradition ever act or speak quite literally? In this narrative, only when he is depicted as explaining himself — but these explanations, the commentaries agree, are the easiest to attribute to ecclesial inheritance or Mark himself.

The form-critical difference, then, between some mysterious *logion* or acted parable and its translation for the disciples would then correspond rhetorically to the difference between revelation in the third category and teaching in the second. For Mark is a teacher, not a prophet, a transmitter and explainer of the gospel he passes on, not its originator. For him that is Jesus alone.

3

The possibility of faith, parabolically implicit in the understanding evoked by the parables, surfaces explicitly in the next major section of Mark's narrative, from 4:35 to 6:6. The disciples in the boat are said specifically to *lack* faith in Jesus' power to curb the storm. Instead they are afraid. The case of the Gerasene demoniac which follows is still obscure in the previous style: did this man want to be cured, and is that desire the analogue of faith on the level of the unconsidering flesh, or is it that the legion of devils hopes for a safer home in the swine? His townsfolk at least are afraid; which the storm episode has just shown is the opposite of faith. The cured man is however told *not* to follow Jesus, though he is for a change free to spread the news. Jairus though has faith in so many words when he follows Jesus into the house in spite of the report that his daughter is dead. And the woman with the issue is cured, Jesus tells her, because she has faith. In both these contexts faith seems to mean strong desire combined with an exceptional trust in the face of physical and social discouragement. It is a committed orientation towards Jesus; and as before is polarized against fear in both cases. "Do not fear," says Jesus to Jairus, only have faith: *me phobou, monon pistou.* Here at last would be a negative and a positive commandment that could go neatly into the usual covenantal structure: Do

241

not fear *but* have faith — and I will cure your child. The little girl's obedience to the command to rise, so exactly repeated in its original Aramaic, may also be taken as a mode of "following" that applies under the circumstances, and therefore as one more instance of faith. And in negative confirmation of the import of all these stories we have the visit to Nazareth, where Mark frankly tells us Jesus could work no miracle because of their *lack* of faith. His townsfolk could see in him only the carpenter's son with the usual mother and brothers and sisters: a Jesus, that is, altogether after the flesh.

The next identifiable section, from 6:14 to 8:26, is easy to define, dominated as it is by the two miraculous feedings, each forming the principal unit, the commentators point out, in a distinguishable sub-sequence which includes a voyage in a boat, a conflict story, and a cure. Faith is certainly well hidden in these miracles. On neither occasion does the crowd, Jewish or Gentile (if that is the intended difference between the two stories) even become aware that a miracle has taken place. They take what happens as a matter of course. Jesus is again "sowing" the "seed" quite randomly and indeed literally — though in terms of the *other* end of the grain-to-bread spectrum. Everything that occurs is once more the solitary work of Jesus: there is nothing for anyone else to do except eat. We are once more in the atmosphere of the first cures and exorcisms.

The controversial episodes in each sub-section do

though contribute to the elucidation of faith in the negative at least. The Pharisees go wrong because they substitute knowledge in its place. They make too much of the "tradition of the elders," and turn even this into an occasion for remaining in possession of what they pretend to give up. Or they seek a "sign;" that is, some piece of evidence that would allow them to know for certain who Jesus is. But *knowing for certain* is by definition a worldly procedure which cannot reach as far as the acts of the Spirit. Normatively or cognitively, then, the Pharisees introduce irrelevant positives where they do *not* belong. Faith though in all its species is an appropriation of the negative; and so a clearing of the way.

The most interesting cure in this section is that of the Syro-Phoenician woman. When Jesus refuses her original request, she makes use of his rude image in a second try: the "dogs" under the table are at least allowed to eat scraps of bread which the children do not want. Thematically this is one more repetition of the "bread" talk which as Quesnell has pointed out runs through this section. Dramatically, it is *chutzbah,* as a student once called it. *She* is the one who displays "spirit" in a double sense, and Jesus is the legalist. But unlike the Pharisees he can be turned round: her daughter is cured. The initiative she shows accordingly amounts to a version of the faith which most recipients of a cure need not develop.

The two boat episodes are still more illuminating. In the first Jesus comes walking across the water after a night of heavy rowing. The disciples think he is a ghost; that is, an after-image of the flesh. They are terrified. Jesus replies, "Have courage! It is I! Do not be Afraid" (Mk. 6:50). As before they are *not* to fear *but* have courage (in the Greek two parallel verbs in the imperative: *tharseite . . . me phobeisthe.)* Between these commands, positive and negative, comes a specification of the authority behind them: "It is I!" that is, *ego eimi.* The Greek phrase is presumably meant by Mark to have behind the colloquial idiom the full force of the absolute I AM in its traditional Septuagintal sense: it is Jesus' ultimate identity in the Spirit that is revealed in these absolutely sacramental words. Mark appears to intend the *ego eimi* quite as parabolically as John, who uses this expression so much more elaborately to punctuate his gospel. On this occasion it serves as a verbal analogue to Jesus' own miraculous presence upon the waters, or to the bread multiplied in the feeding just before. Characteristically the disciples fail once again. Instead of having courage, which would be faith in this context, they are "utterly and beyond measure put out," a deliberately emphatic superlative of fear. The disciples do not respond, says Mark mysteriously, "for they had not understood about the breads; their heart was closed up" (Mk. 6:52). Quesnell has taken this verse as a point of departure for an ingenious explication of the gospel as a whole. What the disciples have not grasped is that the miracle of the "breads," like the miracle they have just seen, or for that matter the phrase Jesus has just used of himself, is a third category demonstration of the Spirit in terms of the flesh. The crowd could only eat; the disciples might conceivably have appreciated the parabolic character of the extraordinary meal. If they had, the implication would run, they would not be terrified: faith as understanding and faith as courage would have supported each other in the presence of either act of God. The bread is of course the type of all third category events because it can be understood to have functioned as such on the hillside and because it continues to function as such within Mark's church and that of his believing reader. In the light of the Eucharist, understanding and courage may in principle awaken with respect to *any* manifestation of God's presence. Such an awakening would amount to a perfect faith, capable of applying across the board to all possible encounters with the third category — which would indeed, under such circumstances, take in the whole of creation. But that does not happen on this occasion.

4

Paul believes that Jesus' third category identity begins with the resurrection, when he was "appointed son of God in power according to a Spirit of holiness through resurrection from the dead" (Rom. 1:4). The sacramental deeds of Christ therefore take place as far as the apostle is concerned within the Church, where indeed he has personally enacted some of them. For the authors of the narrative gospels, though, Jesus' third category identity commences with the baptism if not before; which means that there can be a relevant "Acts of Jesus" to compose as well as a (theoretically interminable) Acts of the Apostles. Both sorts of evangelist though agree that Jesus has only one serious action to perform within the second category. As the passion begins to loom upon the horizon, then, Mark's narrative comes closer to rehearsing the themes which dominate Paul's argument.

This accommodation begins with the crucial recognition scene at Caesarea Philippi. Placed at the halfway point in the narrative, the episode makes an emphatic climax to the slowly developing theme of faith. For Peter, the chief of the disciples, shows most explicitly that he does have faith — up to a point. He can profess that Jesus is *not* John the Baptist, or Elijah, or any of the prophets (who would be figures corresponding to the Law obeyed by the Pharisees or to the sign they expect) *but* "the Christ" (Mk. 8:29). If he understood that title in a third category sense, a covenantal moment would be completed within the story — which would in effect complete as well the literary intention with which Mark evidently began, to bring a representative character within the tale up to the point of view of the best possible reader of the tale.

But in fact Peter is only "beginning to see," like the blind man in the episode immediately preceding. Jesus at once starts to explain what the presence just recognized properly entails. "The Christ" turns out to be a hidden pun: the new third category sense of the term presupposes, it turns out, an implicit second category meaning as well — which is the reverse of what Peter seems to have in mind. The Son of Man, says Jesus, will *not* reign as a king in this world *but* must suffer, be rejected, put to death, and only then after three days rise again. All but the last item in this series must be passed through within the second category *instead of* conquering the Romans. Isaiah 53 should be read as applying not to some ancient prophet but specifically to the *true* Messiah. This could be sobering for the reader as well as for Peter, for the announcement exposes the extent to which Jesus has so far presented himself (for those who have eyes to see) entirely within the third category. We might say from a Pauline perspective that he has as it were anticipated his resurrected identity while still in this life. Jesus has stood in for God on the scale of the exceptional individual at a certain time and place. Faith has therefore been some recognition of this pneumenon. But now we are told of the action within the second category which will as it were retroactively validate these eschatological anticipations. This action, though, like any other in this world, must in the nature of the case be accomplished by Somebody — not by Somebody Else. It is therefore Jesus as the "Son of Man" in the earthly sense of that ambiguous title who will have to suffer what is now predicted, in order that the Son of Man in the heavenly sense may eventually appear; that is, in order that the kingdom, already "near" in the miracles of the ministry (and soon to be near again in the miracles of the community) may finally "come" completely. The deed Jesus is now to do is thus complementary to the faith he has been inviting from others. He is not only the object of faith but its model. The passion will be *his* act of recognition and trust; which because it is his, and he knows what he is doing, can be unqualified — as Peter's, so far, cannot be.

Implicitly, then, faith is once again being defined as the collaborative working out of a possibility which must in the nature of the covenantal case be traceable in common by Jesus *and* by others. Mark emphasizes the connection immediately with a stringent re-definition of "following" in the same language Jesus has just used about himself: "If anyone wishes to come after me, let him deny himself and take up his cross and follow me"

(Mk. 8:34). The revelation of what there is still for Jesus to do is thus at the same time a final disclosure of what could be meant by faith in others. As there are many laws to specify the Law, so there are in principle as many varieties of faith as there are situations and persons to be in them. But the key to them all is the deed upon which we now see Jesus deliberately embarked. And about this deed Jesus can be presented as speaking openly, *paresia*. For as an action in this world the passion is intrinsically *un*ambiguous. Carnal negatives are as obvious as spiritual positives must be mysterious.

We can now realize too that the seed parable, which could be read in context as rehearsing Jesus' work within the third category, will also make sense within the second. In the third it alludes to the gifts provided. In the second category the sowing of the seed must allude to the act of faith which justifies these gifts. A benefit in the Spirit presumes a service in the flesh. This is the "rule" of the new covenant, which Jesus will reveal by demonstrating both roles — it does not matter, the narrative would appear to be telling us, in which order. So he becomes indeed the "word" between God and man and between man and God: one word, but with two opposite meanings, which the passion and the resurrection separately spell out.

The story of the transfiguration, which follows directly, balances the extreme negativity just disclosed with an anticipatory positive as glorious as the passion predicted is hideous. It represents a chance to see everything plainly and distinctly, as Peter's confession has represented beginning to see. What Peter and James and John are shown on the mountain occurs within the third category, not the fourth. There is still a fleshly element: garments are garments, though extraordinarily white; it even makes a silly kind of sense to build booths. But there is proportionally less of the flesh in this vision, and more of the Spirit. Peter and James and John are brought into the third category *with* Jesus, who has been there all along. So for a moment they can *see* what they must otherwise believe. Vision, or audition, is as it were a kind of sacramental sensation. But presently the moment lapses; they see nobody but Jesus, and he only in the flesh once again. And by the time they rejoin the other disciples and the crowd, they are back in the world at the foot of all mountains, where it is hard to cast out evil spirits, and such faith as one has must be helped.

The sayings and small episodes that complete this section represent detailed applications of the rule that the disciples must indeed take up the cross in one context or another in order to become themselves. The instruction to act as a servant or as a child, for instance, or to abandon a limb or eye, are gnomic repetitions of the action exemplified by Jesus in his suffering and by any one else in his or her faith. Perhaps the most explicit instances of what this might mean in specifiable contexts is provided by the discussion on marriage and the tale of the rich young man.

Both episodes throw into relief the difference between the old and the new covenant. Some Pharisees ask Jesus, is it against the Law for a man to divorce his wife? They know it is not: Dt. 24:1 says a man may divorce his wife "for some impropriety." The "house" of Shammai, we are told, interpreted this to mean only for adultery. The "house" of Hillel, (supposedly) more liberal, interpreted it to mean that divorce was permitted for incompatibility in general. Both schools were of course obliged to insist that adultery on the part of the wife made divorce compulsory for the husband. Otherwise he would become guilty of complicity in her sin. The Pharisee's question, as Mark renders it, would appear to imply that some contrary views of Jesus' were already known. He now advances an alternative instruction explicitly: in marriage God unites man and wife, so they become one flesh. And if God has united them, man cannot afterwards divide them. It follows that divorce is not possible now for any reason — which indeed we find Jesus reported as affirming in Lk. 16:18 (though Mt. 5:32 demurs), a *logion* alluded to as well in I Cor. 7:8-11 and Rom. 7:2-3, and elsewhere in I Tim. 3:2 and Tit. 1:6. The double instruction was evidently a well-attested portion of Jesus's teaching. The effect is to change marriage from a contract within the second category to a sacrament within the third — which is exactly how we found it defined in Paul's gospel according to the body. This is why the reference to Genesis is relevant, for creation is already a third category idea. Marriage is thus ranged with the other miraculous deeds of Jesus — though in this context, the author of the sacramental sign is specified as the Father rather than the Son. Jesus does not marry anyone himself. Instead he offers a new *torah* defining its eschatological character for all times before and after. Within the ministry, this instruction is therefore proleptic. It applies within the community to come — which has always had its difficulties with it. For if a sexual union could be an instance of the eschatological Israel on the scale of the dual, the complimentary response of the parties would have to include a species of faith as unqualified as that of Jesus. The cross would have to be the rule in this context too — which a life-long fidelity would certainly have to be!

The episode of the rich young man, which follows immediately, can serve to specify what a *crucial* faith could mean in economic terms just as the discussion of marriage will indicate what it could mean within the sexual life. There is a parallel contrast between what is required under the Law and what is asked within the new version of the relation, though in this case the Law is not done away with altogether but conceived of as a first step. Asked how eternal life may be obtained, Jesus reminds his inquirer of the commandments. He is assured that these have been practiced. Apparently the young man expects some sectarian super-law over and above those he has already been accustomed to obey. Jesus, we are told, "having looked at him loved him;" his questioner is after all a possible subject for faith. Go, he says, sell everything you have and give it to the poor; then you will have treasure in heaven — and can "afford" to follow me. The covenantal structure is clear and simple: financial self-sacrifice is the species of faith that applies under these circumstances; for the young man, we are told, is rich. But this particular camel does not pass through the needle's eye.

Such a conclusion to a story is not unusual in Mark. As the possibility of discipleship becomes clearer, the actuality becomes rarer. It certainly fails to include any of the official "disciples;" marginal victims, on the whole, seem to do better at exhibiting faith in this narrative. The reason is not, I believe, because Mark is carrying on a deliberate though cryptic vendetta against the actual Twelve, as Weeden has argued. It is because he is addressing other would-be disciples, who are his readers. He needs to show them that a truly crucial faith is humanly speaking very difficult indeed. The original disciples evaded it, we learn. That should be a warning to all future "believers." For Jesus is rightly recognized, and the Spirit received, on no other terms than the cross indeed.

B

You know the way where I am going.
— John 14:4

Mark's rendering of the ministry virtually concludes with the revelation of the passion as the open secret of Jesus' messiahship, for with the entry into Jerusalem which follows the passion narrative proper may almost be said to begin. What Mark has composed so far then is a sequence of traditional stories which gradually disclose the latent structure of the covenant they announce. At first everything seems a gift: the good news would appear to be that the eschatological promises have now been fulfilled without any complementary requirement. But the truth turns out to be one degreee less apocalyptic than that. Understanding is introduced as a minimally appropriate response to parabolic word and parabolic deed. This *gnosis* presently deepens into *pistis;* and faith in its turn is eventually defined in terms of a dreadful death which may be required of all believers because it has already been embarked on by the paradigm himself. The narrative so far ends with some key instances of faith in just this least qualified sense within precisely the contexts where any such possibility is bound to seem most impossible: sex and money. We may gather accordingly that to accept the gifts conferred within the third category is therefore in principle to accept an invitation to share in the sacrifice they already presuppose. The different varieties of faith would then balance the various kinds of gift. Together the several matched pairs would exemplify as many occasions of the same underlying structure.

Once the pattern has finally been developed in full, Mark's narrative can take its place alongside Paul's argument. Both evidently proclaim the same gospel, however different the literary kinds. And both illustrate the persistence of the fundamental structure through a variety of contexts; a key point, for the new covenant must establish its ideal universality by showing the unlimited range of its application. Obedience has to be limited to some specific set of laws, in the nature of the case; but faith, if it is to seem plausible as the sole human element in the absolute relation, must be shown to be as various in form as there might ever be human contexts within which to enact it. The new covenant is thus for the "Gentiles" in a phenomenological as well as a national sense.

Which leaves, one might think, only the event which constitutes the new covenant to entrust to narrative. But first there is a briefer ministry in Jerusalem. The emphasis here is no longer on what Jesus can do (that has already been demonstrated) or what others might do in response (they have had their chance) but on the absence within the "holy" city of that *dynamis* which Jesus has been exhibiting in the countryside. The contrast between him and the actual Jerusalem is established immediately by the entry and the cleansing of the temple. Ezekiel 43:1-9 is a useful guidebook to these verses: the prophet envisions the glory of God coming from the east and taking up its seat within the ideal temple which is to be. In that vision the glory filled the house. In actual history the temple was indeed rebuilt and then rebuilt again most splendidly, as Ezekiel had once hoped; but the glory did *not* take up residence there. So much of the promise had not yet been fulfilled — and could therefore still be expected. Jesus climbs up from Jericho, says Mark, which is to the east. So are Bethany and Bethphage, in which his disciples look for an ass on which to ride. The eastern gate of the temple area was in fact both literally and symbolically blocked. But it is now *as if* he had entered through it, we seem invited to imagine, so as to come into the temple at the one point where its wall coincided with that of the whole city. Once there he looks about, reports a mysterious verse; and then, without doing anything more, retreats for the night to Bethany. What is he supposed to be looking for? Matthew and Luke both leave this verse out of their versions, which suggests they do not know. In the light of Ezekiel, we might guess that Mark intends us to understand Jesus to be looking for the glory which Solomon is reported to have seen on a previous occasion of a similar kind (I Kgs. 8:10-11). The aboriginal promise had been that the "tent of meeting" would

256

be "hallowed in my glory" (Ex. 29:43) and that "I will dwell in the midst of the sons of Israel" (Ex. 29:45). Solomon's temple had once seemed the fulfilment of this. Jesus' gesture might then constitute one more parable. If the glory *had* still been present, Jesus' work would not have been necessary. But as it is, the Spirit is not to be found either in this vulgarly "new" temple of Herod, that other "king of the Jews," or among the people whom this temple and city represent. They are none of them in the third category. Instead the Spirit is with Jesus — and Jesus alone. In his own person he therefore represents the whole of that eschatological Israel for whom the promise has been entirely kept. The task he now assumes would then be to transfer the Spirit from himself as a single individual to the community to which it properly belongs. This is the deed presently to be accomplished. Meanwhile Mark shows him demonstrating in detail that the city is indeed as Spiritless as the country has proved to be, and so in need of just the service he has been called to render.

The tumultuous entry has already demonstrated that the people in general are without the Spirit and incapable of recognizing it in Jesus. The Zechariahan ride upon an ass is a parable that is *not* understood. The crowd sees only a would-be monarch. Their adulation is accordingly an irrelevant substitute for faith. The temple, once Jesus arrives there, is obviously empty of the Spirit and full of the flesh, a den of thieves rather

257

than a place of prayer. The cleansing which Mark places on the following day also seems to have Ezekiel in the background: "on the top of the mountain the whole limit thereof round about is holy of holies: behold, this is the *torah* of the house" (Ezek. 43:12); in which case it should follow that no buying and selling could occur even in the outermost court. From an eschatological point of view the city is one with the temple, as the temple is one with its most holy sanctuary filled with the presence of God. Jesus is practicing apocalyptic geography. By the standard evoked — is the Spirit present or not? — the figtree is indeed barren of fruit. The authorities who challenge Jesus' authority could not recognize holiness in John the Baptist. It is *a fortiori* useless for Jesus to "explain" himself, as if he had not already done so — parabolically, which is the only way possible in this world. His enemies "do not know" how to take in what he has done. Their attitude is rehearsed in that of the husbandmen in the allegory of the vineyard, who destroy the slaves sent by the owner, and finally the son as well.

All the "branches" of the "figtree" are severally given their chance to prove their barrenness. The Pharisees and the Herodians try to trap Jesus with a question about the poll-tax. If he answers yes, it should be paid, he will lose (the commentaries point out) the support of the nationalists; if he says no, it should be withheld, he may please some among the Pharisees but he will declare himself a rebel against the Romans. The answer he finds distinguishes God from Caesar, which is precisely what the questioners will not do. They assume that the honor of the nation is identical with the life of the Spirit. Thus they exhibit their inability to distinguish one from the other.

The Sadducees are guilty of a parallel confusion within the private life. Their question about who shall have the much-married wife in heaven assumes that the other world is just like this one. Jesus repeats what should be obvious, that there could be no marrying or giving in marriage once everything whatsoever has either disappeared or become Spirit altogether. The Pharisees confuse the life of the Spirit with the life of the nation. The Sadducees confuse the life of the Spirit with the life of the family. Thus each party confesses in its different way that it cannot understand the Spirit at all, since in each case they identify it with a possibility of the flesh, public or private.

The first exception to this wasteland of Spiritlessness is one of the scribes. He at least acts as an individual, and not as a member of a faction. And his question is honest, not a trap: "Which is the first commandment of all?" Deuteronomy supplies the first half of the answer: thou shalt love the Lord thy God with all thy heart, soul, mind, and strength. This much is perfectly consistent with a scribal understanding of the tradition: the *Shema* is at the heart of Deuteronomy, as Deuteronomy concentrates the Law. Leviticus supplies the second half: thou shalt love thy neighbor as thyself. This commandment too was often chosen as an epitome of the Law, as anecdotes of Hillel and Akiba will prove. The scribe has asked a single question, so we must take Jesus' double answer as essentially single in intention. If the two commandments are combined "love" must mean what they imply under each other's influence. If I love God within a context of loving my neighbor, the temptation to idolatry is checked; if I must love my neighbor within a context of loving God, my tendency to exchange on a level of interest alone is checked. The commandments taken together are thus potentially the cure of each other's fleshly parodies.

More positively, the combination implies a third kind of love into which the other two might be converted. God and the neighbor are *both* present in any complete human love. What that love might be in its own right we do not learn from Mark. His emphasis throughout is on faith. Instead we are given two angles of an ideal triangle, from which the third might be calculated. Which the scribe does, apparently, when he consents to the combination: well spoke, master, he says; and repeats the gist of what he has understood in such a way as to enforce a consequence: to love God *and* one's neighbor in one and the same act would indeed be more than any holocaust or communion sacrifice.

The scribe *can* recognize the Spirit, then, in Jesus' words, and understand the right response as a species of love which would put them into practice. To that extent, as Jesus says, he is "not far from the kingdom of God." What then would take him the rest of the way? We must suppose something equivalent in this context to the sacrifice the rich young man was invited to. Nothing of the sort though is proposed to the scribe then and there. He is left as it were on the edge of an unqualified faith, still caught in an argumentative admiration.

The rest of the scribes as a party though are as untouched by the Spirit as the Pharisees and Sadducees. They interpret the Messiah as David's carnal son merely, rather than as his spiritual Lord. Their conduct too betrays a practical ignorance of the Spirit, for they are ambitious for honor, and willing to exploit those who might support poor scholars. They do not know the Spirit, and do not know that they do not know the Spirit; so they cannot have faith. Meanwhile the crowd enjoys Jesus' criticism of its betters — but only out of the underdog's inevitable *ressentiment*.

But a second exception does appear. This is the widow whom Jesus sees putting two mites into the Temple treasury. She throws in the whole of her life, remarks Jesus. Here then *would* be an instance of entire faith: not in Jesus personally, who is not involved, but in God — which is after all what counts in the end. She

261

accomplishes the sacrifice which is indeed more than any merely perfunctory holocaust or communion sacrifice, since in giving her money she gives herself — as Jesus is presently to do. She is not just "not far" from the kingdom: she enters it. Her gesture then will represent the action required to complete the admiration of the exceptional scribe.

2

Chapter 13 or the "apocalyptic discourse" contributes little to the covenantal question of faith and Spirit. But in context it may be read as revealing the fate in store for a city and a temple the Spiritlessness of which has just been exposed. A community without God in its midst can only be carnal by definition, and so inherently subject to annihilation. A house of worship which consists of no more than so many big stone blocks piled one upon another is sure to be overthrown sooner or later in the nature of the case. There can be no absolute future for such things, nor does it take a prophet to say so. Apocalyptic, however fantastic, can only repeat a philosophical and historical truism in cosmic imagery. So much is anticipatory reason, not yet faith; which does though appear towards the end of the discourse, where attention is commended: "Watch!" This instruction is evidently most obviously applicable to Mark's own generation, caught between the portent of the Jewish revolt and an imminent return of the Messiah in glory.

There is more to the point in the last section of the narrative. For Mark, it should be remembered, the three final chapters devoted to the passion and resurrection would have been the original nucleus of the whole. Its "pre-text," if Mark really is a Roman gospel, would have been the passion narrative of his church, as that

263

body was accustomed to rehearse its belief liturgically. Some version of this source, already amplified perhaps by the addition of a few subsidiary episodes, may have formed Mark's immediate working text and so his inspiration for the larger gospel. He would have begun composing his own narrative backwards, elaborating a history of the ministry out of oral tradition and informal collections to serve as an "introduction," as it has been called, to a passion story already largely fixed in writing. It would presumably therefore have been this final section that suggested a structure for the previous sequence of stories. It is not surprising, then, that when as readers we approach this conclusion as the fulfilment of the history we have just been reading, we find the covenantal equilibrium which has been gradually becoming apparent through the earlier episodes still more absolutely emphasized. In this section what has for the most part appeared previously as absence of faith now darkens into anti-faith, or unqualified violence. The enemies of Jesus not only ignore, mis-interpret, or reject but betray, deny, and kill. Judas betrays: this is portrayed not just as *in*fidelity but as anti-fidelity, a deliberate repudiation of an allegiance once deliberately assumed. Peter denies the very identity he had once most positively professed his faith in. The crowd which had cheered a king now demands the death of a scapegoat. The soldiers abuse a parody emperor. And Jesus himself feels terror and distress, though unlike the others he is still capable of following the will of God.

And the other side of the covenantal polarity is similarly reinforced. When Jesus stands before the high priest he is shown as declaring himself openly, which hitherto he has not been willing to do. Are you the son of the blessed one, they ask? And he replies, *ego eimi*. But he is heard as a blasphemer: the Spirit, then, is not merely not recognized as such but interpreted as its own opposite, the power of evil. In the same way the man who might have been released as politically innocuous even if not acknowledged as an eschatological king is condemned by Pilate as a rebel, the antipodes of what we are to understand he is in truth. The crowd count Jesus less than Barabbas, who is even lower on the same fleshly scale: a real rebel who has failed. Crucifixion is the fate of a criminal slave. Absence of faith has everywhere turned into conscious or unconscious commitment to evil — except for the centurion at the cross, of all people, whom Mark allows to *say,* this man was the son of God. Coming from a pagan killer, this must represent faith under the circumstances; indeed the most perfect instance of faith, we are obliged to understand, that anybody has shown so far.

Both sides of the ministerial pattern, then, are present in the superlative. But these manifestations are of course not the most significant version of the basic structure in this context. What counts is not what others do but what Jesus does; which is to carry out the essen-

265

tial task on the human side of the new covenant. Jesus no longer evokes faith; he exemplifies it. Thus he retroactively or by anticipation renders absolutely relevant the faith which has been or might ever be asked of anyone else. Jesus acts, and we *can* believe that he has done so. Together these responses amount to the whole of what Somebody might do. Sacrifice and faith are revealed once again as two sides of what is in the end a single deed. What is sacrifice in him is presently faith in us; what is faith in him is presently sacrifice in us. This is the human side of the new covenant.

Thus Jesus typifies the completion of what may be done within the second category by using up all its possibilities except those which repeat his own actuality in faith and practice. This empties the world *of* the world; which leaves God entirely free to act. Whereupon, very early in the morning of the first day of the week . . . but Mark is reserved about the divine half of the covenantal story in this context. Only the emptiness of the empty tomb is reliably attested for the gospel as we have it. There may once have been at least one resurrection story to conclude the original narrative, for a meeting in Galilee between the risen Lord and his followers is powerfully predicted twice in 14:28 and 16:7. If so, it was detached early, for reasons unknown, leaving the abrupt ending of 16:8. It seems to me quite unnecessary to suppose with Marxsen and his American followers that the prophecies of 14:28 and 16:7 refer not to a resurrection vision but to the parousia. Nor would it be necessary to conclude that because the present text of Mark omits a positive resurrection story the author intended to disparage the visions of the apostles or the traditional conviction that the risen Lord was present to his Church. What is not literally included is not necessarily denied. Mark says explicitly that the Church has the Spirit (Mk. 13:12), which is all that is needed to confirm the possibility of other third category manifestations in this or any other context, for in Mark's theology, the Spirit *is* the Christ, as much for the community after the resurrection as for Jesus after the baptism. Something is held back in the present text, to be sure. The "messianic secret" has many manifestations, and this concluding reserve may be the last. It is tempting to adopt Jeremias' alternative suggestion, that the resurrection visions might have been esoteric as far as Mark was concerned (or perhaps his church) in which case they could have been purposely left to the tradition, which the preacher employing the text up to this point might have been expected to repeat for those who were entitled to hear. The original listener or private reader would in any case have had a liturgical repetition of the essential gift to share in. The Easter Eucharist in particular may well have represented the third category event which would have corresponded most directly to a reading of at least the passion narrative in Mark's church. There have to be many "mights" in any speculation of this kind. We need only understand, as readers of the existing text, that the Spirit, which had been missing in Israel, has finally been restored. But now the Spirit endows Israel once more on the scale of a community instead of the exceptional individual alone. To "have faith" then becomes to repent, accept this good news, and be baptized into that community.

For on the divine side of the covenantal structure, the resurrection is a change in the mode in which something transpires within the third category. According to Mark Jesus is in that category from the baptism. Whatever he does throughout the ministry must accordingly be understood as parabolic or sacramental. But he is only one man at one time and place. If the third category is to be reconstituted as a constant possibility for any time and place (for as long as there shall ever be times and places at all) the scale must change. The resurrection demonstrates that this transition has in fact been effected — for those who believe. The community of believers is to that extent in the same situation for all ages that Jesus was in for a short time, and with the same power and privileges. For the Church, or Israel after the Spirit, is in the third category too — as long as it functions as the Church at all. The ministry of Jesus as a whole could therefore be understood by the evangelist and his readers as an enacted prophecy of the possibility which the Church continues to represent. Jesus is then himself as it were a parable of the inspired community to come. The narratives concerning him are therefore the gospel indeed insofar as the reported presence of God within the various episodes is understood as indicative of how the actual presence of God may manifest itself ever since — to those who have faith now as some did then. And Mark's ending presumes a reader who understands this because he or she is already a member, like himself, of the community which understands it too. In this way the "secret" is passed on.

C

Going, he goes in tears, bearing the seed
Coming, he comes in joy, bearing his sheaves.
— *Ps. 126:6*

Mark can represent what might be done to preach
the gospel at all in terms of a narrative of the ministry.
A recapitulation of his work can represent in turn what
might be done to recover a covenantal structure within
the episodes assembled and in the sequence of their assembly. Together with Paul, Mark can therefore illustrate the NT witness as a whole; if these texts can be
read covenantally, so could the rest at leisure. To that
extent there would be no need to labor the same argument through the other authors. Two alternative or
supplementary versions of the basic structure though
are worth mentioning briefly, for they contribute something additional in each case to the content of the new
covenant.

The first of these would be Matthew, the obvious
test case for the possibility that the new covenant could
be expressed in *almost* the same terms as the old. His
major contribution to the idea of a narrative gospel is
the teaching material he introduces in great blocks into
Mark's order of events. The central instance of this ex-
pansion would be the Sermon of the Mount, which as
an inaugural address parallel to the Decalogue certainly
comes as close in form and manner of presentation to a

270

direct repetition of Sinai as the author can make it. Jesus is portrayed as a new Moses upon another mountain, delivering dicta which should constitute the core of a new "Law." The collection of pronouncements that follows is similarly parallel to the "Book of the Covenant" in style of assembly and local structure. Matthew's gospel, an encyclopedia of Christian *halacha,* comes as near as may be to a second *Deutero-evangellion* to match Deuteronomy: here too are explicit commandments, negative and positive, to which obedience is required on pain of punishment and in hope of reward. This is very much the work of a scribal intelligence, or Ezra *redivivus.* The latent contradiction to Paul's version of the gospel can seem very strong.

But this new "Law" is in fact meta-legal. "Happy are the poor in spirit," begins the key sequence, "for theirs is the kingdom of heaven" (Mt. 5:3). Unlike the Decalogue, the mood is indicative rather than imperative. Instead of an order being issued a situation is declared. This emphasizes the paradox, for in this world the rich are happy and the poor, insofar as they are *not* rich, are unhappy. But here the poor are invited to re-interpret their own indigence so as to make of it a poverty "in spirit," as Matthews' special addition puts it, and not just a poverty after the flesh. They are invited to appropriate a deficiency as a species of detachment. If this is possible, the poor would no longer be merely deprived of the first category. They would be free within

271

the second. The Kingdom, then, is being offered not to those who trust in wealth, whether they already possess it or still miss it, but to those who are ready to interpret the absence of riches, however that has come about, as an opportunity to transcend their reliance upon them. We might clarify the offer by putting it back into the imperative form after all. Then it would become: do *not* trust in riches *but* let yourself become poor in relation to the Lord and *then* you will receive the goods of the Spirit. Poverty thus appropriated becomes the equivalent — and more — of justice under the Law. It becomes a specification of faith within the new covenant.

The other members of the first half of the Beatitudes work in the same way. Meekness, loss, hunger, and thirst are not by themselves good things but the absence of good things. As long as powerlessness, suffering, and deprivation are defined as the absence of the fleshly positives they presuppose, they remain as irrelevant religiously as their carnal opposites. If though these negatives are deliberately appropriated, they can be understood as indicating the way to the Kingdom. They become aspects of a universal passion. The mode of relation thereby introduced is clearer in the second half of the sequence: "Blessed are the merciful, for they shall be mercied . . . the clean of heart . . . the peacemakers . . . the persecuted for the sake of righteousness . . ." (Mt. 5:7-10), for in the various contexts these titles invoke, negativity is more obviously the way to a third category end. The Beatitudes begin with the hardest cases, where the negative in question is physical and so most intractable to a religious interpretation, and end with the moral instances, which are easier to comprehend in these new terms. Such an order of formulation is itself paradoxical.

The choice recommended, moreover, is not commanded but asserted to be blessed or happy *already*. The behavior reprobated is not condemned (in Matthew; in Luke it is) but omitted altogether. Indeed it is omitted so entirely that it could even be mis-understood as present after all, as it has been by those who have assumed it is the poor-who-would-be-rich who are declared blessed *in their need* — and have drawn revolutionary conclusions. But judgement is altogether replaced by blessings here. We are once again in the atmosphere of the earliest cures in Mark, where nothing is required and everything is provided. What is provided in this context though is not a natural good but the possibility of a moral conversion. It would indeed take such a turning around of the soul to reinterpret deficiency as transcendence and the absence of the flesh as the transparency of the Spirit. Such a re-apprehension could only occur as an act of faith.

On the divine side of the covenantal exchange the "rewards" for undergoing this *metanoia* are summed up as the Kingdom of Heaven. The phrase is Matthew's expression for the regime of the Spirit as a

273

whole; which is to say, the third and fourth categories taken together. So the comfort, satisfaction, forgiveness, and intercourse with God which are promised "in return" for the conduct advocated are altogether spiritual in character. The Beatitudes are carnally speaking remarkably severe. They promise no worldly compensations for any obvious losses; only the one sure way to work through loss — which is to lose as it were, on purpose. But that is what makes them a true repetition of the gospel, and so covenantal after all.

In the light of these new "commandments" one can go on to make evangelic sense of Matthew's "Book of the Covenant," which follows directly, and of the other blocks of teaching. The Law is fulfilled, Matthew affirms, not abolished; all directives from God, old or new, are to be obeyed in the hope of reward and fear of punishment. So the instructions which follow the Beatitudes take up the language of the original Decalogue: you have heard it said, the formula now runs, you shall not kill, or commit adultery, or swear falsely; but I say that you shall not cultivate anger, or look with lust, or swear at all. To this extent the new commandment is presented as an intensification of the old. On the *negative* side, that is, the Mosaic structure would be reinforced rather than abandoned. The difference is in what is explicitly or implicitly recommended. You are *not* to hate your brother — but become reconciled to him. You are *not* to lust after other women — but remain faithful to your wife. You are *not* to swear by this or that outside yourself — but confess what is so. You are not even to hate your enemies, as might seem implied in the Law (though not literally to be found there) but love them too without qualification or limit. You are, that is, to be perfect, even as your heavenly Father is perfect. To become perfect in any of these ways would be to act out the "rule" of faith. In Matthew's version of the evangelic equilibrium, then, the sin to be rejected is still the old sin, though raised for emphasis to the second power, so it may be all the more vehemently repudiated in the old style — but the "virtue" encouraged is new. The rhetoric is still legal, but the invitation is as much beyond the "works of the law" as it is in Paul. And Paul too, we can remember, is obliged to employ the language of the theology he wished to overthrow in order to describe what overthrew it. That is the burden of the scribe and the Pharisee in any age.

2

A covenantal reading of John would require no such penetration of a contrary language. The core of the new relation as that author understands it may be found in Jn. 5:24: "Amen Amen I say unto you that he who hears my words, and believes in him who sent me, has eternal life, and will not come to judgement but pass from death to life." This recognizing faith is explicitly invited from the characters within the stories and implicitly presented as a continuing possibility for the reader, who is not assumed (as he is in Mark) to be a believer already. Nor is there as in Mark any gradual exposure of this faith: it is possible from the beginning, and always in the same way. The narrative is a series of tableaux, each with the same import, rather than a development. John's eschatology, it has been repeatedly observed since C. H. Dodd put the term into currency, is preponderantly (if not entirely, as Dodd supposed) "realized" rather than futural; more, for him, is to be experienced in the third category and less need therefore be prophesied for the fourth. But all that can be experienced now or in the future is Jesus, alive or risen; for John, "eternal life" has no *other* content.

John's initial addition to the modes of faith is the idea of witnessing. Witness is how the possibility of faith can be passed from one person to another. So John the Baptist witnesses to Jesus before his own disciples, who immediately leave him to follow their new master. Then Jesus' disciples witness to each other — "We have found the Messiah" (Jn. 1:41) — and presently the Samaritan woman witnesses to her townspeople. The works Jesus does are also called witnesses to his true identity, like the scriptures, for those who can read these *semeia* the right of way round. The Father himself witnesses to his Son, and the disciples are told they will witness to others in time to come. This promise is fulfilled in the composition of the gospel itself, which witnesses to the reader — if he or she is able to accept the evangelist in that role. Witness is the socialization of faith, and as such a proof of its intrinsic universality.

The chief contribution John's gospel makes to the other side of the covenantal relation is consistency and clarity. This is most obvious in the great series of I AM declarations which fill up the central portion of the narrative. Each of these is decisively sacramental in structure. The *ego eimi* represents in each case the spiritual element in a declarative proposition of which the predicate represents a fleshly element: that is, the particular sign in terms of which the divine identity is revealed in the episode in question. Thus Jesus is presented as revealing successively that he is the bread, the living water, the light, the good shepherd, and so forth. Once the pattern has become clear, it is possible to apply it retroactively to the story of the miracle at Cana, where an *un*spoken "I AM the wine" seems to preside over what takes place. In a similar fashion the story of the cleansing and the predicted destruction of the temple *almost* includes an "I AM the temple." All these sacramental formulae, explicit or implicit, repeat in as many contexts as the tradition will supply fresh evidence of the initial proposition of the prologue. For John's affirmation there that the word was made flesh may be understood as a summary generalization of the relation asserted in each "I AM the _____." The *ego eimi* IS the *logos*, then, to the extent that this presence can be summed up in a word indeed. The predicates it accumulates in the course of the narrative may then be understood as so many *logoi* translating the word into one fleshly language or another. The final and most literal *logoi* would then be the words of the gospel writer himself, most typically as these occur in the long speeches which typify this author's special method. It is evidently the *risen* Christ, speaking through the inspired author, who might say "I AM these words." Unlike Mark, John *is* a prophet. All these modes of manifestation, then, demonstrate a Jesus who acts within the third category as he does in Mark — but still more unconditionally so, if the last mode of presentation is counted among them. And like Mark too, the narrative shows Jesus entering the second category only twice, once (indispensably) for the passion and (as an anticipatory sign of that) for the washing of the feet, the Johannine equivalent of the Eucharistic offering.

278

But the idea of witnessing, impressive as it eventually becomes, can seem almost a secondary explication of the possiblity of faith within the new covenant next to the idea of love. "This is my commandment," says the Johannine Jesus in the last long speech to his disciples. The stress is clearly meant to be on the possessive pronoun, to distinguish this commandment, of which there is only one, from all the other commandments of the Law, of which there are so many: "This is my commandment, that you love one another as I have loved you" (Jn. 15:12). The verb is *agapan* in both uses, which may or may not imply that the love both exemplified and required is in either case ultimately one with the love that God offers, whether through Jesus or among the disciples. But proximately it is clearly something that can and should be done within the second category by human beings — of whom, in this contest, Jesus is still one. If the brothers around the table are to love each other with the *same kind* of love as that with which Jesus will shortly prove he loves them, this must be a sacrificial love; a *thusic* love, we may call it, after the Greek for "sacrifice," to distinguish it from the purely *agapic* love of the sort which would occur, strictly speaking, in the third category alone. There need be no confusion of ideas, though, whatever verb is used; the love I enact for my "neighbor" (to pick up the appropriate term from the synoptics) is bound to be thusic on my side and agapic on the other — provided he or she receives it as a gift from God. Love in the sense commanded must then be a species of faith, like every other sacrifice.

We needn't of course think this possibility exclusively John's. The "Double Commandment" in Mark is, we have already seen, another presentation of what we must consider fundamental Christian *torah,* as V. P. Furnish has pointed out in his useful *The Love Command in the NT.* The Beatitudes are another instance, in a different rhetorical style. Luke's parable of the Samaritan is a celebrated third. The connection of faith with love is made explicit in Gal. 5:13-14 and 6:2. The idea that faith is most truly itself with respect to other human beings when it "works through love" is held peacefully if variously in common throughout the early tradition.

John's rendering though allows us to be sure that love (in the sense proclaimed) *is* faith — and so covenantally relevant — as soon as another human being is counted in. Love is as it were the content of which faith is the form. It is the concrete of sacrifice in a version of the relation within which the other modes of that cultic action can seem either obsolete or reserved for Jesus himself. Through this specification we are reminded that the commandment of faith does not imply a solitary flight through an empty world to the bosom of the Father, or even a world inhabited only by Jesus and the believer. The new covenant allows for the actual pres-

280

ence of every other human being as well; by orienting our relation to each other on a religious axis. Somebody Else of whatever sort is thereby defined as the sacramental representative of Somebody Else to the infinite degree. To love one's neighbor is to practice one's love of God — which is faith by definition.

The Kingdom is "near" whenever this is done. For if I intend the being of the other without counting either merit or cost, then God gives through me. If man acts *as* God acts, God acts. It is impossible to imitate God without making him present. Keeping one side of the covenant in the mode of love means that the other side is kept too. This need not imply that the other human party will necessarily recognize what is happening. We can read in the gospel narratives that this is just as likely not to occur. But that is not the responsibility of the *thusic* lover. The seed is to be sown regardless.

BOOK THREE
The Church

As an apple tree among the trees of the wood
So is my beloved among the sons.
In his shadow I delight, and I sit;
His fruit is sweet to my palate.
He has brought me to the house of wine
And his banner over me is love.
— Cant. 2:3-4

PART VII
The Eucharist

We have just seen how the last section of Mark's narrative can be read as depicting a shift in the disposition of the Spirit. When Jesus comes to Jerusalem, where the Spirit might have been expected to tabernacle rather than on an amateur rabbi from Galilee, it is shown as absent, together with faith, its human counterpart. The name of the restored city, the last verse of Ezekiel had promised, would be "The Lord is there" (Ezek. 48:35). Jesus is shown as proving that this is *not* true. Instead the Lord is with *him*. He is in his own person the eschatological temple, city, and therefore nation on the scale of the exceptional individual. Which makes him the (spiritual) Messiah indeed. But this third category presence is necessarily limited to a certain time and place as long as he remains a single individual.

283

So we see him acting to transfer the Spirit from himself to a new version of the community, which *as* a community will be capable of acting in many times and places, in the expectation (as any NT author would have understood it) that this new Israel after the Spirit would soon grow to include all peoples in all times and all places — which would be the Kingdom absolutely come. The passion could then be interpreted as the appointed means through which this change of scale within the third category could be achieved. And (though outside the limits of the Markan narrative, if just inside the scope of the Johannine address) this enterprise would have be understood (by the believing reader of either narrative) to have succeeded. For a community does in fact appear which understands itself as having received the same Spirit which Jesus gave up. This community is still the eschatological Israel, as he was: but an Israel in principle and in practice open to members of all the other nations.

Jesus and the Church may therefore be understood as alternative re-presentations within the third category. Jesus is the Christ (the *spiritual* Christ) on the scale of the single individual at a certain time and place. The Church, or Israel insofar as that body has once again received the Spirit, is the same Christ on the scale of a community which, simply because it *is* a community, can manifest itself at any time and any place for as long as there are times and places at all. Jesus concentrates the eschatological Israel; the eschatological Israel universalizes Jesus. The passion is that action which mediates between these alternative modes of what is in the end the same spiritual identity.

It follows that the fundamental structure of the new covenant is not essentially altered by Jesus' death. *Because* it is the Spirit which has been given, it cannot matter religiously whether this is provided through an individual or within the community; or whether, therefore, the signs of this gift are wonders occuring at a certain time and place or acts of love in many times and places. The Spirit is by definition eternal and universal. The faith invited from those who (are reported to have) encountered Jesus in Palestine once upon a time is therefore the same faith which is invited here and now. They had no advantage over us, the contemporary believer can think; and we have no advantage over them. The centuries make no covenantal difference, however tedious or impressive culturally. We are still potentially in the era of grace; which is to say, exactly "one generation" away from the fullness of the Kingdom; as near, that is, as anybody could be then — and as far.

So the structure of the new covenant does not alter. But the characteristic mode of its third category element does, drastically. The passion effects this change in action. The last supper effects it in ritual, both in our narratives and (we are obliged to believe) in fact. For in either context the last supper has to be the end of the ministry and (proleptically) the beginning of the Church. Because it is *the* moment of translation from one sacramental vocabulary to another, it is not surprisingly a node of specifically covenantal language. The Church, we have already said, is Jesus universalized; the Eucharist, which the last supper originates, is correspondingly a re-production of Jesus' presence on the scale of the community in the mode of ritual. Through the Eucharist one makes oneself "contemporary" with Jesus, and he makes himself "contemporary" with us. It is indeed by way of the Eucharist that one is most likely to comprehend what could be meant by a third category event at all — and so begin to appreciate other manifestations within that order of being. And it is through such an acknowledgement of the gifts of the Spirit that one can begin to understand whatever may be one's proper species of faith, and so begin to take part in the infinite relation after the manner promised. The Eucharist is how the believer can realize where he or she is.

2

In the passion and resurrection, we have said, the Spirit is transferred from Jesus to Israel — in principle. The last supper, we have also said, may be understood as a parabolic reproduction of this translation. What must be presumed to have occurred on the original occasion is repeated in Mark's narrative in the language normally used within Mark's congregation for the corresponding liturgical practice. The same is true for the other synoptics. John omits any version of the event, apparently because it was esoteric for him. It is not for Paul, who rehearses the tradition he had learned for the sake of his Corinthians, who appear to have needed every reminder he could give. We are in all these cases obliged by the claims made for the episode in question to read back through the texts which have come down to the initial act as we may be able to reconstruct that, whether naively or critically. For unlike some other episodes in the ministry, the establishment of the Eucharist has to have already been a fact in order to be meaningful at all; and a fact that can be legitimately repeated within the actual community thereby proleptically announced. Indeed the rite may be defined formally as that which puts into a common structure Jesus, the tradition, oral or textual, and the present moment of any current believer. The Eucharist cannot be an exegetical issue alone.

287

Any analysis of the different versions will make it reasonably clear that the core of what must have happened once, or can be seen to happen within the texts, or may still happen within a contemporary liturgy, is exposed, as one would intuitively expect, in the special interpretation offered over the bread and the wine. It seems equally reasonable to suppose that the formulae embodying these central interpretations should be understood as having once been delivered in the simplest and least qualified form. If that is so, we should have to understand along with J. Jeremias (whose masterful *Eucharistic Words* still remains, it seems to me, the modern argument most worth meeting) that "this is my body" and "this is my blood" are indeed the key propositions. The next step, we should probably also suppose (though this too is contested) would be to understand the word "body" in the first formula as practically equivalent to the word "flesh." The Hebrew *basar* (or its Aramaic analogue) may mean either "body" *or* "flesh"; that is, either *soma* or *sarx*. We have already seen how equivocal this ambiguity can make Paul's rhetoric if not quite his thought. For various linguistic and pastoral reasons, Jeremias supposes, *soma* would have come quickly into use in the Hellenistic liturgies, and thereafter, in the West, *corpus* rather than *carnis*. But the original intention would (it does seem to me fair to conclude) have been to maintain the obvious polarity between flesh and blood, a pair as familiar in Hebrew

288

as in English for human nature taken as a whole; or "body," as we can also say, and "soul." If so, we are free to understand the basic formula as intending respectively "This is my flesh" and "This is my blood."

Religiously speaking Jesus at the last supper is already the Christ; that is, as Mark would put it, the man on whom the Spirit rests. As a man, though, Jesus would still have been simply flesh and blood, like Everybody Else. So we may diagram the Jesus who may be imagined as having stood at the table with the bread before him and the wine at hand in either of two ways, as $\dfrac{\text{Spirit}}{\text{Jesus of Nazareth}}$ or as $\dfrac{\text{Spirit}}{\text{flesh and blood}}$. Either will explicate his sacramental identity within the third category.

When he offers the new definitions, then, as I have been saying we must suppose he actually did, he is in effect changing the whole of himself into the elements made available by the ritual meal. The sacramental structure $\dfrac{\text{Spirit}}{\text{flesh and blood}}$ is translated into its equivalent in terms of food and drink, that is, $\dfrac{\text{Spirit}}{\text{bread and wine}}$. The "tenor" of this parabolic repetition remains constant, that is, the Spirit. The "vehicle" changes from the flesh and blood of the carnal Jesus of Nazareth to the flesh and blood of the equally carnal bread and wine. One sign is exchanged for another with the same meaning. In either case the signifier is a creature; and the signified, as always in a sacrament, is God.

Meanwhile and simultaneously, the two halves of the vehicle themselves make up a contrastive pair which is also expressive of the same difference between the flesh and the Spirit. Bread equals flesh, and blood equals Spirit. We may therefore understand the ratios $\dfrac{\text{Spirit}}{\text{flesh and blood}}$ and $\dfrac{\text{Spirit}}{\text{bread and wine}}$ as in their turn equivalent to $\dfrac{\text{blood}}{\text{flesh}}$ and $\dfrac{\text{wine}}{\text{bread}}$.

Finally, the bread is eaten and the wine is drunk, according to instructions. This last portion of the ritual is the equivalent on the side of the community to the act of interpretation on the side of the individual. The transfer is completed, that is, by another translation, this time from symbols back into human beings. $\dfrac{\text{Spirit}}{\text{bread and wine}}$ or $\dfrac{\text{wine}}{\text{bread}}$ now becomes, through the act of consumption $\dfrac{\text{Spirit}}{\text{Israel}}$. Eating and drinking the alimentary form of the spiritual body enacts a conversion of the participants into the same spiritual body on the scale of the community. Thus most literally does the Lord come to tabernacle in the midst of his people, constructing thereby a temple not made with hands. The old covenantal promise is kept once again — in parable

290

at least.

It will be helpful I suspect to have all the stages of this apparently complex but really quite simple metamorphosis laid out on a single chart:

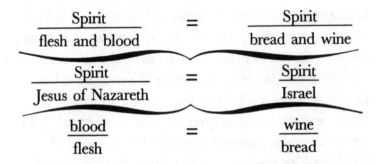

$$\frac{\text{Spirit}}{\text{flesh and blood}} = \frac{\text{Spirit}}{\text{bread and wine}}$$

$$\frac{\text{Spirit}}{\text{Jesus of Nazareth}} = \frac{\text{Spirit}}{\text{Israel}}$$

$$\frac{\text{blood}}{\text{flesh}} = \frac{\text{wine}}{\text{bread}}$$

All these exchanges, it must constantly be recalled, are between "spiritual bodies" in exactly Paul's sense of that phrase. For all are bodies of which the soul is the Spirit and the flesh is something in this world, whether that something is an individual, or food and drink, or a community. Each stage in the transfer, then, is equally sacramental. The parabolic action at the last supper accomplishes a change from one state of affairs within the third category to another state of affairs which is also in the third category. The chart may be visually deceptive, therefore, if it is read as if it could lie on top of the other charts we have used to display the covenantal structure as a whole. It should instead be mentally tipped on its side and placed on the right hand side of any page devoted to the covenantal relation in its entirety. For the presumed element within the second category is still as always faith — either in Jesus *or* in the presence of the Spirit within the Church; which is, covenantally speaking, the same thing.

An analysis of the sort just offered can rehearse the Eucharistic intention in terms of what must be presumed to have happened at the last supper. It is an argument, that is, in place of a narrative. But the last supper, we have also got to remember, would have had to be rather a dress rehearsal than the performance itself. It may even have been quite literally a rehearsal. I am attracted to the suggestion, which I find repeated in J. Jocz' book on the *Covenant* (p. 191), that Jesus, finding events moving faster than he had anticipated, may have anticipated the Passover by one day. In which case the last supper would have been a paschal meal *without the lamb.* This could make good sense theologically as well as chronologically. For it would reinforce the extent to which we are obliged in any case to consider what was done at the supper as an imaginative prefigurement for those actually involved as well as for ourselves of what could happen in full only after the resurrection.

At the supper Jesus would have still been present as a living individual; which for the purpose at hand was not an advantage but a concession to the anticipatory character of the rite. At the supper itself therefore communion in the flesh and blood could only indicate a willingness on the part of those present to share in the

292

sacrifice to come; a commitment from which, as events proved, all involved retreated. The bread and the wine could have had an immediate meaning, then, only within the second category. Their strictly sacramental meaning was still necessarily futural. Within the Eucharistic action though as this could be celebrated after the resurrection and has been celebrated ever since, the center of gravity has shifted decisively in the direction indicated by the underlying intention. We can now be altogether the community endowed by the Spirit. Jesus as a single human being has disappeared. In his place is an apostle, or the spiritual "descendant" of an apostle; that is, some member of the community sacramentally deputized for the purpose. The literal passion is now recollected rather than predicted; it must therefore repeat itself chiefly within the faith of the congregation. What was once his individual presence has long since become his passion as that passion in turn has now become our faith. So the bread and the wine can stand out all the more unconditionally as the flesh and blood of the *risen* body. They are altogether in the third category, like the community within which they find their meaning. At the last supper the Church was still represented by Jesus alone, for the disciples could represent only the failure of Israel after the flesh. In the Eucharist, though, the Church, or Israel after the Spirit, has become present as herself — at least in ritual terms. The intention is to that extent fulfilled.

293

3

To follow the theological trajectory of the Eucharistic intention by way of its minimal constituents the two "words" of institution, and these in their most radically reduced form, is in the nature of the case to neglect other elements within the texts or the historical situation they reproduce which should of course concern a careful student of the matter. The problem of the word of *anamnesis,* for instance ("Do this in remembrance of me") we have already presumed solved by the nature of the intention detected. We therefore presuppose without argument a Jesus who expected his own action to be repeated within the community which that action began to establish. The universally attested reference to a "new covenant," though, requires a little more attention. The clauses referring to it make grammatically clumsy interpolations in the formulae for the wine in the texts as they have been handed down. But that very clumsiness, which may in the first place betray a degree of embarrassment on the part of the tradition, may also testify to the originality of *some* reference to covenant within the initiating situation. There seems good reason then to agree once more with J. Coppens that the primary source for all the covenantal language to be found in the NT and thereafter in the Church's understanding of itself should be located in a reference made by Jesus at the supper and thereafter passed on, however awkwardly, in the language employed for ecclesial repetitions of that event. If so, we would also have in such a reference the justifying occasion for any retroactive reading of the OT in terms of covenant as well — and so incidently for this project among all the others. If the bread of the Eucharist is the flesh of precisely that sacrifice which constitutes a covenant, and the wine is the blood, then that mode of relation is once and for all confirmed as unconditionally authoritative for Christians ever after.

That Jesus would have understood his own death as an expiatory sacrifice is attested indirectly by the Church's acceptance of this interpretation within the earliest proclamations of the gospel and by the "Servant Songs," which we can read as well as he. That he also understood his death as an inaugural sacrifice which established a thoroughly novel version of the new covenant promised in Jeremiah 31:31 we may infer from this reference within the Eucharistic tradition. The principal pre-text is presumably Exodus 24:8: "And Moses took the blood and sprinkled it on the people and said, behold the blood of the covenant which the Lord has cut with you according to all these words . . ." Israel is thereafter committed to the covenant. The equivalent is evidently true of the last supper. Drinking would then be the "sprinkling" of this new rite, which as a whole would anticipate an offering incomplete since the day Abraham did *not* sacrifice Isaac. An un-metaphoric sac-

295

rifice, a new covenant, a new disposition of the blood — the various elements seem to come together of themselves. And once the primary pre-text from Exodus has been recalled, others from remoter contexts can be brought forward to reinforce a connection between one covenantal moment and another.

The Eucharist in fact allows us to mark the exact difference between the old and the new covenants by means of the place of the blood in the two dispensations. Leviticus 17 is very solemn: the blood of a sacrifice is *not* to be consumed. On the face of it Jesus would seem to be contradicting this key commandment directly. The potential scandal was apparently obvious enough to influence the language in which the word over the wine was cast in the churches of the first generation, as we have seen. More carefully understood, though, there need be no scandal. In the Priestly repetition of the Sinai covenant, the blood of the sacrifices was not to be consumed but poured out at the foot of the altar. It therefore played no role in any communion in the roasted flesh which might follow. In other words, the blood exhausted the whole of its ritual function within the second category. It could have no existence within the third category at all — though the flesh, roasted in the fire of the Spirit, could. The same is true of Jesus' fleshly blood, which is (in principle) poured out upon the cross. There is a sense, as we have noticed, in which he does ask his disciples to drink the ritual analogue of this blood at the Supper; that is, to profess their willingness to accompany him in his passion. This they do not do; the wine, in that sense, fails of its meaning. But outside that immediate situation, there is no intention to ask anyone to drink this blood, symbolically or otherwise. The intention is rather to invite future believers to drink the blood of the future *spiritual* body. He asks us in fact, to drink the Spirit, period. And within the Church, which is the flesh of that spiritual body as much as the bread is, this *is* possible — sacramentally. Through the Eucharist, then, the congregation of believers are enabled to act out their own identity as a community endowed with the Spirit. Their drinking repeats parabolically the very condition into which the deed of Jesus has placed them. They testify thereby to their existence as a living body within the third category. The difference between the literal blood and the sacramental wine then becomes a revelation of the difference between the second category and the third — and so of the difference between one version of the covenant and the other.

The two apparently opposed commandments might therefore be reconciled theoretically by understanding them as applying at different points along the categorical continuum. A combined formula might run like this: do *not* drink the fleshly blood, either of animals or (*a fortiori*) of any man, but instead offer it as that which is most entirely equivalent to the act of sacrifice itself

297

either at the altar or on the cross — literal or metaphoric. *Then* you may drink the blood of the spiritual body which shall be manifested ritually as the wine, as you may eat the flesh of the spiritual body which shall be manifested ritually as the bread. The change from the forbidden blood of one category to the commanded blood of another will thus exemplify exactly the eschatological significance of the deed which is accomplished in Jesus and which the Church understands itself as entitled to proclaim and repeat. Jesus would then not contradict Leviticus but re-place it — to just this extent.

This privilege by way of the wine should probably also be understood as paralleled by a complementary privilege with respect to the bread: though the Western tradition did not pick up the opportunity. Bread in the first category is leavened, we know, yeast being its "life," as blood is the life of a living creature. In the Passover rite, this leaven is burned and *un*leavened bread eaten, to manifest the necessary sacrifice. There is no way however within that rite to present the third category in terms of bread — nor would Jesus have needed anything of the sort at the last supper, if we are right in thinking of it as a second-category rehearsal. The possibility in question would most naturally be exemplified by the presence of *re*-leavened bread; which suggests that the bread of the Eucharist should in fact be leavened, as it is in the Greek tradition. The legitimacy of such a liturgical decision would seem confirmed by the parable in Mt. 13:33 comparing the Kingdom of Heaven to the yeast which a woman mixed with a large amount of flour until it was leavened all through, an image which implies there could be a good or eschatological leaven as well as a bad or sinful leaven. The same difference appears to govern the curious remark in Mk. 8:15, in which the disciples are warned to avoid the yeast of the Pharisees and the yeast of Herod; as if the unspoken alternative were the yeast of Jesus — which the "breads" of the boat and the hillside would exemplify as well as the Eucharist. Ideally, a liturgist might argue, the rite should exhibit its meaning within the elements employed. That is how parables work.

The bread and wine together, we know, amount to the flesh and blood of the body — in the mode of ritual. And because this ritual like the individual and communal body is in the third category it can perform a most significant function. It can serve as the "document" of the new covenant. In the old covenant this document is a literal text. Exodus invites us to think of this as the Decalogue, inscribed on a pair of stones. Some written proof of the kind is virtually demanded by the very idea of a covenant, as M.G. Kline has pointed out and we have repeated in connection with the event of Sinai. And we may if we like follow him too in understanding the successive stages of the OT itself as in effect revisions of this indispensable record, from the possible "J" or "JE" to the actual Deuteronomy, and from there not just as far as the Pentateuch but all the way to "the scriptures" as a whole, complete with history, prophecy, and wisdom. If so, we would also have to realize that any version of such a text would have to exist within the second category, though it might include or be authorized by inspirations which as such would belong to the third. The covenantal document is not supplied by God but composed by men, as a testimony to the obedience they have sworn.

But (and here I would part company with Kline) there is it seems to me no equivalent *text* within the new covenant. A "New Testament" has indeed been brought together as if it were the Christian analogue to what thereby becomes the "Old." But the resemblance is perhaps more superficial than is usually supposed. The NT texts illustrate the new covenant as argument or narrative, as we have seen. But (except perhaps for the speeches in John) they do not as such constitute it. This should not be surprising; in the new covenant there could be, strictly speaking, nothing at all within the second category but faith. The gospel is essentially *post*-textual. And faith — it is Paul's great point — cannot depend upon *any* textual specification, for that would be to convert it back into the Law.

Within the new covenant every positive is in the third category. It would follow that any equivalent to the old treaty document for this eschatological version of the relation would also have to appear within that category in the mode of a sacrament — which is exactly what we find the Eucharist to be. Instead of a text within the second category, then, we are offered the body within the third: in the place of stones, bread; instead of written orders, the presence itself. We can realize accordingly that the last supper is indeed the founding event of the new covenant, as Sinai was for the old; that the Eucharistic ritual is the renewal rite of this covenant, as the oaths sworn at Schechem or in Jerusalem had been before; and that the Eucharistic body is therefore the "document" which testifies to the prevalence of this version of the relation. We need not be surprised. Nothing less could seem consistent with all the other claims put forward. For if Jesus himself is in the third category, and so is the community he establishes, it would follow that the sign which witnesses to just this state of affairs would have to be found in parallel with what it mediates.

PART VIII
Marriage

There is no such thing as "freedom," but
only the relations between persons.
— George Dennison

The Eucharist renews the new covenant in terms of food and drink, which the body needs and we can give each other. It thereby constitutes the eschatological community in ritual terms. The corresponding completion within the dual or sexual context would be marriage — whenever that too becomes a third category pneumenon. The New Testament affirms that this is indeed possible within the new covenant, as we have seen in connection with the gospel according to the body in Paul and the Markan pericope on marriage. In a truly sacramental marriage, these texts would enable us to say, the act of intercourse amounts to the equivalent of a celebration of the Eucharist within the gracious community. It too would pre-present a ritual body of which the soul was the Spirit and the flesh was — the united

302

identities of the lovers. Orgasm, like the birth it anticipates, would be the *epiclesis* of this re-creation, and so
indeed a repetition, as Christian tradition has also held,
of the relation between Christ and his church.

Not every marriage, obviously, could be the Church
repeated on the scale of the couple in such a way. Most
sexual combinations make sense enough within the categories of the flesh. There might, for instance, be innocent couples within the first category. Everybody certainly trusts to that possibility as the myth expressive of
Our condition. Paul, of course, would vehemently deny
this; for him all sexual relations are either sinful or gracious, damned within the second category or hallowed
within the third. Presumably there might also be, even
in these anti-Pauline times, pornic couples, who would
know that what they were doing was sinful. There are
certainly nomic couples, who would define themselves
or be defined in terms of one version or other of the
Law. It is even conceivable there might be philic or simply friendly couples, individuals exchanging sexual and
domestic positives without ever becoming "one flesh."
This too is a contemporary dream. But none of these re-
lationships would be sacramental; all are fully definable
(including the first) in terms of the second category.
What we can learn from Paul or Mark (and therefore
from Jesus behind them both) is that marriage *may* be
understood as occurring within the third category as
well — by way of the new covenant. And this would be

as true now for our generation as it was for their generation within the Church, which is *the* generation between Jesus and the end of the world; for Mark and Paul and modern believers are all members of it. The new covenantal "moment" has been indefinitely but not infinitely prolonged.

Within the old covenant, with its many generations, marriage remains a human contract. It takes place between a man and a woman in the presence of God but not as a function of their relation to him. That is entered into only on the collective scale. Therefore the sexes need not be equal, for only males are obliged to swear the military oath required by any national version of the relation. Covenantality within the dual is accordingly impossible — except between friends, as with David and Jonathan. And without covenantality there can be no sacramentality. But there *is* room for divorce; which may indeed be not only permitted but under certain circumstances commanded. Divorce can be a way to repudiate sin, as marriage is normally the way to practice virtue.

But if marriage does not reach as far as the third category under the old covenant as a theological possibility, it could and did as a prophetic metaphor. For Hosea most prominently, with his sorrowful comparison of an unfaithful wife to unfaithful Israel, but also for Jeremiah (chapter 3) and Ezekiel (chapters 16 and 23) marriage becomes an image for the relation between

304

the Lord and his people. Thus adultery in one context becomes equivalent to idolatry in the other. The presence of the same language in both situations endows marriage with at least an imaginative degree of the holiness proper to the state of affairs it illustrates. And if marriage can be a way of talking about the collective covenant and its vicissitudes, then the private relation becomes an index to the public one, even if not yet positively covenantal in its own right. So on the return to Jerusalem Ezra can insist, for instance, that all foreign wives be divorced, the better to maintain the purity of the nation's devotion to its God.

This undernote becomes dominant in the New Testament, as E. Schillebeeckx (to whose book on *Marriage* I am here indebted) has pointed out. In Revelation especially but also in the parables of the synoptics where a wedding feast figures marriage is the image of choice for the relation of the risen Christ and his Church. The story of the marriage at Cana in John makes the comparison implicitly sacramental as well: the Eucharist, marriage, and the Church are brought together within the same discourse. Ephesians 5:21-23 is the most explicit and best known development of this line of thinking: husbands are enjoined to love their wives and wives instructed to obey their husbands on the ground of the ecclesial analogy. To be sure the distinction here between "love" and "obey" is still Jewish (or Gentile) rather than Christian. For within the new

305

covenant the sexes would have to be equal with respect to their obligation in the second category. Circumcision is necessarily limited to males; but baptism is open to members of either sex, like the faith of which it is the ritual equivalent. A dual version of the relation thus becomes theologically possible — and marriage can be fully sacramental. In that case a comparison between the communal and the dual versions will hold without obliquity: both marriage and the Church are in principle third category events, and may therefore peacefully mirror the truth of each other. The likeness is spiritual as well as imaginative.

If the new covenant offers a species of marriage within the third category, it follows that it must also include a species of faith within the second category. It is clear too what this would have to be: an unqualified mutual fidelity. For those who marry within the new covenant, their fidelity to each other would *be* their faith in God — in terms of the dual. And if that fidelity was broken, what then? Divorce, according to the other half of the dominical instruction, would no longer be possible without implicit apostasy; nor could it be, logically, if the union in question is no longer to be thought of as established by human beings within the second category but by God within the third. The answer does not seem difficult to work out: as faithfulness would be faith within the marital context, so forgiveness would have to be the appropriate repetition of fidelity under

306

the condition of sin. Within the old covenant, it is necessary to repudiate sin in the person of the sinner, in order to avoid becoming guilty oneself. Within the new covenant, one is instead invited to forgive the sin — which might obviously involve a repetition of the passion sufficient to balance the apparent presumption. We are, after all, additionally informed in another text that we shall be forgiven *as* we forgive others, a recommendation which will also fall into the covenantal structure. The new covenant, then, like the old, contains a secondary strategy to encompass breaches of itself. If the commitment is maintained, on the other hand, in the mode of that fidelity which is simultaneously a species of faith, the new covenant promises that God will be with the couple — in the first place by recreating their union as a spiritual body, and so as sacramental on the scale of the dual as the Church is on the scale of the community. This then would be the eschatological possibility.

2

Matched against this ideal of a completely covenantal marriage, the one I shall be relying on as my exemplary history for this chapter must seem very imperfect, like most actual marriages in these times, "Christian" or otherwise. It never became sacramental either legally or truly as far as anyone could tell. A social version of the promises traditionally repeated was indeed exchanged, once upon a time. But these could not be altogether confirmed in the years thereafter. The positives proper to the relationship would have to be understood, therefore, as occurring within the first and second categories. Within the first category the couple made one flesh erotically, domestically, familially: that is, to the usual extent. Within the second category the marriage seemed a contract of sorts, though differently founded, as it turned out, on one side and on the other. There were more or less overt clauses to this contract, which included the conventional expectations, and secret clauses too which supplemented these with small private bargains. Neither the covential nor the covert clauses were always kept, but that is usual too. The parties were "husband" and "wife." The one apparently unconditional element tacitly shared was the expectation of an indefinite continuance, which both parties held without thinking, in the style of their generation. Meanwhile a family appeared; and preoccupied them both. Within that inarticulate ongoingness, nobody has to think things through. Routine absorbs the sharable life. Men and women have children, one can sometimes cynically guess, in order to avoid having to face each other.

But the possibility that could not become actual in the case at hand may still be used to interpret what did happen. The form of the covenant can explicate the religious significance of a private history now, as it could explain the history of a nation once upon a time. So the story of a modern marriage can stand as the equivalent of a royal anecdote in the Deuteronomic histories or a ministerial pericope in the narrative gospels. History, fictional or real, shows what may be done by way of what has been done. So we may explore by means of this instance what might be discoverable about covenant in this context. The Eucharist, we have said, is the bridge between the world of the New Testament and our own. Marriage, though, is this world itself — on the scale of the couple. Whatever happens within that context should accordingly prove crucial for any repetition of the relation in our time.

How though does one represent such matter without either inaccuracy or indecency? The story of any marriage is invariably "according to" Somebody or other. But so individualistic a form can seem by definition inappropriate to the duality of the content. There is no imaginative provision for the moral stichomythy the case ideally requires. The best literary solution is probably the usual one, in which the relation as a whole is shifted into fiction, where no one need feel morally responsible. The type of the fictional in this context would presumably be the familiar change of pronouns. "He" and "she" have to be imagined together by some third person outside *their* relation. At least such a pair of characters can represent duality, even if only in imagination and so not quite seriously. And "you" and "I," appropriately recomposed, can borrow a degree of distance from the same convention. The other literary possibility is generalization. One makes fun of "one," not to mention "men" and "women," but these faceless figments have their own mythic usefulness. Generalization is after all the universalization of fiction; if the latter is legitimate, so should the former be. Both have accordingly been employed here.

B

Lust is the craving for salt of a man who is dying of thirst.
— *Frederick Buechner*

What happened might be formalized after the fact as a loss of the We, or that sexual being which a couple can share who have ever been strongly attracted to each other; the body of flesh, or Adam in the dual. This loss of the first category, and so of a certain residual marital innocence, did not become clear though for a long time. First came an indistinct period of depression and dissatisfaction. But the routine was maintained, along with the expectations it presupposed. Then the partners went off to different cities for half a year, ostensibly to follow up individual opportunities which seemed too good to refuse. It would make a change, both thought. But when they came back together again, sex was all but impossible. Impotence matched distaste. Which was the effect, which the cause? No one knew; a pause ensued. Whereupon other motives and feelings began to surface. A new phase of the common history had evidently begun: the couple were presently no longer just "having problems," they were breaking up. This was odd; neither could have predicted such a thing, after so many years.

Not long after his mother's death, but before the return home that was to reveal the initial state of affairs, one of the partners had a dream. In it he found himself present at the burial of a woman in a grave which already contained the body of another woman, buried a while back but not yet decayed. This previous body was not underneath but sprawled on top of and across the first. It was dressed incongruously in a white bikini, like underwear, or the marks left when a bathing suit is taken off. Then he found himself masturbating this second woman, who would not quite wake up, though the body was obscurely responsive. It seemed peculiar to be making this kind of love to a dead woman, if that was what she was. Then he woke and thought: what is horrible is not that both are dead, but that both seem alive.

Such a dream, mythically entangling death and life, incest and marriage, concealing clothes and sexual flesh could hint at the profoundest confusions; but the surface tensions might as well have been within the range of its prophetic scope. For the marital relation itself became oddly dream-like. Unconscious seemed to communicate directly with unconscious. *You* feel something, but are not sure what. Neither am *I;* but experience the pressure of an unexpressed message, working below the level of consciousness. So *I* react symptomatically, in a way that cannot be interpreted either. Involuntary response matches hidden initiative. But since neither is aware of the initial condition, the reaction to it seems the first thing that is "said" on either side — and the other party reacts as if that were really so. A false dialogue begins, inhibiting the true. Both parties talk all the time; and both fail to say what they mean.

It seemed best to draw back, and see where things were. But what was there exactly to wait for? Presumably some rediscovery of a common ground in custom, desire, affection, good will at least — or firm evidence that one or another of these was indeed missing. Until this seemed clear, it hardly appeared worth while appealing to the standard authorities, psychiatric or legal. Was there indeed motive enough to sustain an interpretative process in either set of terms? Still, it was also cruel to do nothing. Who would end up proving themselves most in the wrong?

The immediate past was reviewed, almost too carefully. There were grievances on both sides, of course. One had felt fear, for a long time: in this scenario a secret terror matched a cruel complacency. Meanwhile, *almost* unconscious of this melodrama, the other had felt exploited. Suppose one party loses interest in the other, but cannot admit this. Might not such a situation generate exploitation as an accidental by-product? For if sex, say, *had* to continue in the absence of desire, the party that felt the obligation would naturally be inclined to make the best of a bad predicament, by taking whatever could be used and ignoring the rest. That would be exploitation, in any context. But the fact that this was going on would itself have to be denied, if the strategy was to work. Meanwhile the other party would feel obscurely rejected, without being able to identify the feeling in question *as* rejection. Both sides, then, could feel victims either of oppression or enslavement. And now each could begin to realize how the other felt about his or her characteristic distortion of the common possibility. In that double mirror sentimental perversity matched callous greed. This was shocking. Where now was the common ground?

While an erotic We, or the first category in the dual, remains in being, nothing shakes it. Infidelity and violence seem no worse than fatal aspects of its natural history. Crises only call forth new reserves, physical and emotional, which both sides can still accept as relevant to the common life. This underlying union can be immensely reassuring: one takes risks, unpacking old needs; and finds them received as functional, somehow, within the whole. These are dangerous exchanges, but energizing: the big moments go on making reciprocal sense within the unconscious. But once the We starts to go, the elements which had made it up begin to separate. The old resources sink back or prove irrelevant to one side or the other. We are no longer each other's audience. Under the turbulent surface there is less, not more.

Intimacy is the quieter mood of this on-going We. I let myself become intimate with you when I trust you not to take advantage of me because I do not have to take advantage of you. I am sure that whatever we al-

314

ready have is stronger than anything either of us could have with someone else. Ideally intimacy is experienced across the board; we share a way of life, a family, feelings, and therefore quite naturally our flesh as well as the words which accompany all these. There will be limits, of course. We do not usually share a job, though some may, and need not even share the same "values," though it is easier when we do. But these are aspects of the public life. And intimacy is private in the dual.

In the negative, though, intimacy becomes fear. You become afraid to share your feelings or your wishes, even when that would do no obvious harm. You don't want me to find out about you now; knowledge is oppressive as such. My curiosity seems hostile or punitive. Boundaries are set up; a space opens out. We are no longer at home with each other. We are divided by what we used to have in common. What we now have in common is the difference itself. We have lost our right to the garden, if we ever had it.

2

As a genuine We begins to disintegrate, it may be replaced to start with not by the corresponding individuals but by a false We to which both sides contribute. Such a spurious equilibrium cannot yet be challenged for fear of disturbing the fundamental lie: that We are still in being in the same old way. Both parties are complicit, the one it may be, to avoid self-criticism for selfishness, the other, it may be, to avoid self-criticism for cowardice.

But if the necessary wish is really on one side only, and impure there, this cannot work for long. The absence of desire on the other side will surface in due course, however masked to begin with by affection, duty, nostalgia, pity or even lust. These can seem almost enough to the party which must entertain them. But then the contrary intimations emerge, one by one: the unexpected remark, the inadvertent gesture, the forgotten appointment. Both sides are still going through the motions; but without support from beneath the motions accumulate as a performance. In the erotic life a performance is intended to fool me as well as the audience. But in the end the flesh cannot lie. The real negative must surface sooner or later as repugnance, which cannot be hidden even from the self.

At such a time unspeaking voices press within the heart. If I do not want you, I do not want you to want me either. Your desire is a threat to me. If I let it inside me, I shall be poisoned; if I go out to meet it, I shall be degraded. I can't make love with someone I don't want; if you persist I will hate you for reminding me of my own incapacity in a way that makes me feel guilty. And the other voice could answer, but does not, quite: last year you thought the sex which I thought was only for you was meant for us both. I found it hard to undeceive you. This year I thought the sex you thought was only for me was meant for us both. You found it hard to undeceive me. One of us thought need and devotion could make up for the absence of desirableness; the other thought that affection and compassion might make up for the absence of desire. Both strategies turned out to be conceits which could not be accepted by the other except as a lie. Each was subverted as soon as the flesh made its own dumb case known. For the body knows better than the stories we tell ourselves and try to tell each other. What we are actually entitled to is never more than whatever is already positive between us of surface or substance, impulse or feeling. Beyond that is nothing whatsoever. When we force ourselves beyond ourselves, impelled by hope or pity, we are abandoned to fantasy and panic; and begin to hate each other.

You are desirable still, and I still desire. But your desirableness is your own now. So my desire is only for myself too. Your desirableness is proof that you exist, as always, and you are pleased with that. My desire is proof to me that I exist still, and I cling to it accordingly, though now in the mode of suffering. But we exist for our selves alone. You are no longer able to identify with my wishes, so as to satisfy them, or accept them, so as to give yourself back, or even to collaborate with them, so as to get something for yourself as well. Once upon a time I could identify with your wishes, but no longer, for now they exclude me; one cannot identify with one's own exclusion without a species of suicide, and even I do not want that. I cannot accept your wishes so as to give myself back because there is nothing I now have that you want. I cannot collaborate with them so as to get something for myself too, for they presuppose my absence. So we are left outside the circle of each other's wishes, each alone with Myself, positive or negative. We no longer exist together. Which means that We no longer exist.

It becomes possible then for an outsider to say: there was always less between those two than either of them supposed. They were not "made for each other," as some seem to be. And from what still remains the inside, each finds it easier to take the outsider's point of view. Was there not always too much anxiety on one side, and reserve on the other? When he felt attracted, she drew back; when she was attracted, he felt embarrassed, as if she mistook him for somebody else. She feared he would hurt her. He feared she would consume him. And each had such incompatible ways of making up for these deficiencies! So they constructed separate worlds, each with their own history, which they could not tell each other.

Finally it *has* come, and we look back on it and know: the last bad sex. Why couldn't we have quit while we were ahead? The bodies are still present, but as resistant or tremulous surfaces without depth; muscles do not relax. Instead of initiative, there is an idea; instead of a response, passivity. In spite of all this something happens: the connection within the flesh is weak but briefly sweet in a miniature, encapsulated way, like some memory from the remote past. The little burst of pleasure is nostalgic. In the present it is the expression of a lie. "What does it matter!" But it does matter, acutely. Nature can fairly be reconstructed in words, once the simple flesh has been decently left behind. But it cannot be imagined in terms of the flesh itself. That is not just a lie, but a horror.

After that episode came another dream, as if to interpret the earlier one by repeating it. The dreamer found himself in a house; upstairs were two dead bodies, one of which again was his mother's. In the roof was hidden, he knew, a third and older corpse, dried up and wrapped in metal. The house was the one in which he had lived as a child, and from which his father had once died. He had just arrived to carry out some piece of family business; and discovered this macabre state of affairs. A day or two passed. The bodies were decaying; it was necessary to have them cremated. But there was nowhere nearby to get this done. He got on the phone to Boston, more and more anxious, still unwilling to go upstairs and face what he would find. Then he woke: and felt relieved, to start with, that the dream was not literally true of the house he was in. Someone still lay beside him, breathing. Where did either of them go from here?

3

The loss of the We could teach something about it. One could learn as it were out of the corner of an eye what the conditions were for the very privilege one was losing. Psychology is the word formulated in the second category to explain the first within the context of human nature. So it arranges itself as the obverse of theology, which is the word formulated in the second category to interpret the third within the context of human action. Insight mirrors faith. A NT pericope can afford to ignore psychology, since within those stories the first category is taken for granted — except in the parables. The contemporary equivalent though cannot, especially within the context of marriage, which presumes the whole of the flesh. The We *is* the first category, I have said, on the scale of the dual. To have lost it can prompt an effort of recovery within the second category on the scale of the individual. The collective truth of such an effort would be a psychology: that is, the "wisdom of men" with respect to the matter at hand. And this in turn could make a stage in the covenantal dialectic, as we have seen in connection with Paul.

So now the lapse of the elementary erotic being precipitated some notions of its nature. One seemed, for instance, to be reminded, as if of something one had always known, of the aboriginal difference between the sexes; and so of the radical dependence of each upon the other. We are neither of us enough alone, but each contributes one or another element to the whole we mime — which would be Ourselves indeed. Plato's myth of the androgyne is true for the first category, as one would expect, for myths are the old way to map that region, as the hypotheses of science are the new. In which case the sexual act would already be a natural rite, demonstrative of that archaic fullness of being to which actual persons cannot otherwise pretend. The unity we thus act out still eludes us, of course; but at least we can represent what the flesh will go on desiring. We can *nearly* let Ourselves be.

Other speculative truths of what might once have been called the "natural law" (and speculation is only science on the scale of the individual) seemed to glimmer through this experience of their negation. The comparative exclusivity of erotic love was one. If the sexual We could be indefinitely plural, as an orgy, for instance, would pretend, there could be no question of loyalty or the reverse: the immediate bond, in such a case, would hold all the participants together as flesh-in-general. But once the We coheres as a *hetero*-sexual duality, it becomes exclusive. A membrane forms about the couple, excluding others — including old husbands and wives. The partners in effect agree to let whatever is happening between them exemplify the common possibility for the time being. If one or another takes up with someone else in the meanwhile, this possibility is implicitly annulled; perhaps before it has properly begun. The body of flesh has its own conditions, which can be either recognized or denied. Adam and Eve are not quite fools.

"Sophistication" would begin in a presumption that this original duality of being is now *im*possible: all sexual experience would then be pre-defined as either Yours or Mine from the word go. Arrangements founded on this basis can notoriously be quite "happy." In the old fashioned versions she exchanged beauty for security, or feelings for status; in a newer variant, he exchanges good nature for vicarious success. The limits of such bargains would be built into the initial supposition. One party may feel quite comfortable as an autonomous individual playing "fair" while the other still harbors wishes for something "deeper." In old movies, this was apt to be the woman; in recent fact, it seems often to be the man.

One could also be impressed with the life of the We in time. Our sexual experience is regressive, in more than one sense. We hark back to make up. The fundamental wish is to rehearse the risks of childhood but still win through at last. So the wife, say, is physically the opposite of the mother — but uncannily like her in temperament; or the husband is socially the reverse of the father — but cast in a latter-day revision of the same role. Up to a point these repetitions work; one is stronger, after all. For the same reason a second marriage can be easier than the first, if the first drew too closely on these infantile patterns. Suppose I marry to escape the grown-ups; and then you become one. You will gradually turn into someone I have to escape from in turn. Or suppose I withdrew as a child, feeling hurt; and now you hurt me again, and I withdraw again. But you felt rejected as a child, so you experience my withdrawal as rejection, and reject me back, to stay on top; which reinforces the withdrawal. The ancient needs, no longer satisfied in each other, begin to drive Us apart. As a parent to your child, for instance, I seem to you punitive; but as a child to your parent, I seem needy. The criss-cross of old roles no longer combine into an unconscious whole.

And there are other facets of the We in time. It is the story of the We in one's own particular case that one remembers of any marriage or considerable affair, for the past is to each of us the temporal mode of the first category. So the moments that count most in reverie will be those occasions on which the primary possibility seemed either augmenting or diminishing. We recollect increments of life and the corresponding subtractions, not the timeless routine in between. Of course these memories need not to be sharable as such. What I recall as a breakthrough you may repress as a scandal. Individuality has already begun with the selection each makes from the common history. But the trajectory would be the same for both, even if the points on it must be idiosyncratic.

324

So Our first moments of attraction, tenderness or sensuality might represent one series, through which We once became "one flesh." The imaginable completion of this unfolding may never occur, but the hope of it can hover in the air indefinitely. Such a hope is itself a chief source of desire, for desire is the hope of the body, and a body hopes always for more of itself. And the corresponding negative series has its own sadder dates: the gestures unreceived, the customs abandoned, the privileges denied. The two series can of course overlap chronologically. The first hints of the death to come may well occur before all the possible life has been enjoyed. And an event which counts as part of the first series for one partner may be listed in the second for the other — at least retrospectively. What is still courtship for me may be "legal" evidence for you.

To think of the waxing and waning of the We in time can prompt speculation on the natural extent of coupledom within the first category. "Till death do us part" would seem to mean, practically speaking, until the children are grown. The natural lifetime of a relationship would then be a single generation — as one would expect. In which case it would not be just coincidence that so many of our old friends were separating too. We had all lived past the point where marriage made automatic family sense. What counts thereafter has to be what one does with one's time; time which has suddenly become shockingly personal. Of course it is

325

possible to avoid this challenge by starting the cycle over again, directly in second marriages or vicariously through the grandchildren, as Everybody used to do. These can be ways to repeat what has just been lived through in some more comfortable if imaginary version. But Somebody should be able to conceive alternatives to so literal a repetition of the fleshly cycle.

To think about the We is already to recognize the extent to which it has ceased to be present and become part of the past. Other experiences supervene; if of the same kind, they effectually replace what used to be their equivalent. The unconscious does not care *who* serves its functions. And even without alternatives, a body can outlearn its dependence on the old drug. Our habits are easier to change than we suppose while we are identified with them. It is like watching the water swirl between the sides of the departing ship and the receding pier. There they still stand, the wildly waving or incuriously gazing figures; close still, but over for now. The scene we shared has become imaginary to us both, but in different ways, as if we were each making up a separate *roman-a-clef* about the same situation.

Desire too can begin to diminish. For without hope, it has no reason to stay alert, and falls asleep; to stir, it may be, and dream from time to time. Fantasy too, though that does not lapse, at least becomes less intense as its old motive disappears: to do better next time. Now it was possible to recall even the old dream about the

326

dead bodies with a certain equanimity. The dreamer could realize at least that he had read the *Interpretation of Dreams* that summer in the hopes of interpreting it. It seemed to him that he almost had.

C

The "I" of autobiography is always, in one degree or another, guilty.
— Denis Donoghue

One could learn, retrospectively, about innocence; one could also learn, and not just retrospectively, about sin. *Porneia* begins early, as Freud and Paul both knew; and remains as long as *I* do, who emerge in the midst of it. Nature is innocence and society indifference; but guilt is the presence of myself to myself. So sex becomes pornic as soon as it ceases to be *with* you either in assumption or hope, and becomes *for* me — or for you. For it is just as pornic for the other party if he or she "goes along." Pity casts the parties into the roles of hungry child and indulgent parent, which is incest. And if I capitulate to unsharable sex for my own sake, I lose the right to protest the reverse, or maintain what I know: that We must do it together or not at all. Surrendering would concede the hegemony of the corresponding view of the world, which holds there is nothing better than a decently reciprocal selfishness anyway.

That attitude is despair adjusted to the demands of worldly justice, though it can look like common sense. You do what you want and I do what I want, provided neither is what the other doesn't want; or better still, each of us is satisfied simultaneously but separately, doing "the same thing," each for his or her own sake.

There might be affairs in which this sort of collaboration between independent erotic powers could make social sense (which is one reason affairs now seem easier to so many) but in a marriage, where at least the possibility of bodily union, natural or spiritual, cannot quite be discounted ahead of time, the idea of reciprocity seems ugly. Besides, it is sure to become unbalanced in practice: "I shall have mine and meanwhile by great good luck you will be having yours" will presently translate into "I will have mine and forget about yours." Sex is not subject to exchange like the other goods of this world. The body is not alienated enough for that.

Reciprocity is socialized individualism; but individualism within the dual is sin as soon as it becomes conscious of itself. Within the We there can be an unconditional because unconscious giving and receiving, physical and emotional. But individualistic sex is neither giving nor receiving but taking. The man takes the woman, or as much as he wants of her, and ignores the rest. The woman takes the man, or as much as she wants of him, and ignores the rest. Perhaps they collaborate, cold-heartedly if hot-bloodedly, to take what they want of each other, and ignore the rest. More often the taker is unaware that he or she is only taking, not knowing anything else is possible. So he or she interprets the other as a taker too; and is afraid accordingly of being taken. And giving, to someone who is afraid to

329

receive, is like being robbed. It is safest to do neither, but take what one can get — and ignore the rest.

In that case I am masturbating really, whoever else may be present. In masturbation the gift is given to myself. But I can only consume the physical side of any gift I give myself. And in giving to myself I do not receive, I only take — and lose. I use up what I might have given, and am bereft not just of my gift but of what I might have received had I given it away. The masturbation of the introvert is fantastic and obvious; the masturbation of the extrovert profligate and covert. But it is just as real; if there are many lovers, the ego is naturally going to seem at the center of its own experience, for that continues and the others change. They are bound accordingly to become objects of consumption, good or bad. Nor need this attitude be inconsistent with a certain playfulness or friendliness; on the contrary, common justice may still be observed, and common courtesy. The non-erotic virtues can protect the erotic vices.

Versions of this style are in imaginative request in these times, and need not be elaborated here; the media will do that for us. The introverted modes of sex *for myself* are less well advertised. The common note of them all is fantasy, which may obtain as well in the presence of the other as alone. If I "worship" your body, it has ceased to belong to you, or to Us either; it has become an idol in the cave of my imagination. Usually this is resisted; who wishes to become a figment of

330

another's mind? But the indulgence is most itself in solitude, where nothing need interrupt. I go to the pornographic movie, but I sit by myself and want nobody near me. So I exploit images for the sake of needs which antedate them. I am put off if the figures on the screen are too obviously themselves and not for me, or if the style of the erotic book I am reading calls attention to its own vulgarity.

And apart from the words or images of others, there is always memory. At night, alone in the dark, I am abandoned to recyclings of the past, mixing memory and desire without regard for either fate or hope. Without lust, this is reverie; with feeling, melancholy. The composite makes up a condition contrary to fact: if only this or that had occurred, would not a happier result have obtained? So one reconstructs the past in order to generate a future in which it is impossible to believe. Thus one avoids the present: in which there is precisely nothing to do, and all the time in the world to do it.

There can be an emotional as well as an erotic pornicity. One recycles feelings as well as images. The meaning of an image, after all, is feeling. This is a species not allowed for in Paul's letters, where he is dealing hastily with outward behavior. One might call the condition in question *patheia,* with the same overtone of uncleanliness. As with desire, feeling too can be at once indulged and inhibited, cultivated inwardly but forbidden expression. Is this victim still really in love, or

331

only in love with love, and so with the idea of him or herself which this emotion proposes? Pornicity of every kind is implicated with theater: I play some part, and you (or the mirror) are my audience. There is a masturbation of the feelings as well as of the body, which though is incapable of "climax," and so of any clarifying descent into guilt. Instead I suffer and take pride in my sufferings; meanwhile of course reserving the right to seek justification from as many others as possible! The heart too, it must be recalled, is under the same judgement as the genitals. It is the body of flesh on the emotional side, no more. When I cultivate it *for myself,* sin is still the result.

The pornic in all its modes depends upon a special kind of half-unconsciousness. With promiscuity this is straightforward secrecy: the ego knows what others don't, which feels like power. But in fact to keep such a secret is in proportion to conceal the meaning of the fact from oneself. Emotional untruth precipitates outwardly as moral insensitivity, which can persist after the secret is out. Suppose, for instance, that he leaves her and moves in with another woman. He does not feel that what he is doing is wrong, exactly. He *is* aware that his wife is devastated, and feels sorry about that; if he could manage without hurting anybody, he would. This makes him feel a good guy at heart. Meanwhile it seems odd to him that he should ever have thought this sort of thing wrong, though perhaps at one time he considered himself a man of old-fashioned opinions. When it actually happens, he could argue, it doesn't seem like that at all; in fact it is self-enhancing, just like the silly books say. But really he has become ignorant of his ignorance. He feels the wrong he is doing in the mode of *not* feeling it; of not feeling anything, actually. Meanwhile, as if to compensate, the abandoned wife is feeling all too much, as if to assume his share as well as her own. But displaced onto her, the assorted feelings become confused, hysterical, irrelevant: only her own, as his "new life" is only his own. Her pains cannot mirror his responsibility back to him. They are merely a burden: of course she's taking it hard.

The egotist can deny his or her selfishness by attributing to it everybody else as well. Nor is the selfishness of the other, real or imagined, always a threat. In some respects it can even be a comfort. If I have already determined to act *for myself,* for instance, I may find it impossible to be at ease sexually or otherwise with partners who are not unconsciously at least as self-centered as I dare not quite confess myself to be. For unless this condition obtains I cannot be sure the other is not judging me, or pretending to please me, or just dangerously concerned about me. But if the other is clearly egotistic too, I can think: he or she is simply enjoying him or herself. Then I am free to enjoy myself too. When the pornic has become normal, it is experienced as ultimate. One feels "beyond good and evil"; though from a more

333

inclusive perspective one would not have caught up with the difference. To know the Law, said Paul, is to realize oneself as guilty before the Law, and the contrary would be equally true: to remain ignorant of the Law (which would begin as conscience, or the *possibility* of Somebody Else) is to remain unaware of oneself as anything more than just another person trying to get by.

To be sure "guilt feelings" are apt to be confused, like the other kinds. But I suspect that, contrary to popular opinion, guilt is in fact always reasonable in the end. If I feel guilty, I am — though not necessarily of the concrete crime I accuse myself of and so re-indulge in imagination. Instead of seeking to dispel free-floating guilt, one might better attempt to locate the wrong one had in fact committed — or was still committing. But that would mean passing within the scope of Law or Conscience, and so once and for all into the middle of the second category instead of backwards into some private exploitation of the first. And the key to this change would be the realization that the sin which counts is the one that is now being committed. "Confession" is otherwise too often no better than secret accusation — and generalization a species of revenge. The mind too has its proper sin, which I am guilty of whenever I know whatever it is I know *for myself;* which is to say, in the absence of Somebody Else, human or divine, and so outside any truth that might be shared. Porneia can be intellectual as well as physical or emotional: sin still, but as usual disguised from itself. To what forgiveness could one then look forward?

2

Innocence, Sin, the Law: the Pauline (and therefore covenantal) sequence of possibilities seems to follow inevitably. But the Law need not make itself felt only in painful or subtle ways. Neutrally, it is the rules and a knowledge of the rules; which would be sociology or moral theory rather than judgement. To separate, one can realize from this perspective, is to annul the previous bond insofar as it was a worldly contract of some kind, that is, a deliberate agreement between You and Me. This annulment takes place inter-subjectively long before the professionals hear of the matter. Nor need it make any difference whether the contract in question was justified pragmatically or ethically. A pragmatic marriage would be an arrangement within which one agreed to live for as long as it made practical sense: while the children were still young, say. After that it would depend. An ethical marriage would amount to an idea constituted by the choice of the parties. The content of such a marriage would be whatever illustrated the idea, good or bad. An ethical marriage would therefore seem "permanent" (as long as it prevailed) for it would participate into the universality of the idea. But an ethical marriage still depends on mutual consent, as the pragmatic depends on mutual interest. Consent could survive interest. But it cannot be sustained from one side alone. An ethical marriage would therefore drop away of itself as soon as either party disengaged his or her will. The other party would then be left without an idea. For all that is left of an idea when only one party continues to posit it is an act of the imagination in moral disguise. I cannot establish a moral truth by myself. Insofar as a marriage is merely a relative contract between two finite parties, then, it is dissolved as soon as one party determines that the bond is no longer in force, however that bond has been justified. On this level and to that extent, nothing would be left morally; though legally there might be a fair amount of paperwork to do.

So now in this case. Upon separation we had apparently become free persons who need be no more to each other than either of us might be to anyone else. This left us in an odd situation. You were virtually a stranger to me now, I could think, though paradoxically a stranger I knew well. We were no longer joined in a common way of life, nor did I have the right to confront you face to face, as man and wife may in love or anger. I had to see you almost as a third person, from the side. Meanwhile I seemed to have become a relative to you. It might have been thought that the normal private relation within the second category for those who are not literally members of the same family or married or lovers would be friendship. But friends, it turns out, have to be connected by some public concern. Friendship is wholly cultural. So we had trouble relating on

337

that basis, for we did not share the same projects. Our public concerns had always been different; and now, unsupported by a common way of life, we felt the gap. And surely we could not just drop back into casual acquaintances; that would be too absurd.

What we could still do in common was realize each other. We were free for that. Gradually your motives and mine did clarify. A clarified motive is an unambiguous message. Each party has something to say: yes, no. The messages by themselves add up to a contradiction, which in terms of motive is a conflict. In this case the resolution was obvious logically however difficult in practice. If one party says no, then the yes of the other party becomes irrelevant. That leaves the no; but a no which is consented to has ceased to be only the message of a single party. It has turned into candor on one side and acceptance on the other. It has become a mutual consent to the absence of what is no longer present. So understood, separation too can be a species of bond.

Such a mutual acknowledgement would be the ideal adjustment as private persons. The Law presides over these in its benign disguise as the conventions of this world, conventions we are bound to discover as we go along. There are comic aspects to this. One announces a separation, it turns out, like an engagement: first the women friends, then the nearer world, last of all the aunts and in-laws. And such a status is disclosed as not just the negative of marriage but a social positive in its own right. A separated person can no longer "commit adultery," for instance — according to the conventions now in force — for the behavior in question need no longer be defined in terms of the marital bond. Now it is "going out," with its own set of rules. I notice too that we introduce ourselves over the phone with our proper names, now. Once we just said, it's me.

There can be a certain superficial ease to the tones deployed within this order. No one need be upset; often one can laugh, through the loss of intimacy may baffle and retard. Meanwhile there are responses which each must follow up as a distinct individual, strategies reflecting so much of the moral Law as impinges upon the conscience. For these separate selves are each ultimately definable in terms of their response to that pressure. I *am* the Law I obey or disobey, whatever commandments may be concretely involved. So what I do with conscience will report my individuality. An unqualified consent to its authority is not possible outside the absolute relation, where unrestricted acknowledgement of sin and unconditional forgiveness are absurdly possible. Short of that, I must a little manage my conscience. Self respect is self-limitation in this world. Responsibility must be reduced to a scale I can "handle."

Projection and incorporation make obvious alternatives. Within a strategy of denial I refuse to believe in the Law at all *except* as a set of conventions. Subjectively I become my own competence and the energies it

339

serves. I ask no more of myself than freedom, which I hope to enjoy as much as I can. I make sure nobody asks any more of me than I already want for myself. So far so good; I feel my own identity at last. But to ensure this result I must keep conscience at a distance. So I project it upon the relevant other; who thus becomes clothed in the part of myself I have refused. That other will now seem to me a mythical embodiment of the aspects of the Law I have denied — whoever he or she may be in their own right. Of course I am now afraid, not recognizing the other either *as* another or as an alienated function of myself. Relation may then be too dangerous to venture upon altogether; though alliance is more necessary than ever. This is a very American solution.

The opposite to denial would be incorporation; in which case my ego identifies with what can then fairly be called the super-ego, taking sides against the rest of the self; or rather, admitting only so much of that remainder as may befit the corresponding self-image. I become my conscience instead of listening to it, and desire credit from others in support of the high opinion I now feel I am entitled to have of myself. Thus I become so much of the Law as I am *not* breaking. Religiously speaking this would be "boasting," in the sense reprobated by Paul, were it ever realized. But usually this strategy remains half-conscious too, like the strategy of projection it mirrors. And like that it is really an exercise of the imagination in the mode of refusing the truth. One method eludes responsibility; the other prevents sanity. Both manipulate the Law by avoidance or ingestion. So they prevent confrontation with the Law *as* the Law: that is, as the commandment of Somebody Else.

Meanwhile each party has a story to tell, as if for the first time. For the We is essentially mute however talkative within itself, and this silence the world protects with various prohibitions. When the We disintegrates, a first person singular emerges who *can* speak — but only in the mode of imagination. These stories seek justification, of course, as all recapitulations do: a story, by definition, is told under the hegemony of the Law, in terms of which it may eventually be confirmed as true or false, fair or unfair, partial or complete. The imagination is a paid advocate: Someody Else is the judge. All accounts (including this one) participate in the Law by appealing to it — on Somebody's behalf. I rehearse my recollections, I re-write my notes, a history is composed. The result is a *work* of some kind, which at least releases intention from the cycles of memory and fantasy. For the presence of the other draws language out into the middle of the second category, breaking its ties to original experience. Fact becomes fiction, even if fiction "based on" fact, and tips in the direction of a clarification which would transcend them both. No writing can be *just* for me. To that extent expression is already a species of criticism.

341

Beyond imagination, sick or sane, is the truth; of which the work of imagination might at least be an anticipation on the scale of the individual. I may know my experience is parabolic, though I do not know its meaning. The way to that meaning leads through the Law, which incidentally generalizes my own case. A generalization should be the cognitive half of a judgement, as a judgement is the normative half of a generalization. I cannot do without both. By definition the universal universalizes: the generalizations I propose can only be true if they apply to Me as well as to You. The imagination would then be the concrete of which the Law is the abstraction, as in the Deuteronomistic history. When complaint or attack lurks beneath a proposition, its rhetorical balance and intended generality are to that extent falsified, and the ideal other, immediate or distant, will hear only one more voice speaking on its own behalf. But that condition, however inevitable, need not be quite fatal. A parody, after all, implies the very possibility it subverts. Even this first person could conceivably come to conclusions for us both — provided I allow myself to be concluded. It is the actual reader's task to keep any writer to this standard; the reader, as it were, always standing in as attorney for the other side in the case — and so, eventually, for God. Somebody Else is at least *my* judge.

3

Lucidity in freedom might already be the private ful-fillment of the Law, then, between two distinct individ-uals. Then You and I could acknowledge each other as no less and no more than just each other indeed, with-out either projection or fantasy; Somebody with Some-body Else simply and utterly like and unlike him or her-self. Such an ideal meeting and parting in the midst of the desert would presuppose and include reciprocal val-idation of the stories composed to explicate these differ-entiated selves. Each could then be the "writer, " each a "reader"; and the message exchanged would become: goodbye. This might be called the ideal Buddhist di-vorce, or "no-fault" interiorized.

Meanwhile, though, in the real world we still share, there will be some public version of the Law too, "secu-lar" or "religious," with ethical as well as social force. The uncoupling couple cannot help confronting this universal word sooner or later as it once had to evoke the same power upon first coming deliberately together. We do not either marry or divorce entirely by ourselves. Duality is always *defined* in terms of communality. So it could only be in terms of some public law that the "will of God" with respect to marriage could conceivably be articulated. If there could be a religious dimension to marriage, this is how one would know.

A "secular" marriage would be constituted by the

343

parties concerned in accordance with the rules of the prevailing social order. Such a marriage takes place entirely within the second category without evoking any authority beyond it. A "religious" marriage would then be constituted by the parties concerned in accordance with the rules of the prevailing social order on the understanding that the bond was simultaneously endorsed by God. Both Jewish marriage and Christian marriage would be religious in this sense; but in different ways.

The difference is exhibited by the treatment of the problem of adultery. Within the Jewish tradition, I can learn from J. H. Hertz' commentary on the Pentateuch (p. 933), the husband *must* divorce his wife in case of her adultery. (There is of course within that tradition no reciprocal right or duty for the wife; only the male can or need act as Somebody within this version of the relation.) Otherwise, as we observed, the husband would become complicit in his wife's breach of the seventh commandment, and so guilty of sin on his own account. We have seen how this view follows from the ontological status of the marital relation within this mode of the covenant. In the Jewish tradition marriage takes place altogether within the second category. Only the children of the union can be within the third category, where they represent a fulfillment of the promise of progeny to the nation as a whole. The relation between the parties is therefore covenantal only indirectly. Obviously this does not mean it is not religiously binding. *Because* it appears in the Decalogue, adultery becomes a breach of the covenant with the Lord. So Proverbs can speak of the foreign woman who forsakes the husband of her youth as forgetting the covenant of her God (Prov. 2:17), and Malachi can inveigh against those Jews who have put away the wives of their youth to marry pagan women as abandoning the "wife of thy covenant" (Mal. 2:14). But such references do not imply that marriage itself is covenantal, only that both parties necessarily share in the collective version of the relation. Fidelity within marriage can therefore be limited in principle, like the persons between whom it is pledged.

Within the new covenant, on the other hand, a man and a woman become capable of a sacramental relation proper to themselves as a couple. To that extent their marriage can take effect within the third category as well as the second. The fidelity pledged between the parties would accordingly have to be as unlimited as that presumed by the communal version of the same covenant. It would have to become a species of faith, for the relation between the parties would in such a case become the dual mode of their relation to God and so of God's relation to them. Not only the progeny but the intercourse between the partners, verbal and domestic as well as sexual, would then become gracious in principle. Faced with adultery, then, whether of the man or the woman (for in the new covenant a member of either sex may count as Somebody), fidelity would have to take the form of forgiveness. In no other way could it be practiced without qualification and so count as a species of faith. Forgiveness would thus become the ultimate marital command within the new covenant, like repudiation within the old. Both traditions agree that adultery is the type of the worst that could happen within a marriage. But their responses to that possibility diverge in proportion to the presumed status of the bond betrayed. In one case, divorce is a species of *herem;* in the other, it would amount to implicit apostasy.

Any infinite privilege within the third category has in the nature of the case to be matched by an equivalently unqualified response within the second category in order to maintain the covenantal character of the relation. Marriage becomes indissoluble as a logical consequence. The strict view of divorce attributed to Jesus in the *logion* which is repeated in Mt. 5:32 and Luke 16:18 would therefore be entirely consistent with an eschatological redefinition of marriage as a third category possibility. The relevant directives may be re-arranged in the familiar style: do *not* divorce and remarry, for that is adultery, *but* remain faithful — no matter what. The complementary promise that they shall be one sacramental body in Mark 10:2-12 we have already taken notice of in a way that will cover its repetition in Mt. 19:3-12, where the negative commandment is also repeated. Paul repeats the positive command in I Cor. 7:10 as coming "not from me but from the Lord": the parties should not leave each other, or if they do, they must remain unmarried to anyone else for life. The argument in Rom. 7:1-3 presumes the same rule, though the topic there is not marriage. I Cor. 7:8, I Tim. 3:2, and Tit: 1:6 seem to imply that the early Church was accustomed to understand this instruction as rendering even a second marriage after the death of the partner unrespectable if still technically licit: a "fence about the law" for the dominical word.

Jesus' *torah* on the subject thus seems remarkably consistent and clear. But the institutional church has of course found it equally difficult to enforce, or even, it can sometimes seem, to understand. The disciples in Matthew are presented as complaining: if that's how the matter stands, it would be better not to marry at all (Mt. 19:10) — an attitude with which Matthew himself appears to have sympathized, for he introduces an exception clause into both his variants of the fundamental instruction ("except for *porneia*") which it seems easiest to interpret as virtually a restoration of the Mosaic *status quo ante*. Presumably he spoke for his "school." Paul permitted separation if not divorce among his Gentile converts if the reason were some religious difference incompatible with domestic peace. This provision is not as such inconsistent with the original instruction, though by the time it is interpreted by later authorities as permitting a subsequent remarriage during the life of the first partner it has apparently become so.

347

The Matthean exception exhibits the whole development in embryo: what begins as a genuinely covenantal equilibrium between a new gift in the third category and a new species of faith to complement it in the second has been translated back into one more set of requirements, all on the hither side of the relation. Covenant has become (nor more than) Law again, in the familiar "post-exilic" style. Reduced from the third to the second category by this neo-judaizing tendency, the sacramental possibility becomes the rule that a bond publicly and deliberately assumed by two provably baptized persons must be considered indissoluble as soon as sexual intercourse has taken place — at least by any power in this world. This rule in turn has generated the so-called "Petrine privilege," by means of which the supreme ecclesiastical authority has defined itself as capable of dissolving an expanding variety of marriages which could be shown in court to fall short of this degree of indissolubility. What starts as a new spiritual possibility is thus turned into an administrative dead end; which has in turn naturally enough provoked extra-legal evasions and escapes. A subjective opportunity has become an objective fate: "Moses" interprets Jesus. The novelty of the new covenant is thus practically abrogated by the very means adopted to articulate it.

And if that were all there could be to the matter, the "pagan" child in Us will of course resist what the "Jewish" grown-up cannot obey and the Christian adult cannot resolve. In recent years the discipline of the Catholic Church has considerably relaxed. The "Law" now seems much weaker — without, unfortunately, ceasing to be the Law. So Nature substitutes for Grace, in the American way. If one wants to divorce civilly and remarry "within the Church," ways can usually be found. Annulment, which is at least intellectually consistent with Jesus' word, is much more readily available. Virtually anyone willing to agree that his or her marriage never was licit for one reason or another can get out of it. For those who stick at such a retrospective denial of their own history, there is a more informal option, the so-called "good conscience" or "internal forum" method. In that mode divorced and remarried people living decent lives can be invited or invite themselves back to the other sacraments as members in good standing of the communal body. All that is still denied is the quaint privilege of receiving the blessing of the Church on their second marriage. It must remain a second category noumenon. To this extent the ghost of the original relevation is tremulously maintained.

The reason for these changes, of course, is "pastoral" need. Everybody naturally wants to try again. And Everybody wants the approval of the institution too. If We have already understood the situation as one more conflict between Us and Them, We are of course pleased to discover that They are lenient these days instead of harsh. And who could object, if that were the

349

only alternative? The moral theologians are left to rationalize the new mode as once they did the old. Charles Curran, to pick a representative example, has for instance suggested that indissolubility should now be re-interpreted as an ideal or goal rather than a juridically enforceable rule. Then it might still orient behavior without injuring those who could not live up to it. A moral ideal only a few might be expected to act out would clearly be less oppressive in practice than a legal imperative automatically binding on whoever satisfied the objective conditions. But neither legalism nor idealism shifts the possibility of marriage out of the second category. And as long as it remains there, it cannot be truly sacramental. For if an indissoluble marriage is legal or ideal without being covenantal, it is no longer Christian at all, whatever the name; it is merely the equivalent within Christendom of that very absolutizing of the Law which Jesus once found to criticize in the Judaism of his day. The argument between the conservatives and the liberals within the Catholic Church of our own day is therefore intramural, a repetition of the difference between Shammai and Hillel. On both sides a spiritual opportunity has been interpreted in fleshly terms, which both sides accept unconsciously. Both can accordingly seem all too correct in their judgements of each other. The conservative position is indeed painfully "legalistic"; the liberal is indeed a weak capitulation to the powers of this world.

Both ought to be religiously irrelevant. For it cannot be the Law which is absolute even in the "old" covenant, but the relation of which it *may* be the vehicle. In which case obedience to it might in principle become a specification of faith, either in Judaism or (*mutatis mutandis*) in Christianity. But this is possible only if the commandments of the Law are once more replaced within a covenantal framework; which in this context would mean a recovery of the perspective in which marriage is a third as well as a second category event. Once that had become clear (as in the Church it *should* be) indissolubility would become not a totalitarian universal exposing the helplessness of actual men and women or even provoking idolatrous allegiance but simply the objective name for what could be experienced subjectively as an unqualified fidelity. Then even the old conditions, baptism of the parties and a canonically valid ceremony, might conceivably be interpretable as prefigurements of the relevant species of faith instead of as prerequisites to a juridical decision — prerequisites which as such need not presume any degree of faith whatsoever. Grace and faith would then appear in complementary equilibrium once more as they might in any other context open to the possibility of exemplifying the new covenant. But obviously it would by difficult to translate so "spiritual" a possibility into pastoral terms. A certificate of baptism is obviously easier to locate.

D

Wo es war, soll Ich werden
— *Sigmund Freud*

Measured either by the conservative or the liberal understanding of the situation, the particular marriage which has been made the type of the possibility for this argument was imperfect indeed. Neither party was baptized at the time the relation was solemnized. The union was frankly civil from the beginning; which is to say, at least pragmatic and at most ethical. So it could not be sacramental in the technical sense. In the course of time, one party was baptized. Still later, the other party withdrew. This entitled either party to a divorce; and the baptized party, it would appear, to an ecclesiastical dissolution in accordance with the current understanding of what is quaintly called the "Pauline privilege." Such a course of action appeared objectively possible. But it did not seem subjectively relevant.

Measured by the fullness of the covenantal possibility just outlined, this marriage would be unsacramental still, though not because both parties were unbaptized when it began and one was unbaptized still. What would be missing from this perspective would presumably be a mutual consent that the relation should be understood as unconditionally determined. If while still both unbaptized this couple had ever come to acknowl-

352

edge their union as absolutely confirmed, the parties would in effect have found themselves "sacramentally" bound, whether or not they felt comfortable with the term. But nothing of this kind happened, as far as anyone could tell.

Where then would this leave the baptized partner once the break had occurred? Still, apparently, married: though in a sense difficult to explain, for the various institutional languages available seemed to have no name for the situation at hand. Objectively there seemed to be an opportunity to dissolve the bond ecclesiastically as well as civilly. But both opportunities seemed to apply to Anybody, not to Somebody. A legal permission is after all not a personal command. On the contrary: what did seem to take the form at least of an invitation appeared to inhere in the opening indicated by an old conviction that this had somehow already become a relation which could not be denied without apostasy. An irrevocable deed had apparently been accomplished by Somebody, however obscurely. The original choice had been re-chosen, over and over; the chance to begin on a species of love which would have to be unqualified in principle had already been taken up — for bad reasons, perhaps, but still; it felt too late now to do otherwise. A choice had become a vow.

So the marriage seemed indissoluble — at least for the party to whom such a possibility could seem real at all — not because it was sacramental either objectively or subjectively but because it was crucial. The task then became to explore the way in which such an imperative could be interpreted as legitimate within the version of the covenant which had to apply to the case. For it was clear that such a possibility could only make sense religiously if at all. A marriage that could remain in force for Somebody in such a situation would have to become altogether an aspect of the relation between him or herself and Somebody Else to the infinite degree. If *such* a version of the relation could hold, though, it would follow that no human power, individual or collective, would have the authority to dissolve it, whatever he or she or they "believed." It would continue true for whomever it could be true for, regardless.

What though could be the nature of a marriage which existed in such a way only, within the second category still — for sacramentality would still have to be discounted — but at, as it were, the extreme end of it? Ethical marriage, we have seen, would already be dissolved, leaving only religious marriage; but a religious marriage in which only one party was apparently involved. Meanwhile to be sure familial attachment might or might not be left over from the first category; if it was, it might well be felt as a surviving concern. Meanwhile too erotic feeling might or might not be left over from the first category: if it was, it would be felt, obviously, in the form of suffering. But the presence or absence of such leftovers, pleasant or unpleasant, would be neither here nor there. Nor would any philic love, that is, the liking of friends, casual or even intimate; though that would be nice too. Nomic love, the love of a husband for his wife simply because she is his wife, or of a wife for her husband simply because he is her husband, would in such a situation become unreliable because *un*real. A moral relation, left to the individual, becomes, as we have said, imaginary. All that could conceivably be left would be an altogether sacrificial love — which would in any case be the only species of love that could possibly count within the relation to Somebody Else to the infinite degree. I could not love God, in such a case, with the same love with which I might still love you. That *would* be abnormal. But the fact that I did love you might then become the mode in which my relation to God would take place within this context. I would not feel that I loved God. (How many people do, without idolatry?) I would feel that I loved you. But the fact of my love for you would at the same time be the concrete of my love for God. It would still be a specification of faith within the dual.

Such a possibility would presumably seem *in*credible to Charles Curran, who has already been spoken of as representing modern Catholic liberal theology. In an influential double article on marriage in the *American Ecclesiastical Review* for January and February of 1974 (vol. 168, pp. 86-87), he remarks that a "covenant" love of the sort recommended, apparently, by some defenders of indissolubility is *not* plausible. Such a love would presume a "fidelity which commits itself to another no matter what might happen in the future." Curran identifies this as *agape,* using this word a little vaguely. We could more accurately call it thusic love, as I suggested earlier, for sacrifice is accomplished in the second category — reserving *agape* for the corresponding gift within the third , as Anders Nygren long ago recommended. In any case, Curran does not believe that Catholic moral theology "as opposed to some forms of Lutheranism" has ever expected such a thing. "Permanence and fidelity remain radical demands of Jesus" to be sure; but reality must be faced.

From the pastoral perspective Curran assumes, he must of course be right: any objective standards that might be enforced either legally or morally could not by definition include the possibility of an act of faith which would transcend these categories. Curran is speaking as a good "Hillelite" on behalf of generosity instead of rigor. But his estimate of the possibilities once again exposes the underlying agreement of liberals and conservatives. Marriage for both sides is essentially "Sinaitic" still: a version of the specifically Christian response may be remotely admired or gently disparaged but it cannot become part of a definition of the possibility. But this, we have suggested, is implicitly to agree with the Reformers that marriage is not a sacrament after all. For it cannot become a sacrament in spirit and in truth unless it can be found to take place on the divine side of a covenantal relation in which the human element would have to be a species of faith. And if that faith is to be genuinely unqualified, it would have to remain possible for the one to whom it applied in the absence as well as in the presence of any *human* mutuality. Otherwise it would not be faith at all.

A thusic love of such a kind might accordingly be placed at the end of a series of which the other species of love could fill up the rest of the first and second categories. Any marriage might exemplify one or another of these in its time. There would have to be narcissistic love, to start with — which certainly begins as innocent, whatever may happen to it later. There is erotic love, the dual development from this elementary beginning. There is domestic affection, the chronic cousin of them both. There is pornicity in all its fantastic or promiscuous varieties: for marriage too can notoriously be "an occasion of sin," as much inside as outside the bond. There is, one may hope, philic love as well; marriage without friendship is hard. Marriage can also become for the conscientious a "work of the law," through which one or the other partner seeks to save him or herself from something worse. Nomic love though can also have its decent varieties: the sense of responsibility is not all hypocrisy. And on the farther side of the Law the individual's relation to the relation could begin to take on the appearance of prayer. If this element should increase as the other possibilities dropped away, who need really be surprised? Sacrifice, humanly speaking, might very well have to begin as a mere loss which could be caught up with only after the fact. Thus one might eventually appropriate what had otherwise merely happened as a kind of choice. In which case marriage might even become a part of one's religious life — instead of, perhaps, an exception to it.

At the end of the second category, then, love would join with faith, so that either might be defined as a species of the other, depending on the context. For faith too may be understood as the final member of a series, each of which can also obtain within a marriage. The initial member of this series would presumably be what has been called "basic trust," or *animal* faith. This innocent confidence in one's own bodily existence and that of the other is the presupposition for sanity and affection at once. From it would derive all our "natural" powers of giving and receiving, and so at once our physical capacities and our emotional susceptibility. Dependence in its secret modalities would then be the deficient version of all these first category positives. In dependency what should have become an unconscious trust in myself and my world is alienated to some other, who is supposed to make it up to me for the life I have missed. Dependency in matters of love is the other side of *porneia,* as addiction is sin under the regime of necessity. *In*dependence would be the obvious opposite, or that form of self-trust which would correspond to individualism. Autonomy is faith in oneself in a social as well as the natural sense: it would have to be located accordingly in the midst of the second category. The independent person seeks to be dependent on nobody (except society as a whole, which he or she translates into the first person singular) and wants nobody dependent on him or her.

The fullness of adulthood would begin with the possibility of inter-dependence, or dependability. Faith of this kind keeps promises, which is the best *I* can do. Somebody who has become dependable, and allowed him or herself to trust Somebody Else, has to that extent both presupposed and transcended independence. Exhibited in marriage, this possibility simultaneously discloses its complementary negative. Betrayal, or serious faithlessness, is emphatically Somebody's characteristic fault, and so the type of every injury to Somebody Else, for it contradicts relation as such.

So much has always been clear in the abstract. But it should also be said that if fewer now entertain the possibility even of worldly fidelity than this culture is yet prepared to admit, fewer are correspondingly capable of the matching negative. The appearance of *in*fidelity is less often deliberate in real life than in old novels. It is more often the almost accidental result of Everybody's needs. Incipient Somebodies nowadays can reach as far as independence, at least in hope; but are apt to fear the solicitations of dependability as disguises for domina-

359

tion or dependence. For those caught at just this point, egos but not yet quite selves, the trust others seem to be recommending may seem either a demand or a performance. In which case one may pretend back, if the other seems serious, but remain suspicious all the while, unable yet to have faith in faithfulness. A person in this familiar position is not yet capable of trust; but for just that reason, is incapable of more than the appearance of betrayal either.

Faith in the religious sense, that is, faith in Somebody Else to the infinite degree, would then be a third and final member of the series within the second category. Fidelity to another person could come under the heading of faith in this last sense in proportion to its unconditionality. At this stage faith would become indistinguishable from the corresponding kind of love. But neither would make sense unless there were a parallel member of both series within the third category on the farther side of the convenantal structure. For love this is *agape*, the love God has for us. For faith it is the fidelity of God.

This link between the faith of men and the faithfulness of God is neatly revealed in a motto from Isaiah which Paul might have used, though he did not: "If ye will not have faith, surely ye shall not be established" (7:9). The play on the passive and the causative forms of the root *a-m-n* is very Pauline: *im lo ta'aminu, ki lo te'amenu*. There is no English word that will quite re-

360

peat the paranomasia so as to act out the intimate connection between trusting in God and being constituted by him. It is by *af*firming, we might sloppily say, that we are *con*firmed; our fidelity engages his. So the covenant may be articulated in terms of faith on both sides, as it can be demonstrated in terms of love on both sides. For God too, it is fair to say, faithfulness is love and love faithfulness.

If this is so, an unraveling bond of the sort we have been following might still become covenantal even if it had never been sacramental — but only in the negative. The second category would have to be filled with what emptied it: that is, with faith — of a certain kind, and love — of a certain kind. Thus the bond might eventually be changed into a species of prayer. Carrying out such an intention would in principle leave both parties exactly where they were otherwise: that is, altogether free. One partner need not necessarily feel imposed upon; the other need not feel obliged to keep up the idea of a self. The marriage could remain as a form of which the content had dropped away, on condition that the form itself continually evaporated in the direction of infinitude. For only absolutely negative resolutions can be absolutely secure.

It might be possible to think, then, that one had arrived near the point where that "infinite resignation" of which Kierkegaard had spoken could be practiced once again; not, in such a case, as a renunciation ahead of time (the mode in which the same issue had presented itself to him) but simply as resignation, period. One could do on the "farther" side of marriage what he had done on the near side. An eccentric fidelity could match the paradox of a love that had found itself obliged to break an engagement through a series of embarrassing moral somersaults. One could nod — across a generation plus a century. "When I lost her," said Kierkegaard after the break with Regine, "I chose death." One could see what he meant.

PART IX
The Works of Mercy

The Life of Christ is the End of the World.
— *A Shaker Tract*

Within the context of marriage, then, the second category could conceivably be filled up, or rather emptied out; if only on the scale of the eccentric individual. To that extent an actual relation could be assimilated to the structure of the covenant. Faith had come home. The other half of the structure had still to be left open as far as marriage was concerned. There was apparently to be no balancing element within the third category along that line. But this left all the other contexts within which to locate whatever could be meant by the gifts of the Spirit within a contemporary situation. Of these the Eucharist would have to be the most dependable. And that rite could always be shared. But there should I knew be other communal occasions besides ritual ones within which to locate instances of what had to be missing within the dual. As the marriage began to break up, then, I found myself looking for some way to participate more actively than had hitherto seemed possible in the gracious work of the Church. The deliberate practice of *agape,* I thought, might help me recover from the wounds of *eros.* A sabbatical term provided the opportunity, and I settled on a half-year's work in a Catholic Worker house of hospitality in a medium-sized city in Upstate New York.

The house I joined was a comparatively small-scale operation. Physically it consisted of a pair of knocked-together buildings on the seedy fringe of downtown. On the ground floor to one side was a dining room with a kitchen behind, separated by a counter and serving table. On the other side was a waiting room furnished with old school-auditorium benches and a television set raised on a table to distract the men waiting to eat. In back on this side were a couple of lavatories, and behind these again, in the position corresponding to the kitchen, a dark clothing room. Furniture and equipment were all in the last stages of hard wear. One window in the waiting room was half boarded up; the benches were battered and splintered; the runnels in the metal strips which held the linoleum surface on the tables were black with grime; stuffing was coming out of the plastic seats of tubular chairs. The walls of the main room had recently been roughly repainted, but the woodwork in the lavatories and passages was dim with a patina of ancient soil. On the walls hung a couple of straw crucifixes and a bulletin board with brittle curled photographs from a local newspaper story about the house.

On the second floor were large unfinished storerooms with beds for the staff who lived in. The third floor had once been inhabited too, by a band of young war resisters; but that raffish community had passed on. Now there were two "regulars" living in, men invited off the line by the director to help out in return for room and board and ten dollars a week pocket money. The older man, an ex-Army sergeant with many of the traditional traits of the type, served as cook. The younger, a more elusively experienced person, set the tables and washed the dishes. There was also an ex-seminarian staying at the house until he determined what else to do with his life. I had already decided not to live there myself but at the seminary, where I could have a "faculty suite" to sleep and study in, and academic company for supper. That was my concession to a middle class identity. Meanwhile the ex-seminarian and I had to find our proper roles in what was going on.

Our main task was to serve a meal once a day six days a week to whoever came. Depending on the time of the month, between thirty and a hundred men (and a few women) would show up. The meal was basically bread and soup, with whatever else besides we could obtain. We got the food for free, and we gave it out for free. The work amounted to how this was done. It was a very domestic service.

Most of the food came from a teaching hospital and the motherhouse of a local teaching order. Once or twice a week two or more of us would drive to these places. During my time the hospital provided the most ample of our "pick-ups." Late in the afternoon we would arrive at a back entrance with our stack of plastic containers, big glaucous shells placed one inside the other, with rolled up copies of the *Catholic Worker* to keep them from sticking together. We would go down an institutional corridor of bulletin boards layered with notices of staff picnics and posters in English and Spanish on the dangers of bacterial contamination. A shift of chattering kitchen workers would just be leaving: large black women, mostly, in white uniforms with pink plastic hairnets ineffectually pinned on. Sometimes the man in charge would have already put out food for us on racks near the door of the vast kitchen; sometimes we would have to wait until he had inspected the range of walk-in refrigerators, section by section, for trays of food technically too old for the patients or the cafeteria. A neat young professional in a white coat, he was cordial but unenthusiastic: he had inherited the arrangement from his predecessor, and we were made to feel it would be impossible to establish any such extra-legal connection if it were to be done over again. The hospital was increasingly constrained by state and county regulations; besides, they were anxious to save money by reducing waste. The quantity of left-overs was already not what it had been. This was a worry. But the food would have had to be thrown out if we had not taken it.

Usually there was something. The food came in deep metal dishes stacked like drawers in metal frames. We would begin on the meat: hamburgers, each dry disk wrapped in a piece of paper towel; beef or veal slabs, layered in a viscous grey-brown sauce; chili con carne, meatballs, baked spaghetti in meat and tomato sauce, liver, porkchops, pieces of chicken. It wasn't bad food but daunting in such quantities. More or less compatible items would be dumped or scraped out of the big pans into our containers and the lids squeezed down around the edges. Then we would begin on the vegetables, borrowing brobdignagian spoons and tweezers from a near-by rack. There were peas and pale beans and milky corn; potatoes in various forms, mashed, creamed, or baked; and rice, plain or Spanish. There was also squash, but our cook didn't like to use this. The squares of baked fish though, like the fried fillets, we could always use, though not in the soup; the men very much liked a piece of cold fish along with their bread. Sometimes we would find closed tinfoil containers of commercially prepared meats, tuna casserole, or chili, or beef stew, each of which had to be ripped open

367

and dumped into the container. If a load was large it was tedious work, especially after a long day at the house; crouching on one's heels, or leaning over with bent back, balancing the heavy pans on one knee, scooping with a big spoon at food which was sometimes disconcertingly loose, sometimes frozen stiff, hoping that gouts of the stuff wouldn't spill on one's pants or the floor. While one of us finished, the other would search out old cartons to store the little plastic dishes of fruit and salad; apricots or plums in syrup, banana and orange slices, cottage cheese, cold slaw, carrot ribbons. When we had finished filling our containers and cartons, we would borrow a hand truck to wheel everything out to the car. Luckily I had been able to bring the family station wagon with me.

The cook inspected the food as it came in, so as to remember what there was, and stored it in a variety of ramshackle refrigerators people had given us over the years or (during the winter) out back in the shed. Every morning he would fetch what he had decided to use and transfer it gradually to the soup kettle, a big aluminum pot fixed inside an even larger pot holding water, to make a double boiler. The soup took all morning to heat up. The meat was usually boiled again separately, like any fresh chicken that came in, or vegetables. Large pieces of meat were cut into rough chunks. If the nose said something had gone obviously bad, it was thrown out. Otherwise it all went in together: potatoes and spaghetti, beef and pork, every sort of vegetable. There was usually a detectable difference between soup with a meat base and soup with a lot of chicken, but otherwise the principal distinction was between degrees of thickness. Usually the result was nearer a stew than a soup. If necessary the cook would boil up a quantity of noodles to thicken it.

For the most part this soup was almost as good as it was certainly filling, though if a large amount was left over to be re-stored and re-combined two or sometimes three days in a row it began to taste stale to me. The men seemed to have cast iron stomachs. I never heard them complain of the wholesomeness of the food, even when, as sometimes happened, the salads would definitely go off. The ex-seminarian found the soup gave him diarrhea, so he took to making himself messes of brown rice instead. The cook used to eat large sandwiches made of luncheon meat. The other two of us ate the soup, one after the meal was served and cleaned up, myself beforehand, at what the world would consider the usual time for lunch. I felt it a duty to eat what everybody else had to eat. It would have seemed wrong to serve it otherwise. I never had diarrhea. Eating the soup every day seemed to make up for not being able to receive communion at noon time, as had been my irregular practice back home. It was the same thing, in principle.

The door opened at 1:00, and the men came in, sometimes in quarrelsome clumps, sometimes as shame-faced individuals, to pick up a numbered card and then sit and watch TV and gossip among themselves. The waiting time was usually peaceful. But sometimes a loud drunk would carry on, and that would set the others going. The shouting occasionally broke out into combat, once with knives. When this happened we would do our best to evict the principals for that day or at least until the meal began. Our second old hand was very brave and skillful in these affairs. He could manhandle a truculent giant out of the door before anyone quite knew what was happening without fear or hard feelings.

At two thirty the meal was served. The two most experienced hands would lift the doubled pots off the stove and heave the inner soup container up to the serving table, where it rested on a specially chosen iron chair. The method for this procedure, like every other regular "liturgy" at the house, had come to be traditional, and could be repeated without strain or words. Then our ex-sergeant would take his position at the double door which connected the waiting and dining rooms and call out numbers in groups of five: "One-to-five," the men nicknamed him. They lined up to jostle past the serving tables, picking up spoons as they came. The soup was served in handsomely heavy bowls of the sort one used to find in cheap restaurants. Each man got a full ladle's worth, and passed on to pick up his four slices of bread from a tray. It was a rule that nobody got more than four pieces no matter what, though sometimes, as I have said, there would be a piece of fish on each stack besides, or perhaps a doughnut. The bread was given to the house by a Trappist monastery not far away which ran a well-known bakery. Once a week the long-haired delivery man would drop off four or five trays of bread, at fifteen loaves to the tray. Sometimes these were loaves the wrapping machine had mishandled, but the bread was always fresh and of excellent quality. The men like the raisin bread best; it was sweet. Nobody could have more than one helping of bread, but everybody could have as much soup as they liked. Some put away six or more helpings.

The regulars would also leave an old mayonaise or powdered coffee jar on the serving table, and if there seemed enough to go round whoever was serving would fill these up as the men were eating. This gave the provident something to eat at night as well. When the crowd was large towards the end of the month before the checks came in, it took a nice sense to calculate whether there would be enough for all the seconds and the jars too. Sometimes there were fights within the staff over priorities: raised voices over voices already raised, the room jammed and hot, soup spilling over tables and towels. We did not open on Sunday, but tried to arrange paper bags with a loaf of bread, if there was enough to spare, and a package of cold cuts. Someone who ran a local sausage firm used to give us a big box

371

of store returns almost every time we called.

The other main source of food was the motherhouse of a teaching order. The director of their kitchen, a motherly person indeed, would save things for us in big tin cans covered with tin foil. We got milk and butter there too, for the use of the staff. Besides the two institutions, individuals sometimes contributed canned or fresh food. A Donut Delight shop in the city gave us doughnuts pretty regularly. Sometimes there was an orange from a box or a banana from a bunch somebody had brought in, or even a slice of watermelon, to go with the bread. A dentist who knew a food supplier used to bring us sacks of carrots and onions and crates with large cans of "Veg-All," a mixture to which our cook was partial. Sometimes the fresh produce would rot in the cellar before it could be used. A black cook at the local association for the blind brought in turkey carcasses with a lot of the meat still on them, which made a good soup base. A Catholic girl's school sometimes gave sacks of peanut-butter and jelly sandwiches left over from the students' lunch. Our cook had his prejudices, though, which limited our alternatives: he didn't like to cook up dried beans or peas, for instance, which might have seemed an obvious resource. A scheme was presently begun to encourage individuals and families to bring in canned supplies on a regular basis, to make up for what seemed to be a gradual diminishment in the institutional supply. But while I was there the left-overs remained our characteristic source.

It was an interesting process. The food had already become garbage as far as the institutions were concerned. It had died to the world. Legally, indeed, they probably should have thrown it out rather than give it to us; another hospital in town interpreted the new State sanitary code in that sense, and wouldn't play. It was a question, then, whether we were given the stuff or it was abandoned to us. In any event, we received it; and with a little lifting and carrying and chopping and heating turned it back into reasonably palatable food. We handed this out, and it was received again; by us, at least representatively, as well as by the people for whom it was primarily intended. Thus something which had already left the first category passed all the way through the second into the third; where it could manifest the love of God. This was certainly covenantal work, then, whatever else failed to be. The food cost us nothing but the labor, which could be reckoned as an unconscious species of faith. Those we served had their varieties of faith too. It cost some who came in a certain amount of pride to enter the dirty doors of a soup kitchen and sit waiting with a bunch of street people for a charity meal. "You're not a bum if you come here, are you?" one of them asked me once. I said no, which was what he wanted to hear. We are all bums, I thought, really. It is part of the point of such enterprises to expose that truth.

So the food was indeed sacramental, a gift of the

Spirit. It was obviously bodily, as all such gifts have to be in one way or another. It was gratuitous, as they must also be, by definition. And finally it was infinitely significant — for those who had eyes to see. How many did was another question. Some seemed to, on both sides of the serving line. "I appreciate this," one of our Indians used to tell me in drunken confidence; "I appreciate this — not like these niggers here." But in fact most people who came seemed to appreciate it now and then. To be sure this consciousness remained random and private. There was nothing in our daily activity to indicate the meaning of what was going on except the straw crucifixes on the walls and the saint's name over the door. The men could attend a weekly mass upstairs if they liked but this was not required. And for the most part our own minds were sunk in the routine or preoccupied by immediate problems, as one would expect. We were like the crowds in the gospel narratives, whom Jesus had once helped — and been impatient with.

Still, an opening had been made. Through this opening the Kingdom could be glimpsed. To that extent our old fashioned little operation on the fringe of the downtown area of a middle sized city in the industrial Northeast reproduced the miraculous feedings upon the hillsides with the same loaves — and sometimes the same fishes, too. (Once somebody brought in a huge tin of frozen fillets, which I cooked in Crisco and distributed, rough square by rough square, all one hot spring afternoon.) For this was economically speaking at least as much of a miracle in our day as the originals could have been *in illo tempore*. And like Jesus, and not only with respect to food, we were sowing the seed. The bread was that seed, by a reversal of first and last which Jesus too had used. The men who ate it, and ourselves, and the city we were in, were the ground, good and bad. That some seed fell where it might grow we knew from individuals who helped us, self-selected servants scattered here and there within the fabric of this world. For it was always some individual who decided when an institution could be of use. The harvest we had to leave to the absolute future, like Jesus again. We had no advantage over him, obviously; but then in this respect he had no advantage over us. The same act was being done, for the same reason. We had become contemporary with our type to that extent. And my private hope had been fulfilled: here was indeed a communal version of that third category element I had had to miss in the dual. The possibility of faith there could match the actuality of gift here, to make up a contemporary version of the covenantal whole. Here was the Church after all, outside the Eucharist as well as in.

We had a clothing room too, from which clothes were distributed once a week with the help of volunteers from the seminary. It became my earliest task to put this place in order. Heaps of unsorted clothes were piled in drifts against the walls under which rats had nested. It took weeks, working at odd moments, to extract the women and children's clothes, which we couldn't use, and carry them across town to a parish store which could; to separate the innumerable suits into pants, which the men would wear, and jackets, which they would not and which therefore had to be given to the Salvation Army for sale or shredding; to hang the overcoats, raincoats, and heavy and light jackets separately; to put the long-sleeved shirts, the short-sleeved shirts, the sport shirts, and the sweaters into separate boxes; and meanwhile to size and hang enough pants and shirts for the men to choose from. Many never washed their clothes; they wore them until they were worn out, and then got new. So a constant supply was in real demand.

Here too the action performed was covenantal in outline at least. Members of the local Catholic bourgeoisie died; their clothing, otherwise useless, became through our irregular labor of some value to a few members of the local street population. The match was not perfect, for the elderly defunct tended to be short and stocky, while our people were often young and slender. There was always a shortage of jeans of the right size. But a relation of sorts was established. I too obtained a couple of jackets of a quality much superior to anything I would have bought for myself. It has remained a curious pleasure to wear good clothes obtained in this way. But I found I was inclined to choose things that required a little work, some button or seam repair, for I felt somehow that I should earn these gifts after all. Otherwise I might be a looter, and not a guest among the other guests. But this scruple was only my lack of faith.

2

Feeding the hungry and clothing the naked are two of the traditional works of mercy. Between them they absorbed most of our routine energy. We could not house people, except in an emergency, partly because of an old agreement with the fire department when the re-sisters commune broke up and partly because the staff who lived in couldn't manage it. This continued to be an unmet need of which we were often reminded. Sometimes I could drive people to the hospital or the drying-out center, or act as advocate for individuals who had got themselves into a tangle with some agency. I found this fun. We did no politics at all, which suited me: part of my motive for choosing this house had been irritation at the modern Church militant, liberal or "radical." But the deficiency made the young people who still sometimes came by impatient. To them the Catholic Worker meant symbolic action against social evil as well as "band-aid" good works. In other cities the movement did indeed engage in such activities, fool-ish or faithful, but not among us. This was the middle seventies, after all.

One could learn from this work, all the same. One could learn for one thing that nobody can do anything for anybody else in this world. The very idea, it turned out, is only a species of vanity. All attempts to help someone else from oneself are bound to fail in the long run. *My* strength simply isn't great enough to change the world for the better, much less another person's character. In the short run the effort may appear to succeed; but if it does, it has really failed. All that happens is that pride is engendered in me and either dependence or resentment in the other; the first if he wants to transfer responsibility for himself to me, the second if not.

The one offering help has to learn not to offer *himself,* or anything belonging to him personally. If he does, he is not in fact enabling an act of charity, whatever he may suppose, only trying to prove his own power, in the first place to himself. *That* power is illusory. And if the other party believes in the good offered as a possession of the helper, he too succumbs to illusion in the mode of vicariousness. It is invariably an illusory strength on which one becomes dependent. In both parties the illusion provides an excuse for not realizing the corresponding truth, which is that neither side is really strong. Nobody is. Ultimately there is no power that belongs to anybody in particular, nor any goods you or I can own. The second category really is empty.

What the helper *can* do instead is mediate whatever goods already exist within the situation, goods which by some accident are more accessible to the helper than to the helpee. These goods do not belong to the helper. They belong, if to anyone, then to God. They are simply *there,* to be received as soon as the way is cleared. Such a good may be external and physical, as when we provided food and clothing. Or it might consist of some assistance the Department of Social Services was capable of providing, once a few calls were made. Or it might conceivably be internal and psychic, as in psychotherapy, where the resources to be mediated are within the person to be helped; resources which a mediator might assist in releasing and making available to the sufferer. We didn't do this at the house, it was too late as far as most of our people were concerned, but it is conceivable as a possibility. Such acts of mediation are implicit instances of faith.

All the goods mediated are there already, inside or out. It would be absurd for Me to take any credit for them. All *I* can do is facilitate their transmission, the more transparently the better. The recipient should feel throughout that he receives them not from me but from the house, or the "system," or the nature of things; that is, from God. In proportion as he *does* receive the goods in question from God, they become sacramental for him, and so a sign of the Kingdom. They can even be that for me too, meanwhile and as it were in anticipation. Both of us are liberated to that extent from dependency or vanity along with the illusion of power which generates these complementary vices. For one cannot become dependent on God. If one thinks one is, it is no longer God upon whom one is hanging. God draws back from behind the idol: for he desires not dependency but faith.

380

In the strict sense, then, what one can do for "the poor" is nothing. One can naught oneself, entering into the specific negative offered by the situation as the type of the universal nothingness which applies then and there. I must, it turns out, suffer my own version of the death from which the other party is already visibly suffering his. Death is what we *may* have in common.

For the act of mediating the goods which happen to be available amounts to a species of co-suffering with the person afflicted. This co-suffering should be discriminated from other possibilities which may appear to resemble it. The helper need not identify with the person helped in his pain, as if he were that person. This is not true, and no help. Nor should he merely imagine what it must be like to be the afflicted person, though that is some help: sympathy is the beginning of compassion. What he can do ideally is live out the complementary negative, whatever that is within the situation at hand. An abyss has always to be passed through before the eschatological positive which may be available within the situation can be released and become accessible to whoever needs it. Initially this takes the banal form of spending time. I have got to "give up my time" to the person concerned. When I do, I realize presently that I have left behind my own time, which I feared to lose, and have entered God's time; which of course turns out to be all the time there is. But first it is a wrench, since there is invariably something already go-

381

ing on which really does have to be taken care of. The call to help another is characteristically an *interruption*.

One could also learn at the house, if one did not know it already, that there is an intolerable amount of suffering in this world. That fact alone explains why we resist meeting each other. The ego already feels overburdened with its own woes. It cannot take on another's too. So each refuses to "get involved," afraid that caring would drown the self. But to admit that sorrow is already too great for any one of us to end on our own can be an opening into the practice of compassion. It frees one to do what *can* be done, as opposed to avoiding what can't. For compassion is the flesh of charity. In compassion I confess that Everybody is very much like Everybody Else, including me. Somebody is not compassionate on his or her own. On my own, I feel my difference from the other, to my advantage or disadvantage. I was more purposeful than Hassan this morning, and less successful than A. last night. These differences are real enough. Between them they constitute society. But to concentrate upon them is to become once more the victim of illusion, the prisoner of a multiplicity of social selves, including my own, which do not finally exist. Compassion liberates me from this illusion with respect to Our common fate, as imagination frees me with respect to the individual predicament. The sympathetic imagination is thus compassion applied to the particular case.

382

Everybody is really very like Everybody Else. That was another conclusion worth learning. Everybody, it turned out, is more or less idle and untrustworthy, confused and easy to enrage. Everybody wants something good to eat and a place to stay for the night. Everybody wants company, and a drink when he (or she) can get it. Everybody also wants meaningful activity, and recognition from others, and a chance to give and receive love. These needs occur beneath and within the ways in which we can be found to differ as rich and poor, white or black, sane and insane, addicted or comparatively free. These differences remain facts of life, but are not life itself. We are all "human beings." It was easier, in such a place, to live with others in a way that accepted this underlying likeness, and cease to be embarrassed or threatened by the various differences. We could *almost* bracket these, it seemed; they obtained, but they did not hinder relation, for they could not count for as much inside such walls as these as they were bound to out there on the street or inside most of the buildings which opened off the street. To labor for the sake of the third category is to be freed to that extent from the compulsions of the second; and so incidently to become more appreciative of the concrete particulars of the first, which provides the matter for all our sacraments. Reality itself was exposed as illusory; but existence seemed that much more substantial. It could even become creation once again.

I learned then that it was impossible for anyone to do anything for anyone else, and that Everybody is really like Everybody Else. These were two Christian paradoxes. There was a third which I also learned: that the exception is the rule. It was always the man who came in late, after the meal was over and the time to clean up had arrived, who had to be most carefully attended to. It was the man who needed a new pair of pants on a day in the week when the clothing room was *not* open who had first to be provided for. It was especially the man — or more often the woman — who, after being granted one favor, immediately asked for another, who nonetheless deserved the best that could be done.

There were many rules at the house. The meal was served at a certain time and in a certain way. Each person received his numbered ticket in order. The "staff" could go behind the serving tables into the kitchen; the "clients" could not. No drinking was allowed in the waiting room, or fighting, or excessively loud talk. And so on; we were an institution in the second category too, like the rest of the Church. All this was religiously the Law, of course. And it had its effect. Even if the act in which both sides were engaged was in principle an act of grace, it could not be realized as such as long as all the regulations were being observed in the ordinary way. In the ordinary way the meal was bound to seem a chore for the workers and a reasonably good deal to be taken for granted by the regulars. The point of it all was necessarily obscured.

When the special case occurred, though, it revealed the true state of affairs. Exasperation, in such circumstances, became a familiar incognito for vocation. Responding to interruptions turned out to be the central reason one was there. The exception was the truth of the rule, the fulfilment of which the rule was the prefigurement. For one can easily obey the Law for oneself, but the exception cannot help but come from elsewhere. "You're always making an exception," grumbled the legalist among us; justifiably enough, in terms of the justice of men. For common justice is fairness, and someone who asked for something beyond the ordinary seemed to be asking us to be unfair to the others. Besides, as the legalist could also point out, it was better to be consistent; if one went beyond the rule, even if nobody was hurt, one might confuse oneself and others and so invite future exploitation. "They" might "take advantage." Sometimes they did. All the same, the exception proved the rule. And in practice, most of those who found themselves the exception recognized that clearly enough. They did not, on the whole, conclude they could "get away with it" indefinitely. They too recognized that the exception was *not* the rule, in the ordinary course of things. So both sides could fall back upon the rule with relief, as soon as the exception was taken care of. It is easier to live that way most of the time. All the same, more deeply considered, the exception *was* the rule.

For in the exceptional moment we did not meet merely as staff member and client, though of course we met in that way to start with. We entered into relation as persons who were obliged by the nature of the emergency to ask and answer as our actual selves. Somebody had to come forward out of the crowd; Somebody Else had to respond. The first gesture was obviously a species of prayer, however it was formulated. The second began as a prayer too — and ended, if all went well, in an answer to prayer. At such moments, and such moments only, could we consciously act out the intention of the whole enterprise. We could do deliberately what we otherwise had to go through the motions of. *Then* I could go down into the cellar and make up a bag with canned meat and spaghetti and beans for a family, and a loaf of bread, if we had that to spare. Then I could run upstairs and down the other flight into the locked clothing room to locate a clean shirt. Then I could beg off cleaning up to drive someone to the emergency room or the sobering-up station across town. I could even arrange for a bus ticket or a room at the Y or a social worker. There were limits to what I could do, given the nature of the work and of myself. But there were usually one or two resources which were in fact more accessible to me than to the person asking. If the need declared corresponded to one or another of these, I could see to it that the first matched the second. None of this was "personal," of course. One did not become friends afterwards, exactly, though we knew each other as individuals now, and were friendly. Intimacy was *not* possible at the house. But a contact had been transmitted. As with Jesus in Mark, the Spirit was easy to interpret as if it were the flesh. But not entirely; a sense hovered in the air that the house and what could sometimes be done there presented something beyond this world. To that extent then we could realize what was going on, and know ourselves as disciples indeed.

3

Of course one came to know many other individuals as well: the members of the staff, the director and his family, people who came in to give us things or talk or pray, a scattering of exceptional persons who worked here and there across the city, a priest, a nun, a social worker, the manager of a rooming house. The experience was a quick immersion in another universe where for a time it seemed worth living as seriously as one could. The men on the line became clear more slowly, usually as they called themselves to one's attention on some special occasion: M.C., a middle-aged black man who carried a bundle of newspapers with him wherever he went; the self-declared "Chinese Cowboy," actually an elderly Irishman who could not stop talking; John, who drank so desperately even by our relaxed standards; the Indians, Duncan the belligerent and Clayton the tremulous, who we once thought had died; Darrell, with his vast bulk and mordant face. But the one among them who most stood out for me through that winter and spring was someone I shall call Steiger.

Steiger — he was always called by his last name — was one of our oldest regulars. Everybody knew him at the house and indeed throughout the city. People spoke of him in a tone of familiar contempt mixed with varying degrees of affection. There he was: perennial, unimportant, indestructible. He was a stocky old man with

388

short white hair and a grizzle of beard, dressed in whatever he had been given lately. He owned nothing more than he stood up in, even a jar for soup. His hands and feet were dark with ingrained dirt. When I first met him he would always be scratching around his torso, partly I suppose because of the dirt, partly because some kids had recently thrown caustic powder over him for a joke. This habit meant the buttons of his shirt were always being ripped off, which was inconvenient in cold weather. He ate his main meal with us most of the time, and spent the rest of the day downtown, panhandling. He was not strictly speaking an alcoholic, though he would drink his share of anything going. On his face was an expression of quizzical weariness, as if he had seen through most things but still preserved a certain cynical good humor. I never heard him complain, except at the rudeness of people who were brusque with him. He could always remember what they said, though it was usually not clear when the unpleasant episode in question had occurred. It might have been that morning, it might have been twenty years before. He had no noticeable hopes or fears. If you were there in front of him, he responded; otherwise you became "this guy," one more figure in the same old story. He was the only person I ever met who really did live in the present. I found this impressive.

I first became aware of Steiger one day in March when he came in with a wounded foot. I noticed him limping through the food line, and later saw that his sock was dark with old blood. Upon investigation it turned out he had a nail sticking up through the heel of his shoe which had punched a deep hole in his heel. Why had he just gone on walking on it? I needn't have asked; that was how it was with Steiger. I pulled the nail out of the shoe and washed the wound and put a bandage on it, but the heel still looked swollen. He was drunk enough to take to the sobering up station, and I asked the ex-seminarian who was free to drive him there to make sure they had a look at his foot.

The next day Steiger reappeared, sitting on a pile of tires across the street. I went over to inquire. He showed me a sheaf of antibiotic packages stuffed in his overcoat pocket. They had given him these at the hospital. Nothing else had been done. Later I learned from the ex-seminarian that the sobering-up station couldn't provide medical treatment, so he had driven Steiger to the nearby Catholic hospital and left him there. Evidently this contact had not been sufficient.

I drove him back to the sobering-up station myself, to see what was what. They could do nothing themselves; if St. Mary's had failed, perhaps we should try the big teaching hospital where we got our food. Meanwhile we were missing the meal at the house, so they gave us soup and crackers. Steiger stuffed some packages of these in his pocket too. You never knew when they might come in handy. Then we drove to the big hospital and I accompanied him into the Emergency Room. There we waited the inevitable time until he received treatment. His foot had an abcess which had to be drained and properly bandaged. They even gave him a pair of crutches, which he didn't know what to do with. He took them politely, though, abandoning them somewhere along the way later. (Later still I got a bill for all this; such things are not free anymore, if they ever were. But by that time Steiger was on Medicaid, so it was free as far as he and I were concerned.)

Meanwhile I had tried to find out something about his predicament. He had no income at all. Once there had been a check because of his knee, see, and it had come to this bar. What bar? Well, the bar on State Street. Joe's bar. But they told him not to come in there any more. They used to let him sleep in the hallway upstairs. But once he had been asked to sort bottles in the cellar, and had drunk a couple, and this guy had told him to get out and not come back. He thought too he had applied for Social Security, and they told him the checks would be along in two or three weeks. At what address? Well, there was this bar, see . . . Meanwhile where had he been living? In the weeds. Really in the weeds? Where had he spent the previous night? There was this empty store on Main Street the guys used. You could get in a window at the back. There was a bed and a chair. The Indian got the bed and he got the chair.

391

So while Steiger was in back getting taken care of, I conferred with the social worker assigned to the Emergency Room. Where did one go from here? The social worker was knowledgeable and sympathetic. Why not try Social Services? He knew just the man to make contact with. He called for me; it was late on a Friday afternoon, but yes, if I brought Steiger right over, Jim Walsh would see us. So as soon as the medical people would let him go, we drove over to the big new building on the outskirts of the city which housed the county bureaucracy. There were guards in the hallways, and you had to have a pass to use the elevators. It was late; clerks were leaving for the weekend; the clients who remained in the waiting room looked haggard and desperate. But Jim Walsh called us in right away. He proved to be a fiercely bearded young man in a leisure suit who understood Stieger's situation immediately. Here was someone who had slipped through the social net: what could be done? He called the Salvation Army, which could put men up over night if they weren't drunk. (The sobering up station would take them only if they *were* drunk.) But Steiger turned out to be on the Army's black list. Our house couldn't put him up, at least for any length of time, and I didn't like to impose on the other members of the staff without discussion. That left the Y. There was somebody special to call there too. Yes, the Y would take him for a couple of weeks, room and board paid by Social Services. That should give everyone time to work something out. A worker from Adult Protective would come round to the Y and look him up. Meanwhile he could have an emergency check. The banks were open late. We could cash it right away.

I was impressed and relieved to find we were actually going to receive something substantial after being passed from office to office all day. Most of what we had been up to had been translation, the characteristic middle class contribution to the way things happen: from one language to another, and therefore from one building to another. Philosophically speaking this had amounted to marching in place within the second category, a tautology sufficiently indicated by the computer, the typewriter, the multi-copy form, the filing cabinet and all the other instruments for repeating a social word without letting it become true. No wonder, I could think, that the esoteric ideology of the intelligentsia these days could be reduced to the slogan, nothing outside the text! It was all too accurate for their case — and that of the bureaucracies of which our finest criticism can seem no more than an academic sublimation. Outside the convenant, textuality is tautology.

But in our case there was a bodily pay off of sorts. The State could be the Church to this extent. Steiger had his picture taken and received his identification card and his emergency check. Then we drove to a bank, cashed the check, and went downtown to the Y. Steiger signed the form promising this and that, and I

393

took him up to his room and back down to the cafeteria, so he would know his way. He had been given a voucher entitling him to four dollars worth of food a day; not much, but still. Walsh had also wanted someone at the Y to see to it he got cleaned up. I asked about this, naively. The man at the desk laughed. It would be a first if anyone at the Y gave anyone a bath, that was for sure. It occurred to me I might do this myself. But it was late by this time. I wanted to get back to the seminary and have a comfortable supper with people like myself. We seemed to have accomplished the main job, after all. So I left Steiger there, telling him not to leave until the promised social worker showed up.

I did not see him again for a few days. He did not come to the house. That figured: he had a place to eat for a while. I called Adult Protective, to check. The man assigned to the case was timid and rule-bound. In any event he like the others at Social Services was stuck behind his desk. He could not solve Steiger's life. An investigative worker was finally sent down to the Y. Of course Steiger was out. Soon the man in charge at the Y complained: Steiger was panhandling in the streets nearby, and had been found one night sleeping on the fire escape. It was felt that the Y was not the appropriate facility for such a case.

The protective worker made a half-hearted attempt to locate an apartment. But that would have been unsuitable even if it could have been found. What Steiger needed, it seemed to me, was a room near the house, so he would have a place to sleep and a place to eat. If a regular income could be arranged, a pattern of life might emerge which he should be able to sustain. He would have his freedom and a reasonable degree of security too. I visited a smelly warren above the bars downtown. One climbed a steep flight of dirty stairs. There was a kitchen and a heavy woman with a greasy neck. Yes, she had a room, and felt sorry for these old guys, there were several that lived with her. But she had to see him first, she always made up her own mind, she wouldn't take everybody, no young black man, for instance, she'd had enough trouble with that kind. I went away encouraged. But when I called to bring him over the next time he showed up she had changed her mind. I don't want to receive any more calls from you, she said, and hung up. I still don't know whether she meant me personally or the house. A second possibility was a rooming house not far from us, run by a steadier and friendlier man. He accepted Steiger even after seeing him. The room looked all right. I paid the rent out of a second Welfare check, told the protective worker what had been arranged, and felt good again.

The next task was to get Steiger an income. I took him round to the Federal building. Social Security was a vast open room filled with desks. One had to accept whatever worker was assigned at random, which made it hard to follow a case through. But we were well received to begin with. The girl who helped us found there had been no previous application, which did not surprise me. She made out applications for regular Social Security and for SSI too. Of course he had no proof of age or any other papers. But he knew his birth date and Social Security number. People had been asking him those for years. And he could recall the name of the church where he had been baptized, in Chicago. She could take it from there. The State would be the Church again.

The next step was to get him examined medically for his disability application. The Social Security people assigned a psychologist for the purpose. I called and explained that an appointment was useless for someone like Steiger but that if and when he turned up I would call and see if I could bring him in. This worked, and I drove him round to a neat little office where a pair of young psychologists had just started a joint practice. One of these set Steiger to work drawing circles and squares. Meanwhile the other man conferred confidentially with me. It is easy on such occasions to fall into a professional complicity. The diagnosis was "simple schizophrenia." That would not have been my term, but after all the name did not matter. At least it was officially agreed that Steiger was beyond looking for a job.

Meanwhile though the other half of the package was beginning to come undone. Steiger could not become attached to his new home. The manager continued sympathetic, which seemed very lucky to me. But Steiger rarely used his room, and never on his own as far as we could tell. If he came to the house I could drive him round or point him in the right direction. But if he headed off downtown instead, following his usual routine, he was lost. He could not find the way from any other direction, and could never remember the address. Once or twice he was arrested for going into the wrong house and frightening somebody. He did not like admitting he could not find his way. Indeed it seemed odd; he knew the city so well otherwise. But his knowledge was wholly by association. If some place were right before him he could recognize it and remember he had been there before. But he could not plot his new room on any mental map. There was none in his head. So he would go back to the empty store to sleep, or climb into a truck at the brewery, or sleep under a highway bridge. A couple of times he spent a week in jail. Once he was allowed to sleep in the hallway of the police station itself. The cops all knew him, like the rest of the world. More than once I would pass him shambling along, shoulders doggedly clenched against the wind, as I drove by on my way from here to there. I would stop: where are you off to, Steiger? And would take him back to the house, or to his place. But if he really could not find his way about, the room was no use. I became concerned; what else was there to do?

For a few weeks he received checks from Social Services. This paid his rent and left something over for cigarettes and wine. He lost thirty dollars once in a bar. After that I used to keep ten or twenty secreted in an envelope at the house. Then a large check arrived from the government, the first installment of his SSI. With that I established a savings acount for him. By this time though I had begun to worry about what would happen once I left town. Who would take care of Steiger's affairs then? It was unwise to have his checks come to the house indefinitely if there would be nobody around to take an interest. Besides, Social Security had received a report from the dapper little psychologist saying not only that Steiger was incapable of working but also that he was incapable of managing his income. They wanted a "fiduciary" to take over. But who would that be? There were members of his family still in town, apparently. But they had disowned him long ago. The Adult Protective Unit was unwilling to assume responsibility as an institution; Steiger wasn't the right age. And the individual worker was too vague and uninterested.

Presently a second large check arrived from the government. This was regular Social Security, and included what had been due him since his sixty-second birthday. It was over 1500 dollars. Steiger was rich; if only there were some reasonable way for him to enjoy his wealth. The room had clearly not worked. I wondered if a proprietary establishment downtown would do, and went round to inquire. Once again I struck an intelligent social worker. Yes, they took in such people. SSI raised the monthly payment; the establishment took all but twenty dollars, which was left over for spending money. Nobody could bring liquor into the house. Would they accept Steiger? The social worker paused, and proceeded carefully. If there were twenty free beds open, probably yes; if there were only two, probably not. They'd have to see him first anyhow. But it did not sound like his kind of deal. These old guys, they like their freedom, said the staff member who had known him best in the old days. But he did not know him as well as I did now. Steiger could not manage freedom as well as he had. His street days were almost over.

Then came another accident. Steiger failed to appear for our usual visit to the bank, and then again the week following. Where had he disappeared to? He had not shown up at his room, needless to say. I thought he must be in jail again, and called to ask, but he wasn't a prisoner either. Finally I heard indirectly: one of our other regulars who had just got back from a stay in the alcoholic ward at the local state mental hospital mentioned that he had seen Steiger there. I called and located the right ward and the man in charge. He had been taken to the State Hospital from the sobering up station some time before. They knew nothing else about him and were glad to fill in some gaps in the story. I should talk to the social worker. The social worker told me they were just about to move Steiger to a "facility" in a nearby suburb, a proprietary home which was willing to receive him. In fact he was just about to drive him out there to see if he liked the place. The social worker sounded energetic. I was relieved; though skeptical by now of the chances that Steiger would stay anywhere long. Meanwhile what should be done about the money? Take it out of the bank and put it into an account at the hospital, I was told; even if the proprietary home didn't work out, Steiger would be brought back there, and they would take responsibility for him. This was what I wanted to hear.

I drove out to the hospital, a military-looking collection of buildings on a wide campus. Ward 67 began as a locked dayroom with the usual collection of people sitting around the walls, not looking at the flickering TV. A mental hospital is the same everywhere. Steiger though was quite changed. He had been cleaned up at last and given a haircut and shave. His clothes were fresh. The smile on his face was sly, as if he had got away with something. I signed him out and we went to the bank to withdraw his money. Did he like the idea of going to the proprietary home? He shrugged; he guessed he might as well. I think he meant he was tired of the alternative. I was relieved again: maybe he would stay this time. We returned to the hospital and I said goodbye. I won't be seeing you again, Steiger, I said; take care of yourself; you've been one of my favorite people in this city. It was true. But I didn't have to worry that he would be upset to lose me. He knew who I was when I was there; otherwise he forgot me. There had never been any danger of dependence in this case. From his point of view I had given him nothing, and now I was taking nothing away. That was how it should be.

This was just before I left the house to return to my ordinary life. The last I heard of Steiger was a telephone call from the social worker at the State Hospital. Steiger had wandered away from the suburban proprietary home. The local police couldn't find him. I laughed; this was what would happen. We thought he might walk into town and reappear at the house again within a day or two. But he hadn't by the time I left.

I have told this story in the past tense, as if Steiger were dead. At any rate he did not show up at the house, and the people there I consulted some time later had heard nothing of him. But I find it easier to imagine that his story is still continuing somewhere, with new helpers playing the role I was cast in for a few months, as no doubt still others I never heard of must have been involved in previous years. Steiger was the representative man of his kind, the margin which really does expose the center. As such he made a good test for all those programs and agencies and methods with which society

401

bothers itself. Could Steiger be "rehabilitated"? Obviously not. He was too much a sheer fact for that. There was no way to "work with" Steiger. He defied the very idea.

But he was also a test of the apparently less demanding fall-back postion that if the world or the individual cannot make someone "normal," at least they might help him or her survive. Steiger could not take care of himself, apparently; but did he not in fact take care of himself rather better than all the others who were trying to take care of him? Through all our failures and half-successes, Steiger continued on his way, always getting something to eat, invariably sleeping somewhere, meanwhile wearing whatever it was he happened to have on. And he found company too: his street companions, the staff people of a dozen agencies, the woman in front of the bank one day who exclaimed, "What are *you* doing here, Steiger?" She was not really surprised to see him. Nobody ever was. Steiger was humanity unadorned and mysteriously sustained.

To any of us he could become accordingly an occasion of faithful action whenever there really was a chance to release some evident good from the store of things for him. He always appreciated whatever came along. One had only to ask: do you want to go to the bank, Steiger? Would you like a lift to the house? And he would nod: sure, these were things he could use. Did you have a cigarette, while you were at it? The very simplicity of his acceptance exposed the extent to which any act of charity was also partly spurious, one more expression of one's own need to be useful, to solve problems, to take responsibility; to "give of oneself." For he let all that go by without reacting to it in the least; which amounted to exactly the necessary irony. Whatever was left after all such egotism, personal or institutional, had been purged away could therefore be trusted as the truth of the matter indeed. What we provided had to be contaminated with ourselves in the nature of the case. But what Steiger received came directly from the hand of God. Presumably he did not know this, though I could not be sure; but he didn't have to. I did — which sufficed to complete the covenantal demonstration. The house had already proved that *agape* was possible for people in general. Steiger showed this could happen on the private scale too, as one more exception that proved the rule. Steiger was an individual and so was I; if he was to take in all there was, I had to run about. That was my unprofitable service to our joint participation in the absolute relation. Grace and faith had once more been enacted. It was not a bad deal.

B

Only faith is certain of the future.
— *Rudolf Bultmann*

The experience of marriage had opened up the last possibility on the hither or human side of the covenantal relation within that context. It had become possible to learn what faith as love might mean in a given case; which universalized that case to this extent. It had *not* been possible to experience the complementary gift on the farther or gracious side — as far as anyone could tell. In a parallel but opposite fashion the experience at the house could be read as illustrating what was possible indeed on that farther side within the context of community life. And it had incidently opened up opportunities for an appropriate private response now and then. On the other hand it left any collective version of that species of faith which would correspond to the release of *agape* comparatively incoherent. It seemed possible for the individual to appreciate what God was doing in the midst of what we were up to. But it did not seem possible, at least while I was there, to work out what we might be doing in response to that as a group — except keep busy, which was in effect to allow God to go on doing what he was doing already. This could not be wrong, but to some of us it seemed incomplete. We were not yet a band of disciples. We did not know how to be. And this in turn seemed to mean that our individual discipleship had to remain random and a little fantastic, like our selves.

For the house functioned religiously but it was not run religiously. It was run like a small business. The director was the absentee boss and the staff who lived in were the employees. Our guests then were not so much "clients" of an "agency" as customers. The volunteers did not really count in this scheme of things, which some of them resented, feeling exploited — which in terms of this model they were. Indeed we all complained in one idiom or another. As the young people said, there was no "sense of community"; by which they meant no purposeful collective. We could work together and did; but we did not eat or think or pray together. We talked on the level of men passing the time of day on the job: jocularity modified by arguments. This sort of language amounted to the verbal equivalent of the "easy listening" music which played in the background all day long. So we were not yet a real Catholic Worker house — through what would that be? We were a soup kitchen run under informal Catholic auspices.

What was missing, it seemed to some of us, was a core of committed believers who could come together deliberately for the sake of the gifts we were already transmitting but also for such other purposes as might serve to uncover the Kingdom. There had once been such a group, I learned. The house had been founded over thirty years before as the project of some friends who had come together to read the social encyclicals. They had been inspired to action by a visit from Dorothy Day. The survivors still lived, most of them, in and about the city. They still enjoyed coming in for meetings and suppers. But they were getting old; they were involved in their own lives; their friendship could indicate what was now missing but could not reconstitute it. More recently there had been the group of war resisters. That had been a purposeful collective while it lasted, with an enthusiastic young leader, chaotically generous attitudes, and the usual instability. Presently it had disintegrated; not without a little help from some of the old hands, who objected to tendencies that seemed to them more counter-cultural than Catholic. They may have been right. An activist commune would not necessarily have done any better as a specification of faith on the scale of the collective than a small business. But it seemed an opportunity had been missed.

There was a cerain apparatus of religious practice. The monthly Friday night meetings, for instance, began with Compline, as in the good old days. Once a week a priest came in from the Office of Human Development to say mass. Once a week too the seminarians who helped with the clothing distribution held a prayer service. And once a week a pair of volunteers from the Legion of Mary arrived to say the Rosary with whoever

406

was willing to stay after the meal for that purpose. All these modes of public prayer felt like obsolete social duties to me. The priest from Human Development, an earnest and sensitive man, eventually stopped coming. He couldn't figure out, he said, who he was coming to.

Nor could we make plans, the normal mode of institutional action in such a situation as ours. At meetings it was easier to criticize nostalgia than avoid it. The efforts to arrange new ways to bring in food to replace the dwindling supply from the hospital had an air of desperate complication which boded ill for their lasting success. There seemed no serious common language in which we could talk either among ourselves or to the public at large — not to mention God. The traditional efforts at "clarification of thought" had to be inhibited because they could not involve real self-criticism. Our separate vested interests were too mindlessly strong and tender for that. The paid staff were not in the same predicament as the volunteers; the old friends of the house had too little in common with the young activists; the pragmatists were out of sorts with the ideologues — and the ideologues could not agree among themselves.

Obviously we were not alone with this problem. Most institutions within the Church (which is to say, the Church of the second category) have had to struggle with much the same questions in recent years, in and out of the Roman allegiance, and all too often with other versions of the same results: division, contention, the mindless repetition of inherited modes competing with hasty borrowings from the surounding culture. Projects of either sort would obviously be substitutes for a true specification of faith on the scale of the collective, — if that is indeed possible at all within the new covenant. In the absence of the real thing, whatever this would be, it cannot be unnatural for the restless or serious to cultivate "works" of various kinds, in the process re-defining so much of the Church as they thereby constitute as one more repetition of Judaism for the Gentiles — as if we needed *that.* Meanwhile the rest of Us are tempted to coast; that is, to give up without going to the trouble of slamming the door. Within the Catholic Church the religious orders have at different times seemed to represent the possiblity we were not enacting. The Catholic Worker is not an order, but it has been a movement. In our case it seemed more like a memory.

In fact things were to improve drastically not long after I left — in part, perhaps, because I had been there. After a further interval of drift, the most serious of the seminarians who had been assisting us committed his new priesthood to the fortunes of the house. That was the unqualified offering I had not been able to make. It made all the difference. New leadership provided a focus for latent energies, as always. Fresh volunteers assembled to reconstruct the place both physically and morally. A cooperative of action and service has since been living as well as working there, with the power to offer shelter as well as food and clothing. The problem that almost choked us has been solved — for the time being at least. While I was there, though, all this was still invisibly ahead.

2

In the absence of a true specification of faith on the scale of the collective, the individual is tempted to make up for the deficiency on his own. My will was exerted at the house, I noticed, to see that things went "right." This was my version of the laziness of one person, the fantasticality of another, the obstinacy of a third. Such wilfulness led to anxiety, of course. Would the crazy lady, or the sleepy man, still be there when we got back from the pick-up? If so, what was to be done about them? In fact such people usually took themselves off. Yet if they or their equivalent were still around, I would press too hard for definite answers to practical questions. Where will you sleep tonight? Who do you know in town? I would feel I had to "solve" their "problem." This assumption, I knew, did not correspond with the facts. The crazy lady and the sleepy man had not come to the house to see me. That was only my conceit. And conceit in the deficient mode *is* anxiety.

One day a man who had once been on the staff turned up. He wanted a place to stay. The director happened to be present and in an expansive mood. Sure, he said — for one night. The man had been fired for drinking and general fecklessness. And ordinarily the house did not take people in, except in an emergency. This was not quite that, but still; for old time's sake it seemed reasonable to let him stay one night. Which he did, and left next morning. But a day or two later he turned up again, hoping to spend another night. He claimed he had not been told he could stay one night only, and wanted to speak to the director about living in the house again. His blue Irish eyes were guileless, his manner deferential. I felt an instant and powerful distrust, and great relief that the director was absent this time. I could put my own decision through before the other members of the staff got wind of what was up. No, I said firmly. That won't be possible. You had your favor and your time here; that's over now. He wavered, hoping still he might appeal over my head. No, I repeated; you couldn't stay unless everybody agreed, and I don't agree. He could not know exactly what my authority amounted to, except insofar as I exercised it then and there, but he was not the sort to make a fuss. Where else then could he go? The Salvation Army wouldn't have him. He hadn't been drinking, so the sobering up station was no use. He had only one dollar. What about the nearby city he had come from, I asked. Would they take him back there, either at the Salvation Army or the house which corresponded to ours, which ran a hostel in the country? He thought they would. Okay, I said, here; and gave him money enough to cover the bus fare. If he got back before 11:00, he said, he would be all right. And he went off into the rain, wan but willing.

When I explained what I had done the others were

puzzled but acquiescent; they didn't want him hanging around either. The director, when I told him the story, was surprisingly undisturbed; he too wasn't really sorry to see the guy go. But I was sick of my own will. I knew I would make the same judgement again, in the like predicament. But it was clear all the same that I had acted not as a person of faith but as a man of the world. I had summoned up my resources, I had exerted power, I had seized the time. I was justified politically but not religiously. It was not the true Church I was defending but one more carnal institution in the second category — which absolutly speaking could not possibly be worth defending at all. So it was not the will of God I was following but my own will.

This was not to say that I could tell what the will of God should have been in this situation. I could not even suppose that it would necessarily have entailed a different decision. It would certainly though have taken more time. I should have had to listen to the man's story, and let him talk to the others. I should at least have given him a ride to the bus station in the rain — which incidentally would have insured that he bought a ticket. I should have had to give myself up to the whole of the situation he brought with him, instead of using money and will power to get rid of both. That had been an act of war: it represented fear, not faith. In faith there would have been some way to wear out both my own impulse to take over and his to cling — which of itself

412

was certainly no more revelatory of the will of God than my own wish to dispose of the problem. His motive had been no better than mine. But his presence was, in a way I had not acknowledged.

I had behaved as the director of the house in this emergency, as I often found myself obliged to do in other contexts. Yet a certain fictionality hung about this identity, which corresponded to the force of will that was required to sustain it. I was after all a visitor, who would presently return to another way of life. That meant I could not quite take myself seriously, nor could the others with whom I had to do. I could "learn," I could "contribute," but I could not really act, for action presupposes an open future, which only an unqualified commitment could uncover. Someone truly "married" to the house was needed; and I could not be that.

As time went on, then, I came to feel that I was neither working nor living quite as myself. At the seminary where I boarded I lived in a faculty suite and ate supper with the priests who taught there. This was pleasant; but really I was not a priest teaching at a seminary, though I could see how, in some other life I had not lived, I might have become just that. Really I was a professor on sabbatic. To be sure I did not feel altogether at home with that label either, though ready enough to take advantage of the duties, money, and freedom it brought with it. Nor, I could reflect, was I altogether a married man, at least in the usual sense. Meanwhile I

413

was "filling in." I could take up the jobs that had been let go, one by one, driving for the pick-ups, replacing broken windows, trying to set up an alternative food supply, and so on. But this did not seem strictly speaking my proper work, whatever that was. If I was not just deputizing for the old director, I was only prefiguring the new leader the place so badly needed, Somebody who did not exist yet that the likes of me could not become. So I felt imaginary to myself; and guilty. It is the characteristic predicament of the ego.

3

During the time I worked at the house I was also reading books for the sake of the book my own reader is now coming near the end of. There was scholarship on the covenant to catch up with in the libraries of the seminary and a Protestant divinity school across town. But the text which made the strongest impression at the time was neither academic nor explicitly Biblical. It was on the contrary a specimen of old fashioned spiritual direction — which though seemed uncannily relevant to just the questions which had come to concern me at the house and as an individual. J.P. de Caussade has never been a "popular" spiritual writer, though his name is mildly familiar to those in the know, and a new translation of his principal work is now available in paperback. The older edition of *Self-Abandonment to Divine Providence* I encountered included some letters of spiritual advice as well as the little treatise for which the author is best known. I read and re-read this volume in small doses through the remainder of my time at the house. It seemed the best of guides under the circumstances.

Jean Pierre de Caussade was a Jesuit schoolmaster in France during the early years of the eighteenth century. His outward life, the editor could tell me, was quite uneventful. The records of the order report an ordinary career as a teacher and administrator at various posts in

415

the provinces. Virtually nothing else is known of him except what emerges from the pages of *L'Abandon*, a few minor essays on the spiritual life, and the letters he wrote to some nuns for whom he acted as director. The first French edition did not appear until the middle of the nineteenth century. An English translation by Algar Thorold was published in 1933 and the fuller edition I used in 1958. In 1975 a new translation of the "Abandonment" alone by John Beever was published by Doubleday in the Anchor series. It seems unlikely that his message should ever become either official or fashionable, even within the circle of those readers who might be concerned. But it may now reach a few more of those to whom it might appeal.

That message is extraordinarily simple, so much so that the obscure history of the text and the usual problems of translation scarcely seem to matter. De Caussade affirms that the spiritual life consists entirely of giving up one's own will to the will of God. And the will of God, he proposes, can in fact be found in the midst of whatever is here and now going on. It is made evident in the duties and inclinations which already meet every soul in the course of its daily experience. This double focus on the simplicity of the fundamental invitation and its simultaneous obviousness and unpredictability is the whole of what he has to convey. There is no need even to quote: all the sentences say the same thing, and none of them, at least in translation, could be called

416

memorable in their own right. His is the least "textual" of texts. The letters of direction, sinuous and fluent in the style of the period, are equally repetitive. The invitation to follow the will of God instead of one's own, and the self-evidence of that will in the intimations which are bound to reach Somebody in the midst of his or her ordinary life are constantly the burden of the instruction. He seems to have felt no need to supplement or complicate his basic intuition.

The clarity and subtlety of this rendering of the covenantal situation was most impressive to me. Here was no method or technique, no detailed recommendations — no goal, even, for the will of God cannot be somewhere to get *to*, like some elevated state of the soul. It seemed too a remarkably un-Baroque and non-Jesuit spirituality, almost the last advice to be expected from that time and place. But it seemed to fit perfectly into the Biblical way of structuring the relation with Somebody Else to the infinite degree, either under the old or the new version of the covenant. For "self-abandonment" was clearly a specification both of obedience and of faith, and so one more name for what could in the end be done in this world. The will of God could become in just this formulation of it the way to precisely that unqualified orientation within the second category which would lead of itself to acknowledgment of the third. One knew already that the will of God stood behind the Law, rendering obedience to its stipulations covenantally relevant — when this obedience was indeed to that will as revealed in the commandments, and not to Somebody's need to construct an ego out of the available moral culture. One could know too from Paul that conscience could function in the same way for the Gentile — who could always make a similar use of that resource to serve his or her own ends. Law and conscience would both be manifestations of the will of God, then, whenever they were religiously significant at all — and obedience to either would be a version of faith. Would it not make sense then for anyone to respond directly to that will, as this might manifest itself through any combination of outward circumstance and inward inclination that should invite some response within the relation? In which case any situation could become the absolute situation, as soon as it was read as such. The covenants, old and new, would thus be implicitly reconciled; and the relation they mediated brought down to earth for any place or time. Faith would always have its potential specification. The rest, as usual, could be left to Somebody Else.

The immediate fruit of the period of prayer into which a reading of this book led was a retrospective awareness of the extent to which my own life had in fact been dominated by a contrary disposition to the one recommended. Had not my imagination generated a succession of projects for the will to carry out? I had willed my marriage; I had willed a career; I had even willed my own thought — and now I was willing this enterprise of the house.

For the wilful person is compelled to perform even that which he or she may recognize as the will of God as if it were one more project of the ego. So one becomes anxious, and apt to impose interpretations on circumstances, as if to forestall the invitation which might otherwise be found among them. One acts not so much in obedient faith as to get the job out of the way, so as to credit oneself with the accomplishment of another act of virtue. In such a case the pneumatic life has become one more psychic enterprise, which must break down and fail like the others; perhaps in despair, perhaps in some petty collapse into self-indulgence.

The initial effect of reading De Caussade, then, was not to teach me God's will but to expose my own. But I could also measure the immediate future against this yardstick. If I asked myself what actual duties impinged, I could in fact answer easily enough. There was the stint at the house to complete. There was an academic year ahead, back where I had come from. There was the marriage to remain faithful to, in whatever way was still possible. There would be a household for a while at least, and a son to care for. And there would be the literary task I had virtually had to suspend in order to do what I was now doing. My special duty was clearly to get on with this — which nobody else could possibly do. But I did not have to save the house from the threat of dissolution which seemed to hang over it. That was the job of some other person, whom I did not know yet. I did not have to resign my professorship in order to get something similar started back home, out of guilt or lack of imagination. I did not even have to change anyone's heart, though that would be nice. There was less to do all round than I had either feared or hoped. There was, indeed, virtually nothing to do. I should have known it all along.

PART X
Prayer

It is there all the time, and if we give it time it will make itself known to us.
— Thomas Merton

The problem of the Church these days is not, it is possible to guess, whether the Spirit is within her, according to the promise. For some (lucky) reason this has not been an issue for those who were disposed to believe at all. The third category is filled up still, for those who have eyes to see, and some do. The problem has been on this side of the covenantal structure. It has been hard to realize what could count as faith — which is all that could count, we know, within the new covenant. Believers have had no difficulty behaving as the crowd. We have managed to receive whatever we were given, whenever we were given it. But the individuals among Us have had trouble becoming a disciple (though no more, to be sure, than the orginals). The conservative has been apt to interpret the possibility of relation in terms of allegiance to a Christian version of the Law; which confuses an attachment within the second category with the way to the third. The liberal has interpreted the possibility of relation in terms of activity on behalf of justice; which confuses a project within the second category with the way to the third. Both have, therefore, been inclined to stop short of the Church indeed in a posture of defence or attack with respect to some idea of the Church; which leaves them at best in an imaginary repetition of the old covenant rather than an authentic specification of the new. Meanwhile the evangelically minded, who should have provided a sufficiently Bilblical alternative to either option, have been inclined to interpret the possibility of relation in terms of allegiance to the letter not of the ecclesiastical law or some secular ideology but of the gospel itself — which should be a contradiction in terms. The problem remains: to clarify what faith could mean in practice, on the scale of the individual and (if that is possible) on the scale of the collective as well.

To identify the covenant again within the situation of the Church, which is to say, within *our* experience as believers as opposed to that which appears in either half of the Bible, is to attempt a restatement of the absolute relation in terms of what we have to call spirituality. Of that half of this relation which is constituted directly by the Spirit, the Eucharist, as we have seen, remains the authorized type — though there must always be other instances which this type can help us interpret. Of that half which must occur as faith, the corresponding type would seem to be prayer. Prayer would represent faith within the second category as the sacramental flesh and blood would represent grace within the third. The problematic of faith could therefore be reviewed to begin with, at least on the scale of the individual, by way of the phenomenology of prayer. For if I pray, I am sure to be enacting the possibility of faith to that extent, whatever else I may or may not be doing at the time. We have seen how the Eucharist presupposes prayer — in the mode of that sacrifice which institutes it, as well as in the mode of the words and motions by means of which this is reenacted ritually. Marriage, we have also seen, would reduce to prayer as soon as it has become at once solitary and unqualified. And my experience at the house could illustrate the extent to which the individual at work in such a place might be able to experience the demands made there as so many openings into the country of prayer. Labor of the sort we were daily embarked upon could already stand as an instance of prayer on the level of the body. What else was possible on the level of the soul?

It seemed clear in general that whatever prayer might consist of, it could not be just meditation, though meditation might be included within prayer. Meditation may be either physical or imaginative. If physical, it is meant to calm and regularize the body so as to free the soul for whatever is in fact the case. This may be everything, if one is centering oneself upon the first category taken as a whole, as in at least some of the influences extending from Hinduism. Or it may be nothing, if one is leaving oneself open to the second category taken as a whole, as in at least some of the influences extending from Buddhism. In either case one is reduced, as cautiously as possible, to the interface between the first and the second categories on the scale of the solitary individual, there to experience precisely that juncture in one way or the other. Meditation of either kind would then be religiously non-committal as such. It would amount to a reduction of Our condition to *My* experience, without necessarily interpreting it as anything more than just that.

The varieties of meditation which involve the imagination as well as the legs and lungs would in effect supplement the disciplines intended to steady a bodily acceptance of the human condition with words or images intended to hold the mind still too. To that extent these methods would commit the practitioner to a selection from the contents of the second category — though usually a drastically reduced one. In their simpler varieties these techniques would amount to a species of song (as the purely physical practices would be a kind of dance) in which language is made to rhyme with the elementary motions of the body. In their higher reaches they might involve an inner repetition of whatever was al-

424

ready imagined in the language regularly used, as in the Ignatian exercises.

In any case, though, one need not be doing more than rehearsing an act of imagination, simple or complex. And as such this would still leave me short of prayer, which puts me into the absolute situation, and declares me a party to it. For acts of imagination, secular or sacred, can do no more in the end than place me within some relative situation, and declare me the initiator of it — which is a double withdrawal from the absolute situation. This need not mean that meditation, physical or imaginative, could not be incorporated into prayer as a prefigurement of it on the level of the body or the soul — or even as a means to hold the latter in check. Abbot Chapman, for instance, has observed that a meditative formula can serve to keep an otherwise over-active mind quiet, as one might throw a dog a bone to keep it from barking or jumping about. This can seem a little harsh; the imagination should also be capable of anticipating the surrender of the will. And that service need not be quite nothing, as the animal sacrifices under the old covenant or the several modes of the religious life under the new could show. A pilgrimage, say, can remind me of the prayer I have not yet really made. But it remains true that the imagination, outward or inward, cannot reach as far as action; which means that meditation is not yet prayer.

It would seem to follow as well that if prayer is *not*

meditation, it *is* contemplation; and that inherently, whether or not it goes by that name. The idea of contemplation would seem coincident with the very possibility of prayer, and not just of some elevated species of it far off in the mystical distance. But here too there could be a distinction worth drawing. Contemplation may be either cognitive or ethical. If it is cognitive, it is not yet prayer either, or indeed a covenantal act at all, though it may appear within a "Christian" context, but a species of Platonism or gnosticism. For the object of cognitive contemplation would have to be some positive within the second category: not an image (that would still be meditation) but an idea of some kind. But to contemplate the idea of God, say, is not yet to pray to God; on the contrary, it would be to assert power over God, to constitute God as one more thought in the mind. To the extent that contemplation too might still be included within prayer while remaining cognitive, the object of that contemplation would have to be not some intellectual positive within the second category but something negative — that is, the second category itself, *without* content. The intellect could realize God only as his absence. That is how God comes before the mind in this world. So "atheism" would be religiously normal — for this faculty.

But contemplation may also be ethical: and within that disposition it would become entirely covenantal, once again whether or not the label is used. For in

426

prayer I am not strictly speaking either imagining or thinking but acting — which might appear paradoxical, since I am most obviously doing nothing. Contemplative prayer might indeed be defined as what can still be accomplished when nothing else is possible. It gives Somebody something to do at last.

By realizing contemplative prayer as *praxis* rather than *gnosis* one could rescue the possibility from the criticism of such a learned evangelical as the influential Anders Nygren, for instance, to whom the tradition of contemplative prayer within Christianity is an instance of an essentially "erotic" and therefore egotistic attitude towards the goods of the Spirit. If these goods were objects to be obtained, this criticism would hold; and for some they may have been. But it seems likely that the language in which contemplative prayer has sometimes been described has seemed more possessive than the intention it was meant to explain. If prayer is still an action, but that action a passion, then the contemplative tradition might be revealed as no longer a rival to an evangelical understanding of faith but one more version of it. From this perspective too one could make sense of praying for others. I must ordinarily imagine and may think for myself; but I can reasonably act on behalf of others who are not for some reason free to act in their own persons. Indeed prayer is essentially for others already as much as it could be for the person who is actually doing it. For all actions are eventually collective in their import, and prayer would be no exception.

So prayer is not just a private inner directedness, but the acceptance of a situation which in the nature of the case is also the situation of every other person too, and so, *a fortiori,* my own situation whether I am praying or not. For if all otherness is incipiently absolute in any case, as the covenantal relation affirms, then I am constantly on the verge of the situation which is uncovered in prayer, whatever else is happening. When I set about praying, then, it is not as if I were embarking upon something special over and above what I am up to ordinarily but as if I were ready at last to recognize how it is with each of us all the time anyway. In prayer I am in the situation I am in without the qualifications which usually prevent me from realizing it. This is why the concerns which preoccupy me most of the time, "legitimately" enough for the most part, can be exposed in prayer as no better than distractions. So they really were all the time; but ordinarily one is not free to notice.

2

It is prayer therefore that uncovers a true identity. Somebody becomes him or herself in prayer as in no other way. For only in prayer do I enter the absolute situation. And in that situation I have to be myself indeed, for God confronts me, who knows what that is. In any relation short of prayer I can be almost anybody else. I may be lost in the crowd, for instance, and so not yet begun upon myself; or subsumed in some other, and therefore lost to myself; or I may be performing some part, in which case all the counter-players will seem as unreal as I am. Distraction is social before it becomes individual. To avoid living as themselves, whoever that would be, people regularly subordinate themselves to anything else besides. The elderly biographer subordinates himself to his subject. The aspiring critic subordinates himself to the incoming ideology. The conformist subordinates himself to the mood of his peers. The wife or husband subordinates him or herself to the role, until it becomes too much — and then the escapee, it may be, subordinates him or herself to the child in Us all. Thus I become recognizable to others and to myself as an imaginary character — at the expense of losing whoever would have had to begin in precisely that emptiness from which I turn away in fear. So I put myself off, indefinitely.

The practical task is to distinguish whom I act *for*

from who I act *as.* If I act *for myself,* I am wasting my time, religiously. If I act for others in the same way in which I would otherwise act for myself, I am still wasting my time religiously, though I may seem responsible and useful and polite. If I act for God, I shall be obedient to his will. But I can only act for God if at the same time I am acting as myself. If I pretend to act for God as if I were someone other than I am, I am only fooling myself, obviously, and my every action will be religiously speaking a waste of time — though I may humanly speaking seem responsible and useful and polite. For God is indifferent to our fictional egos. He cannot use these to accomplish any will of his, except in the indirect way in which he can be said to have used the obstinacy of Pharoah to accomplish the purposes of Moses. Humility is honesty, then; in prayer I *may* learn this.

In prayer too one may learn that doing God's will as oneself is apparently required once in a while only because it is in fact invited all the time and in general. Prayer is a participation in the situation that in fact obtains within and around all the other situations which in the end do not obtain. Within this actual situation there is only one choice: between doing God's will as oneself and doing one's own or another's will as the person one is pretending to be. It is a frequent mistake, for those who are new to the possibility, to suppose that one could obey God's will in some matter where this seems exceptionally evident or enobling, but that otherwise one is left to one's own devices. Then one is inclined to do what God seems to be asking only when he seems to be asking for something in particular. This may appear heroic at the time but in fact it is at best an imaginative anticipation and at worst an egotistic mistake. God intends his will in general; so that only when we consent to this will in general can we be sure of accomplishing it in particular. For it is only when we consent to that will in general that all the particulars are freed to become disclosures of it. To accept the particular demand as an exception is in fact to succumb ahead of time to the temptation to do what appears to be God's will with one's own will — which as we have seen is religiously speaking a waste of time though I may seem to myself and others responsible and useful and polite. Another form of the same error is to suppose that God's invitation ends when a certain project has been pointed out; the rest, we may think, is up to us. But if God's will is practically speaking ignored as soon as the job is begun, the action in question instantly loses any covenantal relevance. It becomes one more occasion for the demonstration of a person who doesn't exist. When this fictionality becomes clear, there is often despondency: the project doesn't seem to be leading anywhere. If though I consent to God's will in general, in however faint a degree, I need not search out projects to prove my good faith to myself. I shall be acting faithfully regardless, and so remain within the covenant. Romance and hero-

431

ism are thereby excluded as irrelevant. But so are exhaustion and despair. For to do God's will in general and therefore as oneself is by definition to have everything whatsoever on one's side. Gravity and grace will coincide.

The self I can "have" as myself will be the opposite both of what They expect and my ego might affirm; which is to say, it will be essentially negative, whatever accidental positives may have accumulated. By assuming this nothingness before God I come into relation with him, whose will is, to begin with, that same nothingness emphasized. To pray then is to set one's random positives in brackets, as it were, in the Husserlian style; not, of course, to seek their annihilation but to discount them, to admit the usual composite of will and imagination as illusory. Yet on occasion something better has sometimes seemed possible, as when the over-familiar flux of images, usually so bulky, has all of a sudden dwindled far down some equally imaginary distance until they became no more than a jiggle along a thread stretched across the face of the sun. In such an image of the death of images, God would be the bright light — which is in fact the reverse of the usual state of affairs, in which the other party to prayer is realized as a patch of darkness; the negative, indeed, of that candle one may have lighted. The candle is at best oneself, not the other, with its flame burning steadily off the solid wax into nowhere. So might I do, I think, turning one more image against images.

In the presence of the darkness, it is possible to realize that to act *as* myself, in or out of prayer, is in proportion to come that much closer to the paradigmatic case. Somebody is not legion, however many demons there may be, but singular after all. Identities converge as they pass through the fictions of this world, until there is at last one path, for it turns out to lead in the same direction whoever treads it. The *imitatio* has been recommended because nothing else is ultimately possible. It is the innumerable intermediate postures that appear so different from one another. But these are only stopping places within the flesh. Times and seasons do change, but never an unqualified self-abandonment. First there was Us; then You and Me; the crowd, then the disciples — and eventually their leader. But Jesus is on this side of the relation an entirely negative example, as indeed he seems to have taken some trouble to explain. The one way beyond all the other ways is altogether a *via negativa*. Prayer is a recovery of this truth, as sacrifice is the enactment of it.

In prayer I simplify. I need not ask who I might yet become within the second category; the answer has already been provided. But I may still reasonably ask. where am I, for the answer will not be first century Palestine. I will know who I am by where I am. To be somewhere for real is already to approximate the state of prayer; to come, as it were, to attention. *"Hineni,"* say the patriarchs and prophets as they are addressed: "here am I." So in my preparation for prayer — which is apt in practice to be the whole of it — I make myself at home in this actual time, this real place, and not just in one more over-crowded city of the mind. Where my body is, there shall my heart be also. In a perfected attention the contents of that mind too can filter down like turbidity in a pool. To be distracted is to be drawn away from where one is. I pray that I may be somewhere indeed. For if I am ever somewhere, it is sure to be as myself. It is only a fictional identity that lives abroad. *Dasein,* Heidegger's name for human being, means literally "being there" or "being here." To be there is to be here.

Of course I am mostly *Dasein* in the deficient mode, but that does not matter within the relation. On the contrary: we are evidently meant to present our need as well as our fullness, whichever comes first. To be somewhere is in the first place to confess oneself a member of the crowd, who may well require healing in the flesh. The Pharisee would rather faith meant the best I could do than a simple exposure of the worst. But if the best one can do is nothing, whatever remains over after that has been done will amount to where I am for the time being.

Suppose, for instance, that I do not have what I want. To begin with I will entertain this condition as an ache of absence. I will feel unjustly alienated from some positive just out of reach which ought to belong to me. But then I am not at prayer; I am complaining. I want Somebody to make it up to me — which Somebody Else will *not* do. But there is another way of entertaining the fact that I do not have what I want. I can identify, not with the thing which I do not have, but with the not having of it. I can realize myself not just as a deficient positive but as the corresponding negative. I can take part in the irony which has liberated me, as it were, against my will. Then I am afloat upon limitless seas. I still want; but I do *not* have; I do not have at all: there is suddenly nothing whatsoever to qualify the entirety with which I do not have what I want. There I was, driving back into town after taking one more man to the sobering-up station for the night. The homeward bound traffic thickened as the insight grew in my mind like a swelling light. I laughed, raising my hands from the wheel; the grey March day and the cars on all sides looked oddly homely. I am here after all, not anywhere else, I could say to myself; and repeated the major proposition: I did not have what I wanted. Of course I didn't; and why not? *Not* to have what one wants is simply the pre-condition of each first person singular, which is only temporarily disguised by this or that positive gratification. (And after all, I could also think, I had not been without some positive gratifications too.) I did not have what I wanted; to that extent, I had entered into the universal predicament. I was not out of

435

place then, but in the one place there really was to be. And to be somewhere, we have observed, is already to begin upon prayer.

3

What is prayer *like*, then, one may still reasonably ask, knowing that in itself it is — nothing. One may go where the possibility is represented publicly and take part in that. Seven times a day the monks file into the stone-floored chapel and take their places around the altar. The invocation is intoned, a brief hymn sung, and the psalms begin, verse answering verse across the circle. Thus a few of our contemporaries act out what Somebody might still do in the world. They stand on the verge of the second category, as each of us really does all the time. Behind them is primary existence, which for the moment they will have to take for granted; their living bodies, this place, the chores of kitchen and barn from which they come. At the center of the chapel is a stone-built altar, from which the third category is dispensed once a day. But that is not happening now. The space between is visibly the abyss that Jesus once crossed and that each of us still faces, or we would not be here. The Psalter is the text for this *agon*. Somebody is praying to Somebody Else to the infinite degree in the best language for that purpose Anybody knows. The psalms are addressed to God or to other men, but if to other men then not as revelation but as exhortation. They are prayer: the voice of each person as him or herself.

It is relevant that the words repeated come from the

Old Testament, though the monks are assembled in the name of the New. In prayer I look forward to redemption, I am not yet redeemed; with respect, at least, to so much of myself as is praying. We are in Advent still, saying this office. As Hebrews on the shore we look forward over the gulf yet to be crossed. And when the words cease there is also silence, surrounding and washing between the words like so much water.

This is the *Opus Dei*, then: to act out a parable of the absolute situation for whoever may realize that there is such a situation and You and I are in it. The monks play out the role of Somebody in relation. So they can speak for each one of us, all the more completely for not using either their own or our words. They repeat the language of Someody who knows what to say. The little choir is a congress, then, not of one nation or even of all nations but of every person there could be in a world of nations. In it we see what can be done.

Since the work is also a cultic demonstration it must often become a performance as far as the individual monk is concerned, as it may be no more than a spectacle for the visitor. The hours of prayer can become a routine like any other. But God is constantly on the other side of the relation entered into, and God at least is not putting on an act. This consideration preserves a certain decorum. Even if the monk is not always the person he is acting the part of, the part he is acting is in fact who he actually is as soon as he comes to himself.

Whenever he wakes from the usual dream, what he finds he is saying is true. We are each of us before God *anyway.* The monk is in a position to realize this, intermittently. And no one does better than that.

But the private demonstrations of prayer are apt to prove the most convincing. One Sunday during my time at the house I walked along the beach by the lake outside the city. The expanse of water looked like the ocean, for the other shore was invisible, and the waves tumbled in upon the sand in the same old way, leaving the same kind of driftwood behind. Here were no tidal marks, to be sure, and trees would not have grown to the edge of the water by the seashore. Nor was there any salt smell, which makes the ocean real. There were two ducks, though, walking beside the edge of the surf along the wet sand, gleaning, and it occurred to me that they might be taken as making up the difference for the time being. They waddled on, the male with his green plush head, the female with her lavender flash, nibbling what they could find, neither of them paying any attention to me, though I was almost treading on their tails. Even a passing trail biker scarcely disturbed their companionable composure. There, I could think to myself, was a married pair.

Then I sat down against a piece of a driftwood and gazed out across the rough green waves. The spring day was chilly and the beach narrow, for the lake was high that season. The waves curled in to topple and break, indefinitely various, infinitely alike. The hazy horizon and the grunt of a fog horn were ocean-like too. Over my head grew willow, cornel, viburnum. The sky was cloudy, with occasional spits of rain, so few people were about, though this was a holiday weekend and the city was nearby: a fashionably dressed man walking his doberman (named "Brandy," it appeared from his call); a pair of boys exploring; off in the distance, two men mysteriously building a shelter with driftwood. Only one cruiser passed off shore. These were the other projects of the day.

So there was nothing to do but gaze at what was there, as I had so often done before in other places, and so many had done before me. Sometimes my attention was caught by some feature of the moving water. More frequently it was carried away by interior eddies of imagination and feeling. I was not thinking. But the situation was more indicative than anything I could do there, idle or serious. I was alone on the edge of the land, looking out upon the water. Here was a complication of earth, sand, wood, leaves, all randomly distributed and occasionally distinguishable, among which organized accidents I was one more, another creature full of his own particulars, living and dead. Sand, emotions, clothes; I was after all allowed out of this into another realm of which the principle was evidently unity. Water is one thing, the biggest visible entity in this world. Yet there seems virtually nothing to it, compared with the land and all its prickly concomitants: translucent, almost empty, containing, if anything beyond its own minerals and molecules, only a few motes detached from the earth and as it were representing it in this alien medium, like the dust caught up within a breaking wave and just visible through its smooth inner surface as it begins to fall. Water seems meant as pure, however many pollutants may actually tinge its body or concentrate in the flesh of its fish. This lake is my outer space, I could think, the representative here and now of absence, a Parmenidean *to meon* to all antecedent existents. To sit there was then to align myself once again with those "silent sentinels" who figure so impressively in the opening chapter of *Moby Dick*, "some leaning against the spiles; some seated on the pier-heads; some looking over the bulwarks of ships from China; some high aloft in the rigging, as if striving to get a still better seaward peep;" all gazing out to sea from the edge of the city, all searching, thought Melville, for what to him at least always remained "the ungraspable phantom of life."

If gazing out over water is like prayer, is indeed already prayer in terms of the body, then whom is one praying to and for what? In *Moby Dick*, God seems a white whale, swimming far off in the remote depths of that same ocean into which the land-imprisoned clerks gaze. But except as one more living creature and so in his own bulky and far-ranging way a fellow inhabitant

441

of this ordinary earth, Moby Dick is no better than a "phantom" projection of Ahab's post-Calvinist mind, one more figment to kill or be killed by. That God is an idol, and reciprocal violence its appropriate liturgy. Such an image is clearly still imaginary, not the truth yet. Nor is the water itself into which one may gaze so searchingly a sign of God, even in its extremest purity, but simply of this gazing. It is a figure of prayer, not yet of the answer to prayer. The true God withdraws before the intention which seeks him. But that withdrawal is also his invitation. It does not imply there can be no answer from the other side.

The perfection of such an experience would be some still more solitary beach before the real ocean, with nobody in sight to either side for miles. How unusual to find such a place in summertime these days in the crowded East, I thought, walking out upon the strand after much wading through tidal flats. Behind me on the salt pond behind the dunes a catboat moved slowly; out at sea, a fishing boat stood still; otherwise there was nothing. The elements of the scene had been there virtually since the beginning, and cared nothing for mere human being: the stringent light, a mineral sea, the swarthy, knife-edged waves, the astronomical sand. This was nature without qualification indeed, and I looked back at the breezy beach grass a little anxiously, as if to another disregarded brother in life. The sun gave out its brightness without cease, an unthinking

442

star; the waves rolled in to drop upon the beach one after another, driven by mere tide and gravity. The sand that clogged my feet had been worn, I knew, from still older rock, who could say how long before. The beach grass waved its brevity in the wind, the growth of this season; nor was I, a middle-aged trespasser on this aboriginal scene, any exception to the devastating rule. Each element had its date, long or short. The sun would exhaust its shining by and by; and each wave already had its proper fall.

This was an ancient but *un*mystical nature, then, that lived by dying. The being of all these things, I could realize, was disclosed in their passing away. It was the sun's burning up that made it visibly the sun. The sea breathed out its being upon the sand. Each wave was what loomed and fell, no more. The identity of these things was an evaporation or phanescence. That steely glitter on the wrinkled sea was the mountainous wink of a planet and its star. Appearance was disappearance; being, not being.

And more formidably still, I could also think that this exhalation of every single thing in an appearance which was simultaneously its disappearance was at the same time utterly coincident with any perception of it. My consciousness of these things *was* their phanescence. Intuition, I was suddenly convinced, is the direct precipitance of being in us. The mind is already an apocalypse. We are not separate from these things, I seemed to realize, much less the creator of what we see, whether on our own or by way of language working through us. We are merely the last phase of it all, spilling over into consciousness. *Psyche* is only *sarx* at one remove — as after all one had been told. So now this ancient ocean repeated itself as if for the last time in the brain it flooded. Being and nothingness! There was nothing to it.

But if this were so, I could conclude as well that I was not really alone either. If the contents of this world must give themselves up as they go, then everything else besides myself would already be (mythologically speaking) at prayer too. Entropy would simply be faith on the scale of the *in*human universe. The waves, I could think, give themselves up; the sun gives itself up; a spear of summer grass waves out its little life. That endless phanescence would then be the equivalent in the order of necessity to self-abandonment in the order of the will. We need not look backward nostalgically to the life of things, then, as we become aware of losing our own, but forward together with their death, which we share in our very perception of them. These images of my prayer, then, would really be repeating the principle they began by illustrating.

And there was more: for if nature could supply either an image for prayer or, more seriously realized, a parallel instance of the same possibility immensely enacted, it (or rather she) could also and still more profoundly stand as the type of everything we might mean by the answer to prayer. Nature is not only in the first category, as I on the beach had begun by assuming, or even in the second in the mode of being realized, as I seemed to be discovering, but in the third as well, as a gift of God. For though every particular thing exists in the undoing of such being as it already "has," the whole of which each is a part persists. All bodies lapse away, or we should never know they ever were; but *the* body remains present. This is true in a qualified sense even for the particulars, after the fashion of their several kinds. The sun goes on shining, it has not run down yet; the individual wave collapses, but waves are falling still; the sand lies glistening before them, stirred now, perhaps, by winter storms and the scuff of the less frequent visitor. Each season the beach grass renews itself, and the beach pea here and there in the midst of it. I can even return to this beach the day after, or the year following. Repetition, like beauty, is already a hint of eternal life, though the units die. Even the universe as a whole, if some speculations are correct, may eventually cease expanding and contract once again into a compact mass, only to explode outward into some new and unimaginable configuration of elements — as fresh as ever. Being-in-general is *in*destructible.

It would have to be this integrity in any natural thing, or of the cosmos as a whole, that could constitute the spiritual element in it. The evanescence of anything

is the subjection of nature. But the presence of everything is already her glory. *That* puts Nature into the
third category with a capital letter. Existence passes
away in the very apprehension of it, which is that passing away; but creation *will be*, eternally.

In which case "Consent in being in general" would
be not only " true virtue," as Jonathan Edwards once
marvellously defined that elusive principle, but a species
of intellectual faith for which a natural theology of one
kind or another might provide a rendering in public
terms. For "reason" need not be understood merely as
preliminary to a "faith" distinct from and supplementary to it but more simply as faith in the mode of the intellect — which would then have creation as its covenantal complement. "If we perceive finite beings as they
actually are," observes E. L. Mascall in his *He Who Is*,
which rehearses the old scholastic arguments in a modern key, "we shall perceive them as creatures of God"
(p. 74). This realization, he argues, is at the heart of the
various medieval arguments for the existence of God
from the things of this world. It could also be aligned as
a Christian equivalent to the perspective assumed in the
sapiential literature of the Old Testament. Wisdom too
can become covenantal as soon as creation is its proper
opposite. What for the scribes is gnomic declaration and
for the scholastics a logical argument would in these latter days be more apt to occur, perhaps, as an intuition
half way between the aesthetic and the religious, as in a

Hopkins — or a Thoreau. But the truth glimped would be the same in the end. The "God of the philosophers," need not remain just an idea, then, but the true God apprehended, as it were, in the mode of thinking. In such a way contemplation could have its cognitive side after all.

B

When artificial lights are turned off in a windowed room at night, it takes a little time to become aware that the darkness is not total, and the longer we are bedazzled by the after-image of that artificial light, the longer it takes to perceive the subtle textures of natural light and shadow — to realize that we can, in fact, see.
— *Philip Slater*

The type of the covenantal equilibrium then on the scale of the individual might be prayer in the second category matched with creation in the third. In this context the answer to prayer would simply be the presence of being. For in relation being is already the *parousia* of God. God, said Tillich famously, may be defined as the ground of being. It would follow that as soon as being is understood as grounded, God is at least implicitly counted in. And contrariwise: without God, being can only phanesce, fictive as memory, unstable as the ego, as undependable as its names seem arbitrary.

My recollections of the lost world are imaginary, of course. But the future world that is just now coming into being — that is the frontier of the Kingdom. Nothing is missing *here. This* body lives eternally, whatever has already happened to my own or any other. Nor need anyone feel deprived of just this much. It only requires to be admitted. And such acknowledgement, aesthetic or rational or even explicitly religious, is sure to be a species of faith, whether so called or not, as whatever is acknowledged has got to be creation. Creation is then the resurrection *across the board.*

So understood being would become undeniable, though so often denied; but only as a grace. If I turn *back* in search of being with the Romantics or the materialists, it will retreat before my retrospective gaze like Eurydice before Orpheus. Those contemporary thinkers who have insisted upon the impossibility of any experience unmediated by a linguistic structure have a case which cannot be faulted as far as it goes. Such scepticism will suffice to subvert a merely nostalgic metaphysic, and keep us "modern" after all. But any ideology that would absolutize this intermediate uncertainty becomes counter-intuitive in proportion. We trust the world is not just these profane arrangements of it, though it must become that for us to "possess" it — even if we laugh at Johnson kicking the stone to refute Berkeley. The latent conviction that being must in the end prove accessible somehow is the cognitive equivalent of the faith of the crowd. The intellectual disciple may go on to suspect that it would always have had to be in some such incoherent anticipation of creation that any thing-in-itself could ever have seemed worth believing in. Everybody's sanity prefigures Somebody's faith. So even an imaginative responsiveness to the truth that faith confesses could be identifiable as the authenticating note within the asseverations of a D. H. Lawrence, say, or a Heidegger: figures from whom the first category has in effect already become the third, though their respective creeds prohibit the corresponding acknowledgment.

That being is not just primordial but eschatological is precisely the understanding, we can also observe, which informs the first great account of creation in Genesis. In "P's" version of the origin of all things the several features of the world do not simply emerge out of chaos only to sink back into it in due course. Instead they are commanded into being by the Lord himself, who creates them all by an unconditional exercise of his will. Before he acts there is only *tohu v'bohu,* an incoherent darkness upon the face of the deep. But the Spirit hovers: "and God said, let there be light, and there was light" (Gen. 1:3). The Hebrew is still more abrupt and emphatic, as we noticed earlier: *y'hi or, v'y'hi or.* The eschatological point of such a formulation would lie in its dramatic reversal of the normal order. Within the perspectives of the flesh, as we all know, word has to follow thing — and leave it irrecoverably behind. In the Spirit, though, the whole is created by the word breathed out by God. The fourth category evidences itself in the third, in which as we have said the flesh becomes a sign of the Spirit. Creation then is not preliminary to revelation, but revelation itself. Nature is already a third category pneumenon; and the development and positioning of this account attest that the last redactors of the Pentateuch were anxious to establish the cosmos in just that sense within the covenant they proposed to reconstitute imaginatively at least. For if nature is understood as a first category phenomenon only, myth would remain the appropriate interpretation of it in ancient terms, as science would be the appropriate interpretation in modern terms. Instead Nature is asserted as properly gracious: *bara* is the special verb for just this work, which only God can accomplish. And for the "P" author as well as Jewish tradition, it is possible that *Elohim* too had a similar overtone, indicating the Lord especially in his role as creator.

Light is created in a word which imaginatively enacts the Spirit's *ex*piration and *ex*pression (which "be!" can demonstrate as bodily in English as *y'hi* in Hebrew). Only after that is the result called "day" in human language. So also with the firmament and the waters and the dry land. In this account God too differentiates, as U. Cassuto has pointed out: light from darkness, then upper waters from nether waters, and seas from dry land; and then again, to repeat this series in a different but parallel set of terms, sun from moon, creatures in the heavens from creatures in the sea, and finally beasts from man. An original obscurity is discriminated successively into parts of a coherent whole as the Spirit advances upon the indefinite flesh to convert it into a sign of its creator. The third category is orderly too, as we have seen in other contexts. But everything in it is perfect: a condition the "P" author imitates stylistically, as Cassuto has also pointed out, by repeating the number seven in various permutations throughout the description, beginning with the first sentence, which contains seven words. The climatic creation of man shares the same pattern: that which makes man after the image of God is precisely his share in the Spirit which brings him into being. It is not biological man then who has "dominion" over the other creatures of this world but spiritual man only. Creation is already re-creation, the principle of which is indicatively repeated in the apparently "natural" power of generation. The earth puts forth grass, the grass produces seed, the fruit trees make fruit; and man is given the same power: "God blessed them, and God said to them, be fruitful and multiply and fill up the earth and subdue it and have dominion over the flesh of the sea and over the fowl of the heavens and all life creeping on the earth" (Gen. 1:28). Man's generativity and dominance thus reproduce within the sphere of the flesh the spiritual lordship of God upon which all depends. The "P" author can thereby understand this original provision as a universal anticipation of the gifts of progeny and territory which will presently be granted to Abraham as an individual and thence to the nation that will descend from him. In this rendering Nature is already a covenantal gift, then, as I have suggested she constantly remains within the perspective of prayer: the grandest if not the greatest of the

452

magnalia. And so she can remain — as long as originality is understood as metaphoric for ultimacy. Otherwise
this story is as mythical as those it displaces, and might
as well be replaced in its turn by geology or biology or
astrophysics. Within the covenantal structure though,
being is a gift to be accepted in obedient faith. Of that
faith the commandment issued to Adam (in the second
or "J" version of the tale which immediately follows) is
in effect a specification in terms of an elementary Law.
When this in turn is *dis*-obeyed, it is (in that second
story) precisely the givenness of the world that is with-
drawn. Mankind drops down from Paradise into reality;
or, as one might paraphrase the change, from the world
as something to be acknowledged within the third category to the world as something to be labored over in the
first. The "fall" is from the Spirit to the flesh, and the
change in the status of nature registers the descent.

Creation then need not be just a "mythical" background to the covenant but a first and last repetition of
it in terms of contemporary, which is to say, universal
experience — whether one means by "contemporary"
the ideal time of Adam, or the time of the Exile, when
the final version of the Pentateuch was put together and
the first chapter of Genesis set into its place, or the present moment of any individual at prayer. And once the
revelatory character of creation has been read out of
Genesis, it may be found elsewhere in the scriptures; in
the book of Job, for instance, also composed, it has

453

been supposed, during the Exile (that permanently typical "time") — with a hero as un-Israelite as Adam but with the same God as ever. In that book Job's complaint *is* his faith. His friends of course are good Deuteronomists for whom the wicked are sure to be punished, from which it follows that if someone suffers, he must be wicked. So if Job is really just, and his protest a species of prayer, it must be in relation to God alone. Job has no one else to cry out to. But when God does at last say something in return, he does not answer Job's protest in the moral terms in which it was put. I do not argue, says the Lord in effect, either to justify myself or you: I create. Which though disconcerting can seem in fact the best possible answer to Job's question — though not after the manner of men. Job answers Deuteronomy by harking back to Genesis; as Jesus does, we have seen, in the context of marriage.

Job does not provide an answer, then, to the "problem of evil" so much as demonstrate that in the presence of creation there need be no such thing. Those who depend upon the positives of this world, which would also have to include its structures of moral explanation, will die along with them, literally or spiritually. This is already their judgement. The fate of the "wicked" is then most simply a consequence of their dependence upon the flesh. They receive nothing from the third category because they do not allow it to obtain. For them the nothingness into which things fall away is necessarily absolute. Phanescence is evanescence, period. That is why they are so grasping in the meantime, and push others off the raft, hoping to survive a little longer themselves. So the "punishment" of the wicked need not be melodramatic, unless as a parable. The doors of hell, said C. S. Lewis, are locked from the inside. The "just" in that case would be whoever remained open to creation — or rather, to the spiritual possibility of which creation is the universal type. And faith would then be any receptive relation to that possibility no matter how enacted; as prayer, in its turn, would be whatever kept that relation open, before or after the gift which invited it. Beforehand, prayer is petition; afterwards, thanksgiving. In exchange for the gift I can really only offer my acceptance of the gift. Gratitude is prayer after the fact — as complaint may be prayer before it. But the fact, in either case, is typically creation. And creation is the presence of being.

2

What then does one do with such answers to prayer as one may receive? Job gives thanks for his restoration to health and prosperity, which for him are at last in the third category, though they began in the first, and so additional instances of the same power which the Lord has just shown him in the display of battlehorse and hippopotamus. The author of *Job* composed his book — which luckily his fellow scribes accepted into the canon. Covenantally speaking all responses of the kind bear a certain family resemblance.

The *Catholic Worker* regularly publishes letters from men in prison asking for mail. One of these struck my attention and I cut it out and saved the clipping in my wallet. It seemed to require something of me. I did not feel compelled to initiate a correspondence with a stranger which neither of us would be likely to enjoy for long. But I thought I might send him a card, perhaps something he could put on the wall of his cell, if that was permitted. So through the following Christmas season I kept an eye out. On the last day of a visit to the monastery I found just what I had been looking for in their shop: a postcard of a French print, showing a spray of yellow roses, with the botanical name in spidery handwriting underneath. It was one of a series with different species and colors of roses; but the yellow was the best. It was beautiful indeed: exact, remote, and elegant in an old fashioned French style. It would represent perfectly everything prison was the absence of: Nature, art, order, peace. So I bought one for my prisoner, and another for myself, and a couple of the red rose cards as well, for thank-you notes. When I got to the post-office though, I found the clipping I had been saving had in the meantime unaccountably dropped out of my wallet. That problem could be solved; when I got back to campus, I looked up a back file of the newspaper, found the relevant issue, and copied off the address. As I was once again about to send the card off, I discovered a second accident: by some error I had carried away only one of the yellow rose cards after all. I was sorely tempted to keep the remaining one for myself and send the prisoner a red rose instead. What difference could it possibly make to him? Besides, I could tell myself dispiritedly, he was unlikely to "relate' to this sort of thing anyway. But I knew all the same I should send the yellow rose. I had promised. And I did, with MERRY CHRISTMAS for a message, signing it only "a fellow reader of the *CW*," so he would know how it came but not have to answer. Perhaps this was cowardice.

My discovery of this gift seemed an answer to the prayer I had at last been able to make at the monastery. So it exemplified the possibility of grace to me: the beauty of existence returned upon a real emptiness at length confessed. That card and the roses on it stood in a luminous space of undeserved delight. But — and this was its most persuasive attribute — the gift had in the nature of the case to be passed on almost as soon as it was received; like the Eucharist, of which it seemed another repetition on the scale of accidentality. Here was Kierkegaard's rule proved true again: in spiritual things, possession is communication. In the things of this world, possession may be perception, or enjoyment, or theft. But in spiritual things, possession is communication. That card with the yellow roses had not come to me so I might keep it for myself, but in order that I might give it away to another. A sacrament is a hot potato. And I passed it on.